BLACK TOOTH GRIN

THE HIGH LIFE, GOOD TIMES, AND TRAGIC END OF
"DIMEBAG" DARRELL ABBOTT

Zac Crain

Da Capo Press
A Member of the Perseus Books Group

Library of Congress Cataloging-in-Publication Data
Crain, Zac.
   Black tooth grin : the high life, good times, and tragic end of 'Dimebag' Darrell Abbott / Zac Crain.
      p.   cm.
   Includes discography.
   ISBN 978-0-306-81524-9 (alk. paper)
      1. Abbott, Darrell.   2. Guitarists—United States—Biography
3. Rock musicians—Biography.   I. Title.
   ML419.A04C73 2009
   787.87'166092—dc22
   [B]

                                                    2008040662

First Da Capo Press edition 2009

Published by Da Capo Press
A Member of the Perseus Books Group
www.dacapopress.com

Da Capo Press books are available at special discounts for bulk purchases in the U.S. by corporations, institutions, and other organizations. For more information, please contact the Special Markets Department at the Perseus Books Group, 2300 Chestnut Street, Suite 200, Philadelphia PA 19103, or call (800) 810-4145, extension 5000, or e-mail special.markets@perseusbooks.com.

10 9 8 7 6 5 4 3 2 1

TRACK LISTING

SIDE TWO: COWBOYS FROM HELL (1989–1995)

SIDE THREE: THIRTEEN STEPS TO NOWHERE (1996–2000)

SIDE FOUR: NEW FOUND POWER (2001–2004)

Introduction

Blink of an Eye

This was the boring part of Mitch Carpenter's job, telling assholes like the guy in the red Pontiac Grand Am they couldn't park their cars wherever they felt like it. If one were to break it down, what Mitch did, it was like being a glorified hall monitor sometimes.

The Grand Am had pulled to a stop next to the fence bordering the patio area at Alrosa Villa. The low-key, stucco-sided building had been hosting heavy metal shows in Columbus, Ohio, for more than three decades. Albert Catuela and his wife, Rosa—hence the name "Alrosa"—opened the club in 1974 and just about every hard-rock band worth a damn had graced (if that word was appropriate) the stage since then.

The driver of the Grand Am, a burly six-foot-something with a shaved head, had been heading for Alrosa Villa's front door, probably in search of tickets for tonight's show. He'd have to wait. Mitch turned him around and made him move his car.

Mitch walked back to his post in the parking lot. It was only 9 P.M., but he'd already been working for almost three hours.

Having his brother, David, here with him, working security in the parking lot, too, might make the time pass a little quicker, but it didn't do a damn thing about the weather. If winter wasn't here yet, it was at least close enough to count. Maybe later he would duck inside, get out of the chill, and check out some of the show. Two of the guys from Pantera were in a new band that was headlining tonight and—wait.

Christ. *Now* the red Grand Am was parked by Alrosa's sign, which, besides marking the club's location off Sinclair Road, also happened to be a no-parking zone. Dammit. What did he want, valet parking? Mitch waved the driver away: "Hey, can't park there either." The beefy guy at the wheel nodded and—again— eased out of his illegal space without putting up a fight.

Maybe it was going to be one of those nights, a trying shift that found Mitch having to practically hold everyone's hand like a kindergarten teacher. Or maybe not. Maybe it would be a boring night, the kind you hope for when you work security. Whatever. It was cold and getting colder. Yeah, he'd duck inside for a bit later, just inside the door. At least he'd be out of the wind. Mitch noticed the Grand Am's misguided owner was heading his way. Looked like he ended up parking across the street. Why couldn't he have just done that in the first place?

"Hey, buddy. You OK?"

"Yes, sir. Sorry about that."

AARON BARNES was the last guy left on the tour bus tonight, which wasn't unusual. The Abbott brothers, Darrell and Vinnie Paul, hall-of-fame hell-raisers for more than two decades, liked to be out among the fans, buying shots and posing for photos.

Barnes had been with them almost the entire time. The only thing the Abbotts, and Darrell in particular, liked better than having a good time was making sure everyone else had a good time, too—whether they wanted to or not.

It was a few minutes after 10 P.M., and the show was about to start. Then there would be an after-party, because there was always an after-party, and Barnes wouldn't be alone again until he hit the sack, whenever that happened. Definitely wouldn't be for hours.

There wasn't much time to enjoy this rare moment of solitude, but no one really got into the music business for that anyway. It was time to go to work; Barnes, the band's sound engineer, was needed inside. He stepped off the bus, locking the door behind him, and turned into the face of a muscle-bound man in a Columbus Blue Jackets jersey with a hooded sweatshirt underneath. He was bald, or close to it anyway, and anxious about something.

The Columbus Blue Jackets fan wanted to know if the Abbotts were still on the bus, or if they'd already made their way inside the club. Barnes wasn't surprised by the question. People always wanted to hang out with the brothers, before and after the show, and they were rarely turned away. That wasn't exactly standard operating procedure with most bands, but it was in the Abbott camp. Barnes told him the brothers were already backstage, preparing for the night's gig. He shrugged off the missed opportunity, a losing lottery ticket bought with a dollar he found in the street.

"See you inside," the big man said, and walked away.

LIKE MOST rock-show audiences, the crowd that night was acting as a human motion detector. Any hint of action onstage brought forth a chorus of *whoooo*s and/or chants of the band's name, each syllable separated by an exclamation point: *Da! Mage! Plan!* Even though it was only tour manager Chris Paluska arranging water bottles on the drum riser, or security chief Jeffrey "Mayhem" Thompson crossing from one side to the other to set up the band's ever-present video camera.

"If you do get carried away down there, make sure there's no fists swinging or kicking or anything like that" began an announcement over the club's PA system. "It will bother our security. We want you to have a good time. There is no wall of death in this club."

Da! Mage! Plan! Da! Mage! Plan! Da! Mage! Plan!

MITCH CARPENTER was standing just inside Alrosa's north entrance. Damageplan, tonight's headliner, was about to start its set. Another couple of hours and he could go home.

Something caught Carpenter's eye, over by the privacy fence bordering the club's outdoor patio. It was the guy from the parking lot, the one who couldn't figure out where to park his damned Grand Am. What was he up to now? He wasn't trying to . . .

Oh, crap. He was climbing over.

"VAN HALEN?" Vinnie Paul Abbott asked. It was a question rooted in the shorthand favored by brothers, bandmates, and best friends. Darrell and Vinnie could check all three boxes on that list. To him and Darrell, those two words meant, "Let it all hang out there tonight." Or, more to the point, and in their vernacular, "Rock and fucking roll."

Darrell stopped warming up his hands. "Van-fuckin'-Halen," he said, slapping his brother's big hand, the engine that had been driving their shared career since they were teenagers. It wasn't a question that needed to be asked (or answered), but it was their ritual. The Abbotts hadn't played Alrosa Villa in years, not since their previous band, Pantera, was getting off the ground as a national touring act. They'd been playing—and usually filling—arenas since then.

But Damageplan wasn't Pantera, not yet at least, and so it was back to the clubs. Their careers, like so many careers in the music business, had come full circle. The Abbotts didn't seem to mind—"The highs and lows of rock and roll," as Darrell often said. After a few years stuck at home while Pantera messily dissolved, they were happy to even have a band again, happy to be out on the road, happy to be playing onstage.

The set was about to begin. Everything was ready to go. A couple of dozen red Solo cups were lined up on a table just offstage. Their role in the show had been a highlight of Darrell's act for years now. He'd fill the cups with beer and then toss them to the crowd. The Abbott brothers might have been downsized into smaller venues, but they still approached every gig like they were playing in an arena. That's how they did it on the way up, and that's how they'd do it now.

Van-fuckin'-Halen.

PENNY REED yelled, "Fugitive! Fugitive!" when the husky guy in the Columbus Blue Jackets jersey grabbed the top of the fence at the edge of the patio and started to pull himself over the top. She wasn't necessarily trying to alert Alrosa's security staff to the presence of the intruder. Just heckling the stocky kid awkwardly trying to sneak into the gig, having some fun with her husband, Jimmy, and her brother-in-law, Andrew, before the band started playing. So someone was trying to get into the show for free. Guys like that never got away with it.

As a general rule, no one ever stops people from hopping over fences at concerts. This time was no different. A few of the paying customers out on the patio encouraged him. Some even helped him make it over the fence. Still, it didn't appear as though he was going to get away with it. One of the club's bouncers was already on the patio, heading toward him. The warm-up act, such as it was, was coming to an end.

"No way!" the bouncer said, approaching. "No way!"

The scofflaw was undaunted—and quicker than he looked. "What's up?" he said as he darted past the bouncer and into the concert-ready darkness of Alrosa Villa.

His hands were in his pockets as he ran further toward the stage.

MITCH CARPENTER wasn't bothered by the fact that the fence-hopper was running toward the stage as much as he was that the dude hadn't paid. He couldn't have known what was about to happen.

Carpenter hustled after the guy, this thorn in his paw all night, yelling for him to stop. The guy didn't even turn around, because even if Carpenter's words would have caused him to stop, there was absolutely no way they were audible. The band had already started, and like most groups that played Alrosa Villa, they were loud.

Mitch had better luck with Ron Jenkins, one of the club's bouncers. He quickly explained the situation as best he could, but Ron could only understand half of it. Mitch was the one saying it and he couldn't make out much more. It was like a foreign film no one had bothered to subtitle.

Ron picked up the gist, at least, since he picked up the chase, following the guy as he ran toward the left side of the stage. Mitch figured Ron would have some help if the guy made it all the way up front. Beyond Alrosa Villa's own security staff positioned at the foot of the stage, the band had brought its own bodyguard along, a beast of a guy they called, appropriately, Mayhem.

Yes, he would be back in his Grand Am soon enough, illegally parking somewhere else on someone else's watch. If they were lucky, and if he was smart, this guy, not exactly the best representative of the Columbus Blue Jackets, would bail out on whatever it was he had planned to do and just keep on running through the back door.

Wait, where'd he go?

TWENTY-FOUR years to the day from when John Lennon was shot and killed by Mark David Chapman in front of his New York City apartment building, Nathan Gale, a six-foot-five, 268-pound former U.S. Marine and semipro football lineman, emerged from behind a seven-foot-high stack of amplifiers on the left side of Alrosa Villa's stage. Damageplan was less than halfway through its first song of the night, "Breathing New Life." Hardly anyone noticed him, and those who did probably thought he was just a thrill seeker looking for a little extra excitement to add to his concert-going experience. If they were frightened, it was only because they weren't looking forward to catching someone that size once he toppled like a felled oak tree off the stage and onto their heads.

They didn't see the security guards chasing him.

Gale jogged past the bass player, Bob Kakaha, and past the singer, Pat Lachman, moving with the aimless lope of a typical stage diver. He slowed briefly as he made his way past Vinnie Paul and his drum kit. His hands weren't in his pockets anymore.

Walking with purpose now, arms in front of him, Gale didn't stop until he reached the other side of the stage, where Darrell Abbott stood, crouched over his guitar, enraptured, as always, by the power of the sounds he made with it.

Mayhem was a few feet behind Gale, too close to give up, too far away to make a difference. He might as well not have been there at all. It would have been better for him if he hadn't been.

Darrell coaxed one final noise out of his guitar.

WHEN DARRELL Abbott was murdered onstage at Alrosa Villa on December 8, 2004, it was the lead story on every news channel and above the fold in every newspaper. But before that moment, Darrell was more-or-less unknown outside the hard rock/heavy metal community.

So when David Draiman of Disturbed called the murder "the 9/11 of heavy metal" in the aftermath, some might have been taken aback by the comparison. To those who knew Darrell, or knew of him, however, the parallel was obvious. It was a shocking and unprovoked attack on a symbol of everything they stood for. Both a fan favorite and a fan himself, Darrell had something in common with everyone in all corners of the heavy metal universe, from the most insignificant specks of cosmic debris to the brightest suns. People were drawn to him, even those Darrell never could have imagined. He died much too young, but by then, he had already lived out an existence far beyond his boyhood, head-banging dreams.

At his funeral less than a week later in his hometown of Arlington, Texas, Eddie Van Halen, one of Darrell's heroes since before he could even play the guitar, told a story. Not long before the murder, it was announced that a limited-run series of guitars decorated with Van Halen's signature tape-striping would be issued. To sweeten the pot, Van Halen would personally customize the instruments; each would be sold with a certificate of authenticity and a photo of the guitarist performing the task. When Darrell heard the news, he called Van Halen, trying to buy one before they went on sale. Van Halen told him no—he'd give Darrell a guitar the next time they were together and would tape-stripe it right in front of him.

Van Halen told the assembled that he never got a chance to make good on that offer. Then he pulled out his famous black-and-yellow-striped guitar—Darrell's favorite, the one that appeared on the back cover of *Van Halen II*. He put it in Darrell's casket so it could be buried with him.

"When Eddie put the black-and-yellow guitar in the casket with Darrell, I remember thinking, You know what? If back in the old days, when we first started, if you would have told Darrell that, when you die, Van Halen is going to put that guitar in your casket, Darrell would have said, 'Kill me now,'" says Terry Glaze. He was an original member of Pantera, singing on the group's first three albums.

That was Darrell—at the beginning and at the end. He became enough of a guitar hero to be respected by arguably the
biggest guitar hero of them all, and yet he remained a fifteen-
year-old kid inside. He was still awed by the power of rock and
roll, still enthralled by the entire experience, whether he was onstage with his Dean ML in hand or backstage with one of his
customary "black tooth grins" (a double shot of whiskey with a
splash of Coke) instead.

That's why, while most people would say they'd prefer to die
doing what they loved, it's doubtful anyone meant that more
than Darrell Lance Abbott. His death was a tragedy. It would
have been even more tragic if it hadn't happened where it did,
when it did.

But doing what he loved wasn't the reason Darrell's death res-
onated so intensely with so many people. It wasn't the only reason, at any rate. When I covered his public memorial service at
the Arlington Convention Center for *Spin*, everyone I met that
night had a story. Not just about their favorite Pantera concert—
they were far more personal than that. Everyone, it seemed, had
shared a joke with Darrell, done a shot with him, something.

There were several thousand people in attendance, and I
wouldn't have been at all surprised to learn Darrell had met
every one of them.

SIDE ONE
METAL MAGIC
(1966–1988)

1

AND THE CRADLE WILL ROCK

Born Country and Western, Raised Heavy Metal

"A lot of guitar players come up to me and say Alive! *is their rock 'n' roll bible. That's how they learned to play guitar, which I find flattering."*

ACE FREHLEY,
KISS: Behind the Mask

In the case of Darrell Lance Abbott, it happened exactly as it was supposed to. He was born to be a musician; he wanted to become a musician; he became a musician. He was a textbook case, even if nothing else about him—his dyed-red billy-goat beard, his inked-up body, his long kinky hair, his sailor's mouth, his choice of profession—exactly screamed academia.

It started, like most things do, with his family. Darrell got the talent from his father. By the time Darrell came along on August 20, 1966, Jerry Abbott was already a one-stop shop. Jerry was a skilled songwriter, could play just about anything that made a noise, and also knew his way around a recording studio. "He would do these country tracks for people, and he played piano," says Jerry Hudson, who worked as a recording engineer at Pantego Sound Studio with Abbott. "He got me basically to just watch the machine. He'd set it up and I'd watch levels for him. Once he got the rhythm track, he'd come in and he'd take over. He'd overdub acoustics and stuff, and we'd work together on that. . . . Him and Charles Stewart were songwriting partners, and they had some chart hits. He didn't have any No. 1s or anything, but they charted songs with Danny Wood. Buck [Owens] and Emmylou [Harris] recorded one of their songs ["Together Again," a country chart hit in 1979, also memorably covered by ex–Screaming Trees front man Mark Lanegan]." That Jerry Abbott didn't make it in the music business before his sons did had more to do with timing than ability. Because he had a family to support, Jerry didn't have a chance to pursue his country music dreams until later, when Darrell and Vince's success allowed him to leave Arlington, Texas, behind for Nashville, where he set up Abtrax Studio and sold some songs.

Prior to Darrell's arrival, Jerry had already passed his gifts along to his oldest son, Vincent Paul, born two years before Darrell (on March 11, 1964) when the family lived in Abilene.

Vince—as he was known growing up, and as he's still known to his oldest friends; in the music industry, most know him as Vinnie Paul—would choose a different instrument than his younger brother, but his choice of drums made him a perfect jamming partner for Darrell. It also conveniently aped the bandmate/brother dynamic earlier set forth by Alex and Eddie Van Halen, whom the Abbott boys modeled themselves after from the very beginning. Beyond his natural musical ability, Vince also inherited Jerry's knack for recording, which would come in handy later, when Darrell was searching for the guitar sound that would ultimately launch a thousand picks.

From his mother, Carolyn, Darrell received something even more important than a music gene and a fairly easy entrance into the business: unconditional love. Carolyn and Jerry divorced in 1979 after almost seventeen years of marriage, but Carolyn made sure Vince and Darrell had a stable home life. By all accounts, she was the kind of mother that usually exists only on very special episodes of *Oprah*; Carolyn didn't care what her boys did as long as it made them happy. That's what made *her* happy. That's probably why they kept living with her long after they could afford houses of their own. In fact, they kept living with her when they could have bought a few houses of their own. They were mama's boys, and proud of it.

"Every time Darrell came home from a tour, he paid his mom's credit cards off," says Kitty Webster with a laugh. She worked with Carolyn until 1990, and her sons, Buddy and Ken, were friends with Darrell and Vince. "Because she liked to shop and buy jewelry and stuff. He always came home and cleaned up her credit cards."

"She was fantastic," says Buddy Webster, known in the music industry as Buddy Blaze.

She was a foreman in a factory and worked a normal eight-to-five job, or whatever you would call it. To me, from somebody somewhat on the inside looking at the whole picture, Pantera [and its success] without Carolyn Abbott, I don't know how it could have happened. That house was a band house, from the time that Darrell was, like, in the ninth or tenth grade. There would be fifty people at the house and she'd let it happen. She loved her kids and she supported them. And obviously, Darrell and Pantera were doing pretty darn good. They [eventually] reached enough success that they could do things like buy her cars and things, kind of pay her back. I don't know how they would have done it without her. Because a lot of parents would have said, "Get the hell out," and that kind of forces people to figure out how they're going to eat. They had a roof over their heads and they were able to eat regardless of what they did. I think they were really blessed to have a mom like Carolyn.

Even though they were blessed with the right parents to facilitate a career in music, that didn't necessarily mean Vince and Darrell would pursue one. That they did had as much to do with where they lived as it did with whom they lived with.

ARLINGTON, TEXAS, is a small town made big (population just over three hundred thousand) by its proximity to two of the state's largest cities, Dallas and Fort Worth. It hangs in a hammock between the two, suspended by the dual highways, Interstates 20 and 30, cutting through it.

It's fitting that the Abbotts hail from Arlington, since the city's reputation, what there is of it, is based on fun and games. It's the home of North Texas's only real amusement park, Six Flags over Texas (the older brother in the Six Flags chain), as well as Rangers Ballpark in Arlington, which houses baseball's Texas Rangers. The venerable Dallas Cowboys are currently building a state-of-the-art new stadium there and will move in before the 2009 season. Other than that, there isn't much to recommend Arlington. It's a sea of strip malls known most for being the city one passes through on the way to Fort Worth or Dallas.

While Arlington isn't quite as cosmopolitan as its neighbors to the east and west, it shares with them an abiding love for hard rock and heavy metal. North Texas has a long history as a heavy music outpost, thanks largely to the Texxas Jam,[1] an arena rock festival held at the Cotton Bowl every summer between 1978 and 1988. During its run, Texxas Jam hosted day-long, multiact shows featuring the likes of Aerosmith, Ted Nugent, Journey, Blue Oyster Cult, Rush, Ozzy Osbourne, Dio, Boston, and Metallica long before Lollapalooza and Ozzfest and Coachella and Bonnaroo and dozens of other summer rock festivals existed. Vince Abbott was at the very first installment, on July 1, 1978, which boasted a lineup that included Cheech & Chong, the Atlanta Rhythm Section, Eddie Money, Mahogany Rush, and, most important of all, Van Halen.

Given that musical climate, and the fact that their hometown didn't have much else to offer, it's easy to see why the Abbott boys decided to form their own band. It's harder to understand why they didn't leave Arlington behind as soon as they possibly could.

But Darrell stayed. Where he grew up is five minutes and a few miles from where he spent the rest of his days. Almost all the important events in his life happened within the same zip code.

The tour starts at Pantego Sound Studio, where Pantera recorded its first six albums, the first four with Jerry Abbott at the helm. There's little chance one would come across Pantego Sound Studio unless it was the specific destination. Even then, it's hard to find. Located at the ass-end of an industrial park that was probably frayed at the seams when it was brand-new, the tan brick building is completely hidden from view, the last stop before a dead-end street becomes a scraggly mess of trees. If potential visitors didn't happen to notice the lonely mailbox jutting out from behind the fence corralling Cowboy Towing's land of misfit cars, they wouldn't even know there was a building there, much less the creation site of two of the most beloved metal albums of the past two decades.

Those albums made Darrell a rich man. Not obscenely rich, not like someone on *MTV Cribs* rubbing a chamois on his fleet of Ferraris, but he certainly never had to worry about having a little change in his pocket. Wealthy enough, certainly, that he could have easily moved away from that beaten-down industrial park and the studio hidden on a dead-end street. Yet Darrell's home in Dalworthington Gardens, a tiny, tony suburb of Arlington, is just over a mile from Pantego.

The home itself isn't ostentatious; it's one of the more modest homes in the area. It's gated, but other than its position at the bottom of a small rise, it's not away from prying eyes. Had a fan hunted down his address while he was still alive, they would have had a good chance of spotting Darrell rambling around his property, heading out back to record maybe, or deciding where to ignite a fresh sack of M-80s and Roman candles.

"I told myself a long time ago that if I could ever afford to buy a house, I wanted to have a studio in the backyard, just like Edward Van Halen—my very own 5150," Darrell told *Guitar Player* magazine in 2004. "So when I found this house . . . and saw the barn behind it, I knew I was set."[2]

The path to get there began more than twenty years earlier, and less than two miles away, in the bedroom of his mother's unassuming ranch house on Monterrey Street.

ACE FREHLEY stood in the middle of the bedroom, watching him watch himself in the mirror. His guitar was slung over his shoulder. His makeup was perfect. It was showtime. He only needed to ignore a few minor details, such as the fact that he was lacking the rest of the band, the audience, and the ability to actually play the thing hanging from his skinny frame, and, oh yeah, the reality that he wasn't, technically speaking, Ace Frehley.

But that, of course, was inconsequential. So what if he wasn't really Ace Frehley? So what if the rest of the band existed solely on the turntable, and the only audience was the mirror and the occasional family member who wandered by, wondering when Darrell Abbott was going to stop messing around, stop posing with his guitar and start learning how to play it? If he thought hard enough, and turned the music up loud enough, he really was making all that glorious noise on *Alive!*—right alongside

Paul, Peter, and Gene. Really, weren't KISS's instruments more-or-less props anyway?

Posing was about all Darrell could handle at first. The guitar was practically bigger than he was, and roughly as heavy. Darrell was a stick figure with a pulse, the size and shape of a mike stand, a volcanic tangle of curly hair that tapered down to nothingness. It was more fun this way, and certainly easier. All he needed was face paint, a turntable, his guitar, and some imagination.

That was the full inventory of what Darrell required to be happy. He remained that same KISS fan the rest of his days. He had Frehley's portrait and autograph tattooed on his chest, a blood oath that meant he was in it for the long haul. Years later, after he had blossomed into the rock god he dreamed of being in his boyhood bedroom, Darrell still thought nothing of jumping onstage and joining some nobody band to blaze through a cover of "Cold Gin," while the audience—the band, too—looked on in disbelief. KISS came before his first kiss, and before his first love. (His first love: That happened when his dad gave him that cheap guitar.) Vince and Darrell were fans, and from the beginning they made sure their fandom was well known, as indelible as Darrell's future tattoo.

"Back in our tape room [at Pantego]—it was all rough cedar, all finished out," says Jerry Hudson. The boys would regularly come to work with their father. "They had drawn the KISS logo in black Magic Marker—and some of the made-up faces and stuff, too—on the wall. Even though it wasn't my studio, I was kind of, like, 'What's the deal with that?' And Jerry was just, like, 'Ah, it's just my kids.'"

Jerry Abbott never forced the boys to think of his studio as more than just a place for KISS graffiti. He never forced them to follow him into the music business; he knew firsthand that was a hard life. But Jerry never discouraged them either. If they wanted to follow his path and make music for a living (and all that entailed), he could at least point them in the right direction and help them hone the skills they'd need to survive. That's why, when Vince came home from school with a tuba, Jerry bought him a drum kit. ("You're never going to make a penny with that thing," Jerry told Vince. "Take it back.") That's why, when Vince wouldn't let Darrell get much time behind the drums and was already showing proof of Jerry's genes, Jerry bought Darrell a Les Paul copy and a Pignose amp for his birthday.

In the mythology of Darrell and Pantera, that is the extent of Jerry Abbott's role. In most versions, he provided his sons with the genes, a recording studio, some early managerial guidance, and that's about it. As far as Darrell went, well, he was born to be a guitar hero. He didn't have to learn to play so much as he had to decide to start playing. The skill, the story goes, was right there waiting. The legend is more-or-less a parallel to the Immaculate Conception: Darrell couldn't play his guitar, and then, one day, he could. No one knows what really happened, just that Darrell and his guitar disappeared behind his bedroom door for six weeks (or six months, depending on whom you believe), and when he finally emerged, he wasn't good—he was *great*. He was a *Guitar World* cover waiting to happen, only missing the nicknames and the attention. End of story.

This is true in a sense. Darrell did hide himself away in his bedroom, and he did figure out how to turn that Les Paul copy into a weapon, an ax in just about every way you could mean it. That is the Hollywood biopic version of the story, however, compressing the timeline and leaving out crucial characters. It neglects the messy business of learning, the fits and starts, the setbacks. It skips over the period when Jerry would learn KISS songs (and Van Halen and Judas Priest and more) so he could walk Darrell through them. Jerry didn't much care for that kind of music. He was a C&W man, and always would be. But someone had to help Darrell learn how to play.

Had Jerry taught Darrell what *he* knew how to play rather than what his son wanted to learn, Darrell's life might have gone in a different direction. Had the boys never strayed from their father's record collection, Darrell would probably be the most sought-after session musician in Nashville right now, though his skills and personality might not have allowed him to remain behind closed doors. He might have gone on to become a country singer in the outlaw tradition—another Waylon Jennings or Willie Nelson or, even better, David Allan Coe, a talented but underappreciated renegade, a hardcore troubadour acknowledged by a loyal cadre of fans (including Jerry and Carolyn Abbott) and an even more loyal faction of musicians.

Darrell and Vince found a different path, mapped out by the Judas Priest, Black Sabbath, KISS, and Van Halen albums that dominated their turntable. When Darrell was twelve years old and stumbled across the melody to Deep Purple's "Smoke on the Water" by plucking individual notes on a single string, Jerry had to start listening to those albums, too.

"My dad showed me how to play a movable power chord shape, and that made the riff sound heavy as shit," Darrell told

Guitar World's Nick Bowcott, who worked with Darrell on his "Riffer Madness" column for the magazine. "Being able to play a whole song is one of the most satisfying things when you're learning to play guitar."

Being able to play a whole song also allowed him to—finally—jam with Vince, who had been pestering him, leading the charge for Darrell to stop posing and start playing. That first day wasn't much—five or six hours of nothing but "Smoke on the Water," which is probably more than even the most ardent Deep Purple fan would want to hear in one sitting, showing anyone in ten words or less exactly how much Jerry and Carolyn Abbott loved their sons. But it got better. Between lessons from his father and jam sessions with his brother, Darrell's repertoire expanded. Just as important, Darrell had regular access to the guitar players who came through his dad's studio—Texas legends like Bugs Henderson, Ricky Lynn Gregg, Jimmy Wallace, and Rocky Athas. He would hit them up for pointers or, more often, stare at their fingers.

"His dad let him sit, actually, in the studio while we were recording," Henderson says. Henderson recorded his 1981 album, *Still Flyin'*, at Pantego Sound, with Jerry Abbott producing. "He'd sit over by the piano, on the floor or something, and watch. Just kind of soak it up. His dad said he was starting to play guitar and he was just trying to learn everything he could and asked me if I minded him coming in. I said, 'No, I don't mind at all.' He'd been around enough sessions to know to sit there and be still. Real nice kid. Real polite and respectful. He'd occasionally ask me something, but never any big deal. He was more interested in how I'd set the amp and stuff like that."

If all that study didn't translate exactly right when the guitar was in Darrell's hands, sometimes that was even better. "I'd take it home, dick with it to see how many ways I could stretch it," he would say later. "Doing that would always lead me into some new shit."

FROM THAT first marathon version of "Smoke on the Water" on, Darrell and Vince Abbott were always a package deal. You wanted one, you got both, and if you didn't like it, tough shit. The pattern was established from the beginning, in 1981, when a nascent version of Pantera was coming together.

Jerry knew from experience that a good drummer was rarely out of work for long. Vince learned quickly that was the truth when Terry Glaze, Tommy Bradford, and Donny Hart, three kids from school, were trying to start a band. They needed a drummer, and their list was one name long. Vince was Jerry and Carolyn Abbott's original musical prodigy. Everyone knew Vince Abbott was the best drummer around. He was a standout in the drum corps and jazz band at Arlington's James Bowie High School, and beginning to prove his father right that a drummer could go much farther than a tuba player. Vince agreed to drop by Glaze's house after school so the four of them (Glaze on guitar, Bradford on bass, and Hart on vocals—mainly because he had his own PA system) could jam. It went well enough that Vince agreed to join the band, with one stipulation: His little brother Darrell would be coming on board as well, on guitar.

It was a tough sell, mainly because "he wasn't very good," Glaze says, somewhat sheepishly poking holes in the legend. "He had just started. He was a little skinny, scrawny dude. We're in

high school, and we don't want us a young kid. We didn't know."
He laughs. "We're stupid."

Almost a decade later, when Megadeth's Dave Mustaine
wanted Darrell to join his band, Darrell paid Vince back: He told
Mustaine, "Sure, I'm in, as long as you're planning to hire my
brother to play drums." The gambit may not have worked then,
but it did in 1981; it was agreed that both Abbotts would join the
group. With the brothers in the fold, the new band was ready to
go. They called themselves Pantera, Spanish for "panther," a
name suggested by a friend "mainly because it sounded cool,"
says Glaze. But that version of Pantera didn't really go anywhere.
Hart was the first out the door, replaced before it swung shut.
"Donny came in one night when I was in singing," Glaze says.
"He was pissed that I was singing. And that's when it turned into
a four-piece."[3]

Bradford didn't last much longer; that summer, he decided he
wanted try out for drum major in the school marching band, and
he quit Pantera to focus on that goal. In one of the band's early
publicity bios, for their first album, *Metal Magic*, Bradford's and
Hart's exit from Pantera was blamed on the fact that they were
"both suffering from long-standing personal problems." This
may have been slightly tongue-in-cheek; later in the bio, the
band describes being "discovered by Jerry Eld'n, a long-time
record producer for Metal Magic Records" that signed the
"bangers" to his label. Which is just a somewhat creative way of
getting around the fact that the Abbotts' father recorded Pantera's album and issued it on the label he started solely for the
purpose of releasing Pantera albums, something every young
band does to plump up a lightweight résumé.

The band located Bradford's replacement quickly, inviting a local kid named Rex Brown to Pantego Sound to test him out. Brown was, like Vince, a member of the jazz band at Bowie High and had been playing bass with another local group, Lance & the Brew Necks. When he left the studio that night, he was a member of Pantera.

Brown—who went by Rex Rocker during the band's formative years, and later, for a time, just Rex—is perhaps the most overlooked member of Pantera, a fate typical of most bass players. Yet he would, over the years, come to be something of a heavy metal icon all his own. Part of the reason was that his underrated bass playing helped lay the foundation for the band's trademark "power groove" sound. The other part was because Brown, as much as anyone who ever picked up the instrument, just *looked* like a heavy metal bassist, with long, stringy hair, goatee, and backward baseball cap. Brown was so identifiable in this role that in the 1994 movie *Airheads*, Steve Buscemi portrayed an almost carbon-copy version of Brown—a bassist for a struggling metal band who was named, perhaps not coincidentally, Rex.[4] But in 1982, Brown was just another local kid who could play bass and got along well enough with the rest of the group.

About the same time, something more important happened: Darrell's transformation as a guitar player, the result of the increasing amount of time he and his guitar spent hidden away from all outside distractions—including, on a regular basis, school. This period served as the genesis for Darrell's infamous "loogie wall." It was exactly what it sounds like. He would sit on his bed with his guitar and, every so often, lean back, hock up a load of phlegm, and spit it over his head against the wall. Even after he was good enough with his guitar to take his act outside the confines of his room, the wall regularly received a fresh coat. (Though, strictly speaking, "fresh" might not be the best word for it.)

Psychologists might look at this behavior and think they have an easy diagnosis. Most academic studies of heavy metal, most notably Jeffrey Jensen Arnett's *Metalheads: Heavy Metal Music and Adolescent Alienation*,[5] typically talk about the music's tendency to isolate its listeners from society, with all the attendant negative connotations. In Darrell's case, the symptoms may have been the same, but the disease was not present. He wasn't escaping from something in his bedroom. While his parents divorced in 1979, his family life was happy, and he didn't have many concerns. No, when Darrell shut himself off in his room, he was escaping *into* something, a joyful place that just happened to be built—especially later—out of something that sounded a lot like pain. He wasn't distancing himself from the world. He was joining it. By the time those bedroom sessions were over, he was already there.

"When he came out, he could play, like, 'Eruption' and 'Crazy Train,'" Glaze says. "I mean he just *morphed* over the six-month period. Before that, we shared lead guitar. But pretty quickly, I backed into rhythm guitar. The funny part was that's all I really wanted to do. I always wanted to be the singer-songwriter, play a G chord, and do that. That's all I wanted to do."

Glaze had to, at least temporarily, set aside his hopes of being a songwriter. Pantera was birthed into a Dallas–Fort Worth area club scene that had little use for original material. Pantera and the other bands making the rounds would work in one or two of their own songs on occasion, if the set was long enough, but cover tunes were the order of the day: KISS, Van Halen, Ozzy, and whatever else was popular on the radio at the time. Pantera would quickly pick up a following because they were better at the routine than most. It helped that they had a budding virtuoso in their midst.

"Darrell was just like a natural," says Tommy Snellings, Brown's high school best friend and a member of Pantera's crew until the late 1980s. "They always amazed me because they could pick out any song. There would be a new song come on the radio. They would listen to it two or three times and go out and play it. It just amazed me. I was still trying to figure out what the lyrics said. They had such an ear for it. They were just naturals."

By the end of 1982, the first "real" incarnation of Pantera had solidified, and it played its first gig together at a now-defunct club in Dallas called the Ritz. Snellings was there that night with his camera. He worked at a Fotomat in Arlington and lined up jobs for the members of the band there. He usually had a camera with him. That fact, along with his status as a card-carrying pack rat, has made Snellings something of an unofficial historian of Pantera's early days. At his home in south Arlington, Snellings has a dozen or so photo albums devoted to his time with the band, not to mention a few boxes crammed with the rock-and-roll ephemera he accumulated along the way, including a pair of Darrell's impossibly tiny magenta spandex pants. When he digs out his photos from the Ritz, they bear out at least a portion of the Darrell Abbott legend: He was born for the stage. No noticeable nightclub jitters are present in any of the photos. Just a skinny kid who looks like he's already found his home.

2

HEAVY METAL RULES

"Diamond" Darrell Lance, Dime Bags, and Life on the Road

"Have . . . a good time . . . all the time."

VIV SAVAGE,
This Is Spinal Tap

Pantera and the other groups on the hard-rock club circuit in the early 1980s weren't just mimicking other bands' material; they were mimicking everything else, too, down to the last studded bracelet. At the time, it wasn't advisable to get up onstage and play in street clothes, not if you were in an aspiring heavy metal band. The ripped-jeans-and-flannel approach to stage wear was a decade away. It was the still the 1980s, when image was everything.

Darrell and the band didn't have much of an image early on. In Tommy Snellings's photos from that first show at the Ritz, there are no lights onstage other than the club's usual setup, though that would soon be rectified. A few pairs of spandex trousers aside, the group is dressed rather plainly, particularly for the time period; they had as much in common with Bruce Springsteen as they did Bruce Dickinson of Iron Maiden. They appear to be, for the most part, another anonymous bar band. During their initial orbit through local clubs, that's exactly what they were. Their first set of promotional photos underscores that imageless period. They might as well have been taken for the high school yearbook—just four regular, random guys goofing around during homeroom.

All that would change within the next year of the band's existence, when if you saw merely a photo of the band's stage setup— with enough lights to (quite literally) land an airplane, along with the demon-head busts and pentagrams adorning Vince's double bass drums—you would have no doubts that it was the terrain of a heavy metal band and, given the amount of equipment up there, a fairly successful one. Fake it until you make it, as they say. By the end of 1983, a photograph of Pantera would include the era's essentials: Hairspray? Makeup? Spandex? All present and accounted for.

None of that transformed Pantera into a band of pretty boys. On them, the spandex and hairspray and everything else simply didn't look right. "We tried to look tough. You look at those pictures and we look like a bunch of loser girls," Glaze admits. "Guys dressed up like girls with spandex and all those bracelets and things."

Looking like a bunch of ugly girls wasn't (necessarily) something to be ashamed of then. As Vince would say later, "That's the way everybody dressed back then. I've got pictures of James Hetfield wearing spandex. We were young kids when we started. We emulated our favorite bands, like Judas Priest, KISS, and Van Halen. But we were also image-conscious and felt we had to dress the part to play the music. Then in the late eighties we realized, 'Those clothes and that hairspray and all that stuff isn't playing the music—we are.'"

Vince wasn't always so forthcoming, not after he and his brother and the rest of the group had put the spandex behind them. He wasn't alone. This period in Pantera history was a definite sore spot to everyone except Glaze, seeing as how it contradicted the image they later cultivated, when they'd reimagined themselves as so-called cowboys from hell. For years, the members of Pantera—and most of their fans—treated 1990's *Cowboys from Hell* as the group's debut. The 1980s incarnation was a dirty little secret (more or less) shared by the band's original regional fan base, the way things could be in the pre-Internet days.

Some evidence of those earlier years would remain, however, on Pantera's first two records for Atco, the discs recorded after they had ditched their spandex and Aqua Net: Darrell's original stage name, Diamond Darrell Lance, shortened by the time Pantera signed its recording contract to Diamond Darrell.[6] Like most of what the Abbotts and Pantera did in the beginning, the name was partially a tribute to Van Halen.

"Our show, we based it pretty much on Van Halen," Glaze says. "It was just like that—*wild*, jumping and running. I wanted to be David Lee Roth." Diamond Darrell Lance, obviously, wanted to be Eddie Van Halen. He learned how to play "Eruption" as well as the man who wrote it. Between his emerging skills and his cascading mane of brown curls, he looked and sounded the part.

Pantera's reticence to acknowledge their cover-band/hair metal roots—due to image control or embarrassment or both—would come later. In 1983, they were loud and proud, and ready to take over the world, starting in Texas.

DARRELL AND the other members of Pantera didn't have to make up the rock-and-roll lifestyle as they went along. Plenty of bands—Aerosmith, Van Halen, Zeppelin, Sabbath, to name but a very few—had turned the sex-drugs-and-rock-and-roll blueprint into elaborate constructions long before they came of age. Their exploits were legend. By the time Pantera hit the road, they knew how they were supposed to act onstage and off. You got loaded. You trashed hotel rooms. You had a girl in every city. Those were the rules, and Pantera tried to play by them. *Tried* being the operative word.

"The guys, they would always be, like, 'We're rockers. We need to act like it,'" Tommy Snellings says.

First thing they'd do when they walked into a hotel room was turn all the lampshades crooked and the pictures crooked. Jump all over the beds. But they wouldn't do anything that cost money because, you know, they didn't have the money to fix it, right? Well, this one particular time, we were playing with the Leather Angels, this all-girl heavy metal band. Their manager was just a wild man. He was sitting by the door, and he ripped off the arms of this chair—it was, like, a wooden chair. And he beat the door or something. He messed up the door. We tried to get out before they found out. Well, we didn't quite make it out of the parking lot. There was this ol' cowboy that, the night before, we'd given him a ride. He was too drunk, so Darrell and I gave him a ride back to Gainesville—because that was the closest Jack in the Box open at two in the morning. So, anyway, we didn't have the money and they weren't going to let us go. They called the police and everything. Well, this guy comes up to get his truck. He found out what kind of trouble we're in. He bought one of our little amps, and it was such a piece of shit. But it was Pantera and he was really hyped about it. He paid the two hundred dollars or whatever we needed and he got the amp. That's how we got out of that.

As for the other lessons in the school of rock, the band only fared marginally better. "Darrell and Vince were so antidrug," Snellings says. "Especially Vince. Rex and I would smoke pot and they'd get really ticked off."

Rick E. Warden believes this was a front—at least where Darrell was concerned. Vince? That was different.

"I always thought of Vince as the big brother, almost daddy type," Warden says.

Like, "Hey, be cool around Vince." We don't want Vince to bust us, you know? I assure you, though, that Darrell smoked pot, pretty much on a daily basis, from sixteen, seventeen on. But he respected his career, and the talent he had, so he wouldn't out himself in too peculiar of a situation where he would get in trouble. How he was around other people, there might have been kind of two sides of Darrell, to some extent, back in the earlier days, because of him protecting himself from getting into trouble. I would say that that wouldn't fall in the category of being two-faced, if that's the way he was with some other people. That was just trying to play it smart and protect the talent.

Darrell, in fact, had enough of a reputation that he'd already earned his famous nickname: Dimebag.

"All he would ever carry on him was a dime bag," Warden says. "He wouldn't let you *give* him more than that. He'd be, like, 'No, dude, I don't want to have any more than what I can get rid of today. I don't want to get caught.' So he was always aware that— you know, his career was so important, he wasn't going to jeopardize it. That's why he would never take more than a dime bag—and I mean we're talking about people *giving* him the stuff."

Drinking was a completely different animal. No one was shy about knocking back a couple of cold ones. "We used to drink Coors Light," Glaze says. "That was water [to us]. Drinking age was eighteen back then, and that's what we drank. But nobody did anything except that. We were just out of high school. None of that other stuff was around. We were mostly goody two-shoes." Indeed, by the standards Darrell would later set, when he gulped his signature "black tooth grins" by the dozen and went through life with a mostly permanent buzz, those teenage road trips barely qualified as dabbling. There might be a bottle of Jack Daniels or Jose Cuervo around, but more often than not, there wasn't.

When it came to sex, there were groupies, occasionally, but the band all had regular girlfriends (and soon enough, Glaze had a wife), so even that was half-hearted. "We went back to Texarkana so often, everybody had a girlfriend they'd see," Snellings says. "Darrell and Rex and Vince and Terry, we were all sitting over at the Abbotts' house one day, and all the girls we knew from up there came down here. That was the end of that. The guys threw a frigging fit."

But Texarkana was the exception. Pantera wasn't a band that appealed much to the fairer sex. "It was such a *guy* band," Glaze says, laughing. "We were really good, but man, we never had any girls come to see us. It was always, like, *guys*. I wish we'd have had chicks come to see us. And the ones that did were kind of scary."

PANTERA WASN'T a marauding band of heavy metal pirates, though they might show up to a gig dressed that way. They were fairly nice, normal guys who liked playing music, practical jokes, and dress-up. Snellings digs out a photo of Darrell running around the parking lot of a motel brandishing a toy sword, wearing only red briefs and a kid's gladiator costume, complete with fake chain mail, shield, and helmet. "We would go out and they would say, 'We've gotta find some new shit for tonight,'" Snellings says. "So we'd go out to the Wal-Mart or K-Mart or whatever, and they'd buy all these toys."

One can see in that photo what everyone says anyway: Darrell was the ringleader, the instigator, the first into battle. He'd do anything for a laugh, even if that meant one person definitely wouldn't be sharing in the fun. Like, say, Dusty Osbourne, a Pantera crew member who woke up one morning after a gig in

Sherman to find Darrell "standing over him, pissing all over him," Snellings says. "Man, he was so pissed off." Beyond that, they drank, but that wasn't exactly scandalous, other than the sight of a fifteen-year-old Darrell being fed beer bongs. It wasn't *Hammer of the Gods*—though Darrell's golden shower attack on Osbourne comes close to John Bonham's shitting-in-a-purse audacity. It was more like a traveling high school kegger.

Pantera played just about anywhere they could get on a bill. Nowheresville towns like Muenster (where they played at the Ranch) and Denison (Electric Company) were regulars on the itinerary. They played Village Square in Texarkana at least once a month. There was the Ritz and Matley's in Dallas, and the Aragon Danceland, Savvy's, Roxz, and Joe's Garage in Fort Worth; Rock Haven, better known as "Roach Haven," in Grand Prairie. An air force base in Wichita Falls, where a combination of bare feet, a metal dance floor, and an electrical short ended up shocking Snellings. They played on the shore of Eagle Mountain Lake at Twin Points Resort, where it was so hot they had to ditch the spandex and play in shorts. They played house parties, backyard beer busts, and generator parties out in the middle of nowhere, and they managed to score opening slots for the likes of Night Ranger, Dokken, Quiet Riot, and Nazareth. They even played Nolan High School's prom in 1983. They weren't particular.

Before the band could afford a van, they ruined the engines of five of Jerry's cars and two of Carolyn's hauling their gear around the state. "We were playing every week," Glaze says. "We would do a cycle. We would play Dallas, we'd play Houston, we'd play Wichita Falls—we'd play all of those places, and then we would rotate it. We were living at home, playing these clubs, and acting like maniacs. . . . There were some rough places. We pulled into Matley's one day to load in, and there was a chalk outline of a body right there on the sidewalk. It was pretty weird."

One constant remained no matter where they played: Darrell was unquestionably the star of the group. A flyer for a New Year's Eve show at Village Square in Texarkana says it simply enough: Darrell's name and résumé ("Two-time winner of the Q102 & KZEW GUITAR CONTESTS") literally overshadows his bandmates, placed above them like an umbrella in double the point size.

"They had the total poseur hair and all that, and they played Van Halen and all of the poseur rock of the day," says Dale Brock. He first saw the band in Wichita Falls when he was seventeen, when his tastes ran toward punk rock. Brock came around eventually; the band had stopped playing covers and he was managing a club where they were regulars, onstage and off. "Dime was the full-blown Eddie Van Halen wannabe who had his licks down to a tee. Did 'Eruption' live, before everybody else did it. It was just a poseur metal cover band with a *smokin'*, amazing, blow-everybody-away, almost-little-kid guitar player. He looked like a little kid, but he ripped just like he always did."

There was one other constant at almost all of those venues: Darrell had to be accompanied by Jerry or Carolyn, or else he couldn't get inside. He was too young. But that was never really a problem. Carolyn came out to every local show her boys played anyway, and Jerry went on the road with the band, as manager, soundman, father, and whatever else he needed to be. "He was behind us," Glaze says. "He was *so* behind Vince and Darrell. He was wonderful. He didn't mind that, in Houston, we'd play five, six sets. He didn't freak out that it was already late and there would be five more tunes to go. It was no big deal."

"Here's this mid-forties guy going to, you know, Joe's Garage," says Jerry Hudson. "Before you knew it, he just blended in. They had the nickname 'Eld'n' for him, you know. But he was all for it. He loved it. I think it gave him a new youth, basically. And of course, Darrell, he'd have had to wait another three years to even start playing in clubs if Daddy hadn't been there."

Just because his dad was always around didn't mean Darrell didn't partake in what nightclubs have to offer.

"In Texas, if you're kicking ass up there on that stage, people send you shots to show their appreciation," Darrell said. "So, what do you do? Turn the shot down and piss off some big-assed dude and his buds? Not in Texas, bro! You grab the thing, say 'thanks,' down the thing, and go with it."

JERRY ABBOTT served a much more vital role in Pantera than merely allowing Darrell access to the stage. For one thing, he gave the band access to a recording studio. "We could go in and record whenever no one was in the studio," Glaze says. "So that was, like, a big moment. It taught us all to be comfortable in that moment, instead of being in awe of it."

It paid off: Less than a year into its career, when other bands were still trying (and more often than not, failing) to get their shit together, Pantera released its debut album, *Metal Magic*, a ten-song disc recorded by Jerry and released on his newly cre- ated label, also called Metal Magic. Jerry's importance to the band at that time was not lost on anyone, and sifting through the accumulated bric-a-brac of that era, it's somewhat difficult to see how it could have been. In one of the flyers advertising *Metal Magic*'s release, his name is listed right alongside the band's, in the exact same font and type size, as though he was another member of the group. But that billing seems, if not fair, then certainly close enough, since he contributed enough to the band (including a few lyrics here and there) to classify him as a sort of fifth member of Pantera. That would become a problem later. It wasn't yet.

A review of *Metal Magic* in the May 1983 issue of *Heavy Metal Times* illustrates how much Pantera's sound changed over the years. "*Metal Magic* may be considered a well-balanced collection of rock/metal rather than the average slice your face off cuts," it reads, before pointing out that "Biggest Part of Me," the album's lone ballad, "could very well put Pantera across to the top 40 venues as well as the rock and roll public."[7] In the November 1983 issue of *Buddy*, another review points out (rather obliquely) how little changed, insofar as Darrell already had a distinct style: "The solos tend to be asymmetrical in that the old theory of musical thought consisting of statements alternating with appropriate responses is ignored and replaced by authoritative delivery of the player's own concept of what should happen."[8]

To put it more plainly: Darrell Abbott could play.

3

FLAMING YOUTH

Brothers from Another Mother

"We few, we lucky few,
we band of brothers."

WILLIAM SHAKESPEARE

Typically, brothers are exactly the same yet completely different. Such was the case with Vincent Paul and Darrell Lance Abbott. Vince took after his old man (sharing his business savvy and studio acumen), while Darrell was obviously his mother's son (inheriting her warm manner and enthusiasm for life)—but they both lived with their mother well after they had the means to do otherwise. They were in the same band, but Darrell cared most about playing his guitar, playing the shows, and having a good time before and after; Vince, on the other hand, was more interested in the production side, as well as the business. Darrell was the best friend of everyone he ever met; Vince was more guarded, and more selective when choosing his confidants. They looked a lot alike, even though, for most of their time together, Darrell was skinnier than a guitar neck and Vince was thick like a kick drum. They were both naturally talented, but Darrell seemed to have more direct access to his genetic gift. They played different instruments, but that only helped them strive to reach their shared goal: being Van Halen. In other words, they were exactly the same and completely different.

So, too, were Buddy and Ken Webster—the former rechristened (by himself) as Buddy Blaze; the latter dubbed (by Darrell) Pyro. They were both gifted when it came to working with tools and technical matters; Buddy used his skills to build and customize guitars, while Ken was a whiz at rigging stage explosions, as well as skilled with lighting and sound equipment. Buddy was always in bands; Ken was a clean-cut member of the U.S. Air Force. They don't sound much alike, but both do a note-perfect imitation of Darrell—it's actually the same impression, down to the last inflection. Buddy never left the music business; Ken got out early and never went back.

In the early days of Pantera, each pair of brothers found their opposite number in the other set. Darrell gravitated toward Buddy because of their mutual love of guitars. Vince saw in Ken someone who could help Pantera be an arena band even while the group was still working the club circuit. For a time, the Abbotts' story was inextricably linked with the Websters', even though history, such that it is, acknowledges only one side of the partnership of two sets of brothers, close in different ways, bound not only by blood, but by sweat and tears, surely, and beers, definitely. Their mothers were best friends, double dating, working together at Oil States (manufacturing parts for oil and gas drilling and production), sharing tables at gigs. Together, they were the "Pantera mamas," as Buddy and Ken's mother, Kitty Webster, remembers, and that cements them together forever.

"The thing is, Carolyn and Darrell were like family to us," Buddy Blaze says. "We loved the shit out of them. And we *liked* Vince." He laughs.

> We would do holidays together. They would play my birthday parties. I had two birthday parties at my house that Pantera played in my living room. That was when Terry was still in the band. And sure enough, food fights and all kinds of other shit would commence. It was a lot of fun. My mom and dad hung out with Carolyn and her boyfriend. They went out drinking all the time. Carolyn, my mom, and my wife and I went out to see Pantera more times than I can ever remember. We would do Christmas and Thanksgiving at each other's houses. Shit like that. We did a lot together. We were very, very close.

The friendship between the two women faded over time, as circumstance inevitably built one barrier, then another. But the ghost of it remains, and always will. Those times are trapped in amber—or, as the case may be, amber-colored liquid. The relationship between the sets of brothers fared better, even though those same barriers existed. The difference is, the mothers were involved in the war—and taking a band from nowhere clubs to arenas is a kind of military campaign, a metaphor that rings even truer when the band in question is armed with such a destructive arsenal. But the two sets of brothers were on the front lines. Even though they all eventually left the foxhole, the bond formed was indelible, unshakable, unknowable by everyone except those that were there. That's why, though Buddy and Ken hadn't seen Darrell for several years before his murder, it was as though they lost a brother just the same. That's why, though Ken hadn't been around him on a daily basis for almost two decades, he could do an impression of Darrell that conjures his voice precisely.

"You know, they almost grew up together, you can almost say, before they became men," Kitty says.

In each case, the Websters' introduction to Darrell doesn't have the makings of history, even the history of a heavy metal band—or, at least, it doesn't seem to initially. But in the telling, there is the jolt of possibility, as the future unfolds like scenes from a movie. They flocked to the brothers and their band independently, for their own reasons, so it is something like fate that they both ended up with Pantera.

KEN WEBSTER was the first brother to enter the Abbotts' world. He recalls:

A friend of mine and I saw a little flyer on a telephone pole about an outdoor concert. It was thrown by this guy named Jerry Warden. He used to do a whole lot of these outdoor metal gigs. He had a lot of friends in different bands, and he'd get them together, mostly local bands. They'd run generators and bring kegs of beer to the country somewhere. This was in south Arlington. I went out to watch it and was just sitting out in the field. The first band came on. They were all right and everything.

Then Pantera came on and, well, they sounded excellent, but the sound system really sucked. It just sounded horrible. It mostly belonged to Jerry Warden. Now, I'm an air force guy and I've got short hair; I'm really the outcast of them all. I go up to him and say, "You know what? I can fix that. I can get your speakers and your sound system and all that stuff working like it should." He took my number down and called me a day or two later and told me where he lived in Arlington. I went to his house. I picked up some of the pieces and started rebuilding the mixing board. I reconed a bunch of the speakers and everything else. I just briefly talked to the guys in the band.

Warden did another outdoor gig with Pantera. I set up the sound and everything, and it just kicked ass. It was day-and-night difference. And Darrell just blew me away. The guy was just unbelievable—little braces and big ol' 'fro hair and he was skinny as can be. The guy was just awesome. They were doing some Van Halen tunes and stuff like that. So I start talking to them. I said, "You know, I could do a little more. I could rig up some lights for you and things like that."

Before long, Webster had "Ken-gineered" (as he used to say) an elaborate stage presentation for Pantera. The setup rivaled that of most arena bands, even though Webster, for the most part, made it up as he went along, using a bit of homespun ingenuity and pulling a few five-finger discounts along the way. That job gave Darrell the idea for his not terribly imaginative but absolutely appropriate nickname for Webster: Pyro.

"Basically, it was just all out of my head," Webster says.

While I was in the air force, I used to go to the field maintenance squadron and talk the guys into giving me a bunch of lights and stuff they use on the B-52 aircraft. I took some of these 28-volt lights and rigged them to work into the house voltage, but they were landing lights for the B-52, so you can imagine how strong these things are. Had four of those—two on each side. Had the bomb-bay door lights that were real small but they were strong beam lights; I set those up above the drum riser. Set up strobes and all that kind of stuff. I made a little digital sequencer and sequenced lights. They would go out and steal floodlights from lawns. We put 'em all in a row below the drum riser. Then I said, "You know what? We've got to do some fire." . . . I started going down to sporting goods places when you could buy gunpowder. You can't do it anymore, but I used to go down and buy pounds of gunpowder—blue dot and green dot and red dot shotgun powder. And then black powder, like you use for smoke. I'd go down to the army-navy surplus and buy pieces of old military shells to use them for the flash pots and things like that. I wired them up to a rig; I would use the filaments off of flash photography bulbs on the end of wires and run juice through them on this little switchboard that I made. We'd set off explosions and fireballs all over the place. We had a few incidents. It wasn't Great White bad, but it could have been.

He laughs, grimly referring to the tragic fire at the Station House nightclub in Providence, Rhode Island.

"We had a lot of close calls," he continues. "The guys in the band, I'd tell them where it is and when it's gonna go, and be careful, you know? I've seen flames just curl around Darrell. I mean, *curl around* him. But it was, like, this guy—he's impervious." He laughs again, bigger this time.

Webster had more of a relationship with Vince initially, since Vince concerned himself more with the mechanics of becoming a successful band than Darrell did, a mind-set that appreciated Webster's technical prowess and considered how it could further Pantera's career. But Webster was, inevitably, drawn to Darrell. It was hard not to be. In those days, Darrell was already a really good guitarist, though he still had things to learn about his instrument. His personality didn't seem to require much improvement. Everything about him was already in place.

"You never saw him really down or out," Webster says.

He was always upbeat about everything. If things were going wrong, and people were getting pissed off, and the sound wasn't right, he was just, like, "Dude, dude, it's cool." And he'd just go on. He *never* let things get him down. For such a young person to be so positive about life and so professional at what he did, it's pretty amazing. You got your artists, you know, people that can paint and make a *Mona Lisa*. This guy, he could pick up a guitar and paint his own *Mona Lisa*. I always knew. We just *knew* he was destined for greatness. There was just no doubt about it. I mean, yeah, Rex is an OK bass player and Terry Glaze is a good Van Halen singer. I'm not going to take anything away from them. And Vince is a hell of a drummer. That son of a bitch can get down. But Darrell, there's nobody like Darrell. If he'd have been with any other band, he'd have been the difference.

In those early years, Webster was, in many ways, the crucial difference. He gave Pantera something that allowed the band to stand out amid a sea of bands also covering Van Halen, Def Leppard, and Judas Priest. With Webster behind his "Ken-gineered" sequencer, the group brought an arena-level lights-and-pyrotechnics spectacle to the club circuit, as well as a sense of professionalism rarely seen on those kinds of stages.

Even so, after about two years, "I had to finally just say, 'Guys, I can't do it anymore,'" Webster recalls.

Before he quit, Webster had gained enough from his experience with Darrell and the band that he never regretted his decision. He left with a new handle, a new little brother, and a new approach to life.

Every time I saw Darrell after that, it was just like yesterday. He was always the same guy and just full of love. The guy was nothing but good, always approachable. It didn't matter who it was. He used to go around and talk to the kids in high schools and stuff, drive around the high schools, raise hell. . . . He never did anything to hurt anybody deliberately. He never grew up. And nobody would want him to, you know?

. . . Vince was never a very kind, approachable person. I mean he was OK when they were first starting out. Between him and his brother, they were day and night. It's pretty much like my brother and me. I think that's just the natural way of being in a family. Darrell, everybody wanted to be around that boy. Vince, you know, you could take him or leave him. . . .

He laughs.

. . . But Vince was definitely a driving force. He was the meat and potatoes of the business. He was, like, "We're going to go after it big." He has a lot of his dad in him. Darrell, he was all out for the fun. Yeah, I'm sure he liked the money and whatever, the glory and all that. But that was all coming after the fun. You could tell his heart was in it every time. I'm sure Rex's and Vince's were, too. But Darrell, it just seemed like that was what he was all about.

That's what Darrell taught me. Here I am, an older guy in the air force and everything else, and this guy has taught me more in that little time I knew him than most people I know. And it was all about life, and living it. That boy did it.

THOUGH HIS brother was already working with Pantera, and his mom worked with Carolyn Abbott, Buddy Blaze resisted early invites to check out the band. Mainly because those invites were coming from the mother of two of the band members. He tended to see things like that as red flags.

"I looked at Darrell as just some young kid," Blaze says.

Another one of those kids, you know, that Mom says, "My kid plays guitar," and you go, "Oh, Christ." And then you go see this kid, and you go, "Wait a minute. No, this guy really does play." He was amazing. The second time I saw him—because the first time, you know, they were doing a twenty-, thirty-minute set opening up for a band called Savvy. The second time I saw them was at Aragon, where they were doing, like, three sets, so they threw in some of their own stuff, and Darrell put a solo in the middle of it. That changed everything. That's when I could see that this kid really had something. Darrell and I hit it off right away. After that, you know, he'd be calling me up and saying, "Man, we're playing the Aragon Danceland. We need some people to come out. Y'all gonna come out?" You have to remember, this is a ninety-pound fifteen-year-old kid at that time. I mean, the guitar dwarfed him.

Blaze could see right away that Darrell's talent dwarfed everyone else's. "The kid when he was fifteen, sixteen years old had a better feel of the groove and blues than guys that had been playing for 30 years," he says.

He had the tone—and he was playing through crap gear. That's one of the things that made me laugh. He'd put a Marshall stack behind him—he was using one of the 412s—but he had, like, this solid-state Yamaha amp pushing it, one of his dad's studio amps. Like a totally generic, flavorless amp. And he sounded *that amazing* playing through crap. When he got the Randall—a lot of people bag him about the Randalls—but, God, did you hear him? He just took a stock Randall and kicked your ass with it. He was amazing. The kid had the goods. He was so ridiculously good that it didn't make you want to quit, because he was so good that you knew no other human was going to catch him.

So all I had to do was be better than the other 99 percent. I've done stuff with the biggest guys in the world. But I've never, to this day, seen anybody better, especially at his age. What he was doing as a teenager was insane.

Blaze was already in his early twenties when they met, so he quickly developed a big-brother relationship with the fifteen-year-old Darrell, a much different dynamic than the one shared by Darrell and Pyro. "Darrell and I were friends and I loaned him gear and drove him to gigs," Blaze says. "But I never worked for Darrell." He couldn't teach Darrell much about playing guitar that Darrell didn't already know, but Blaze did have plenty of other guitar-related nuggets of wisdom that he could impart. How was taken care of, so they worked on the who, what, where, when, and why. It was the start of a conversation that would continue for the next twenty years.

Blaze had been trying to make a name for himself by playing guitars; *building* guitars was where his true talent lay. "I got kind of famous as a guitar builder more by default and by accident," Blaze says, "because I never really could buy a guitar that pleased me. As I would see a guitar, I would build one and buy another one. I was kind of accumulating guitars. People would play the ones that I built and lose their minds." The guys in Lee Greenwood's band started playing Blaze's guitars, as did Vivian Campbell (who played with Dio, Whitesnake, and Def Leppard) and others. His skills eventually became so in demand, he left Arlington to work for Kramer Guitars in 1987.

His relationship with Darrell was far from over. They didn't live in the same city anymore, but Darrell would need Buddy more than ever in the next few years—as a friend, and as someone in the guitar business.

"I got Darrell his first national interview with a guitar magazine," Blaze says.

I arranged for the guy from *Guitar World* to come out and see Darrell. When I was head of the biggest guitar company, basically, in America, which was Kramer at the time, we'd have meetings about what artists are we going to go after, you know, that we don't already have (and we had most). I just said the best guy out there—and this was before anybody knew who Darrell was—I said the best guy out there is this teenage, snot-nose kid in Arlington, Texas. He was Diamond Darrell Lance at the time. I said Darrell Abbott is the guy. We already had Van Halen. And I said, there isn't one guy we got that, in the long run, is going to be what this kid could be, but he plays Dean MLs and I don't see us making copies of those guitars. And Darrell would insist that we basically made copies of those guitars. So then you start thinking about, "Next!"

I was dealing with some pretty huge acts. In my heart, and especially when I got out and was really in the center—because I had everybody and their dog sending me tapes and things like that; everybody wanted an endorsement and all that—nothing came close.

4

RIGHT ON THE EDGE

Rita Haney, *Ride the Lightning,* and Philip Anselmo

"Well, it looks like I finally found some-one who likes to play as rough as I do."

RAVEN,
Streets of Fire

In 1984, Pantera continued to be, as Terry Glaze says, a "guy band." There was at least one girl who came to see Pantera. Specifically, she came to see Darrell. Her name was Rita Haney, and Darrell had known her since the third grade. Because her mother worked nights, Rita spent her postschool afternoons at the home of her aunt, who happened to live in the same neighborhood as the Abbotts. Rita and Darrell would hang out often, doing what eight-year-olds do. Mostly that entailed riding their bikes to an abandoned housing development known by the kids in the area as "the bike trails"; on their first ride together, she pushed Darrell off his bike. Again, doing what eight-year-olds do. They got over that and became best friends. They had their first concert experience together a few years later, going to see—of course—KISS in 1979.

"I remember he almost cried because he missed Gene Simmons breathing fire," Rita remembered in VH1's *Behind the Music* episode on Pantera, "because some old lady in the back behind us was all stoned, put her cigarette out in his hair."

They fell out of touch soon after. Rita stopped hanging out at her aunt's house, and she and Darrell lived in different parts of town. Music would bring them back together a couple of years later. Both fans of hard rock and heavy metal, they wound up at the same shows and partied with the same crowd. They renewed their friendship, and Rita became a staple at Pantera shows. But it was "just friends" for a long time. In fact, Rita regularly set up Darrell on dates with her girlfriends.

The situation would change one late night after a Pantera gig in 1984, when Darrell gave Rita a ride home. Playing guitar was Darrell's first love, and it was probably his truest. In Rita, though, he had found another love, one that would last almost as long. He didn't have to look very hard to find it. It was right there in the front seat.

"He tried to kiss me, and I was, like, 'Weird, but I think I like you, too,'" Rita told *Metal Edge* magazine in July 2006. They officially became a couple on December 4, at a Malice show. "And we were together from then on."[9]

TERRY GLAZE recalls the members of Pantera being rock stars, at least in their little corner of the world. They were the stereotypical big-fish–small-pond band. How big? Rhonda and Timmy Riley, regulars at Pantera gigs at Joe's Garage, named their daughter Pantera Frances Lynn Riley, which is simultaneously awesome and tragic. If nothing else, it speaks to the level of dedication Pantera inspired.

The group hustled to maintain that devotion, playing as much as seven nights a week and recording at Pantego when they could. The latter resulted in two more albums, 1984's *Projects in the Jungle* and 1985's *I Am the Night*. Like *Metal Magic*, both discs again showed that Pantera could deliver well-balanced collections of rock/metal and that Darrell already had a strong sense of who he was as a guitar player. But they didn't do much else. While each was better than the last, neither could be described as groundbreaking or even stellar examples of the prevailing style at the time. They are patchwork, cobbled together from pieces of early Van Halen, *Shout at the Devil*–era Mötley Crüe, and about a dozen other things. On songs like "Forever Tonight" (off *I Am the Night*), you can even hear a bit of what Bon Jovi arrived at around the same time, thanks to Terry Glaze's pop influence.

Though Jerry Abbott's production is murky on all three albums, one thing already shines: Darrell. His playing isn't inventive, and it doesn't much resemble his latter-day style. What it lacks in originality is made up for by his impressive facility with his instrument. You can hear why he wowed everyone who happened upon him. His playing had the agility and the assurance of a man twice his age.

Still, as good as Darrell was with his guitar, and as hard as Pantera worked as a band, there was something holding them back from finding an audience beyond Joe's Garage. Though they might not have known it at the time, at least consciously, it's plain to see now. For them to succeed, someone in the band had to become "the Pete Best of Pantera," as Buddy Blaze puts it.

The path they were on at the time may very well have landed Pantera a recording contract. It wouldn't have taken them much beyond that. The odds are they would have quickly ended up back where they started, and they probably wouldn't have received a second chance; few bands do. Pantera was good at what it did, but what it did was on the way out. No one could see the end of hair metal coming. It was fast approaching all the same.

I Am the Night, for the most part just another well-balanced collection of rock/metal, did mark a shift within the band, a subtle change, probably imperceptible at the time. It wasn't a left turn so much as a blinker signaling that a turn was coming. Darrell and Vince had long been inspired by new sounds they were hearing in heavy metal's underground, digging on the outrageous amounts of speed and volume on records that mixed punk's aggression with metal's chops. They began immersing themselves in the music of Metallica, Slayer, and other American bands that had a heavier, faster take on the genre. Darrell would do what he used to when he was sitting on the floor of Pantego Studio watching Bugs Henderson and Ricky Lynn Gregg record with his father, studying the riffs until he figured them out enough to try them on his own, then dicking around with them in his bedroom until he came up with something new.

Darrell had seen the light, but it was his friend Rick E. Warden who had his finger on the switch. Warden found religion in the early 1990s, becoming a born-again Christian just as Pantera was becoming a success. Obviously, it changed his life. But before that happened, he helped Darrell find something that would change the young guitarist's life: Metallica.

Warden met Darrell not long after he had been banned from entering any more guitar contests. Darrell invited him to a keg party where Pantera was playing. Darrell was fifteen, and Warden was a year older. Warden had already seen more than his fair share of bands. He went to his first concert when he was twelve. It was a Foghat gig, though Warden might have remembered it as a Judas Priest show if his older brother, Jerry (the same Jerry Warden who later booked Pantera at a few of his generator parties), hadn't made them late. He went to the first Texxas Jam at the Cotton Bowl in 1978.

Which is to say that Warden had plenty to compare Darrell to when he turned up at that keg party. While he was impressed by Pantera's usual mix of covers, it was when they broke out an original, "Rock Out," that he knew he was seeing something special. "Being a big-time guitar freak, I noticed right away that Darrell definitely had the touch, you know?" Warden says. "He had *it*. He happened to be a real cool kid, too, so we just hit it off and became buddies."

Since they had both sold their souls for rock and roll, it's likely Warden would have run into Darrell at some point, even if he hadn't accepted that party invite. Later on, he became the manager of Pipe Dreams, a head shop that doubled as a record store; it was where everyone went to pick up the latest metal al-nity radio station. He took over the Saturday night twelve-to-two metal show from his brother, who had been kicked off the air. "Being the squirrelly little brother that I was, I went right up and said, 'Hey, I'll do it,'" Warden says. "Kind of made my brother mad, because he was, like, hey, if they wouldn't have had a replacement, they would have had to come crawling back and begged me to do the show."

Darrell helped Warden out at both of his jobs, recording commercials for Pipe Dreams and doing show intros for KNON. "We just did them there at his house," Warden says. "Squealing tires in the driveway and smashing bottles, you know, recording it and putting it all together." They became closer during those times than at Pantera gigs and the inevitable after-parties. Working at the record store and the radio station also gave Warden a chance to introduce Darrell—and everyone else he knew—to Metallica.

I'm the first one that I know, period, that knew anything about Metallica, much less had a Metallica song that I was going around and playing for everybody: "Hit the Lights." *Dude, check out this, man—it's Metallica.* It had Dave Mustaine on guitar and James Hetfield singing. [Warden had first heard the song on the Metal Blade records compilation *Metal Massacre.*] Then when the *Kill 'Em All* album came out [in 1983], obviously I jumped right on that, and it blew us all away because it was smoking. It was some of the heaviest, most aggressive, pure metal, period. Darrell was blown away. We all were. It was a manifestation of everything that we wanted to hear in music at the time. No question about it. *Kill 'Em All* is probably the single most vital album to all of new American heavy metal music.

Vital though it was, there wasn't much of a market for what Metallica was doing then, at least not in the Dallas–Fort Worth area. A band like Pantera could maybe get away with a cover or two here and there, but for the most part, the club crowds wanted what they heard on the radio, or songs that sounded similar. "Even at that point, Pantera was already playing Sherman, Texas; Norman, Oklahoma; down in Houston; all over Dallas–Fort Worth," Warden says. "But in order to play those clubs, even though Darrell was into heavier stuff, they still had to play a lot of goofy stuff, mixing Iron Maiden songs in with Loverboy. Definitely some Van Halen. They played 'Jump,' and Terry Glaze would play keyboards."

Metallica didn't play Dallas or Fort Worth while touring behind *Kill 'Em All*, a package show with New Wave of British Heavy Metal band Raven (supporting its third album, *All for One*) that they called, in a synergistic move, the "Kill 'Em All for One Tour." Metallica instead booked shows in Texarkana and Tyler. Warden made the trip to Texarkana and ended up talking about shared musical tastes with Hetfield and drummer Lars Ulrich, a conversation they continued after Metallica played in Tyler.

"It wasn't just cool for us. It was cool for James and Lars, you know, to meet these guys from Texas that were into all the same stuff they were into. You just didn't run into that many people that were like that." Warden told Hetfield and Ulrich about his friend Darrell and his band, Pantera. "I'm, like, 'They play some poseur stuff, but you have to understand it's just the way it is here in Texas.'"

That was beginning to change—or, at least, Darrell's resolve to make it change was becoming steelier whenever he listened to Metallica's second album, 1984's *Ride the Lightning*, which was quite a bit.

"Dude, Darrell *loved* the *Ride the Lightning* album," Warden says.

> I mean, that was like the all-time—at the time it was just the best thing. There was nothing else out there that was even comparable to being as good as *Ride the Lightning*. Darrell used to come over to my house. By this time, I had a house and had a, you know, a rockin' stereo. We had a PA system set up in the living room, and we had bands jamming in there all the time and stuff. Darrell would come over, and we'd get a little loose and stuff, and dude, he would just be, like, "Put on that *Ride the Lightning* again." "Dude, we just listened to it." I remember specifically telling him, "Here, take the album home with you and listen to it, man." That's all he wanted to listen to, over and over again.

Darrell kept listening to *Ride the Lightning*, and Warden kept talking about him when Metallica came back to Texas to promote the album. Warden's friend Rita Haney—not yet Darrell's girlfriend—helped him get some more alone time with the band. According to Warden, Haney hooked up with Ulrich on the *Ride the Lightning* tour, getting an invitation from the drummer to visit him while Metallica was in Arizona. (Haney would say she merely became friends with Ulrich and Hetfield.) She, in turn, asked Warden if he wanted to make the trip with her. "I'm, like, 'I'm on my way. Let's go,'" Warden laughs. When it was all said and done, Warden had succeeded in intriguing Hetfield and Ulrich. Soon, the duo would be headed to Texas, courtesy of two free round-trip tickets Haney had received after she was bumped off a flight.

"Metallica was finished with the *Ride the Lightning* tour," Warden says, "and they called and said, 'Hey, where's that Darrell Abbott guy? We want to check him out.' And I'm, like, OK. So we called Darrell, we called Pantera, and we set up the meeting and for [Pantera] to play up at Savvy's. They ended up playing up there at Savvy's, man, it was at least three nights in a row, maybe five. They would go up there and play gigs at Savvy's and then come home and play in the house and party all night."

The party was just about over for Terry Glaze.

"That was a totally different game all of a sudden," Buddy Blaze says. "And that's really where Terry wouldn't fit in. Darrell would actually get up and sing the heavier kind of stuff"—the band did a great version of Metallica's "Seek and Destroy" as a trio, with Darrell handling the vocals—"but that wasn't Terry. That was definitely a different ballgame."

"On our third record, they were going in that direction, and I didn't want to do that," Glaze says. "I didn't want to play guitar-based music; I wanted to play song-based music. That's why I always thought, you know, it worked good, because with Darrell's music and my lyrics—the combination, we kind of added something, made something new. I didn't want to go that heavy. I didn't like it as well if the guitar was the main thing, like the Metallica songs."

Less than a year after the release of *I Am the Night*, Glaze didn't have a say in the matter anymore. He left Pantera in the spring of 1986. But it wasn't only philosophical differences over the direction of the band that resulted in Glaze's departure. It had to do, like so many disputes in the music business, with money.

Jerry Abbott had been Pantera's manager from the beginning. There was nothing on paper, but there didn't really need to be, not as long as the boys were playing places like the Aragon Danceland and high school proms. Even then, Jerry's presence was a sticky subject, since it meant Glaze and Brown were always outvoted three to two. "The Abbotts never split votes," Glaze says, "so what the Abbotts said is what happened." When Pantera started to reach different levels of success, a sticky subject turned into a sticking point. Jerry Abbott had put a lot of time and money into Pantera, buying the band a PA system, recording all the albums, releasing them on his own label, traveling with the group. With bigger paydays on the horizon, he made a move to protect his investment and had a proper management contract drawn up.

"I had an attorney look at it, and I was advised, *do not sign this*," Glaze says. "I said no, and I was basically told, 'You sign this contract or you're out.' I have a letter at home. I just felt like I couldn't have him as my manager when he was their dad. He was always going to be on their side, and I didn't feel comfortable with that. That's the nicest way I can put it; I could say lots of other things. But I'd probably do the same thing if it was my kid."

Glaze's departure from Pantera turned out to be the right move for all involved. Glaze formed a new band, Lord Tracy (originally called Tracy Lords), that scored a major-label deal before Pantera did, releasing *Deaf Gods of Babylon* on UNI/MCA in 1989. With Glaze gone, Darrell was free to fully develop his boozy, bluesy, bruising take on metal, which would make over Pantera into cowboys from hell and him into King Dime.

If Glaze had signed the management contract, "Pantera would in no way have become what they became," Buddy Blaze says.

If they did succeed, with that being one of the criteria, you would have to look at it as, you know, they would have been a competing hair band, the way I see it. I really don't understand how they would have not just disappeared, other than Darrell being an amazing guitar player. To me, it would have just been a vehicle for Darrell to get a real gig. And that's not putting Terry down at all. To me, it was inevitable that Darrell was going to be a star. It was inevitable; he was too good to be denied. My instinct, my heart tells me Pantera would have never been as big if Terry was in it. I honestly don't think so.

Pantera didn't find someone to replace Terry Glaze right away, nor did they immediately drop the glam look. They tried out a couple of new singers—Matt L'Amour and David Peacock—but neither stayed around long. Even Glaze came back and played a show at Savvy's with them. "It was really good," he says, "but I didn't want to go back to the way it was."

The man who had preceded Glaze in Pantera, Donny Hart, came back, too.

"To be honest with you, Donny Hart looked like he was going to be the real candidate," Warden says. "Donny Hart was the one that, out of those three, stood the best chance. The problem with

Donny Hart was that his singing style was more in the vein of, like, a Geoff Tate. He was a good singer, a real good singer; he could hit those Queensryche Geoff Tate notes all day."

It was a frustrating time for Warden and other Pantera fans. "It was really a situation where, you know, who was the person? Who was going to do it?" Warden says.

They obviously knew that they had to find a singer. They knew that they had a challenge ahead of them. But it wasn't, on their part, a down-and-out, bummed-out time. For the rest of us, I can say for myself personally, yeah, it was a bit of a bummer. Because you're going, "I've seen Eddie Van Halen. I've seen Randy Rhoads. I've seen all these guitarists. And that guy is as good as all of them. What's the deal? How come we can't get a singer that comes close to comparing or can make this thing come together?" They were never bummed out about it. *Bummed out* would be too harsh of a term for anything you would ever put on Darrell. Darrell was the epitome of, you know, everything bounced off of him. Life was just a carnival to him. There was never a dull moment with Darrell. Even back before they were famous. I mean, it was from the time he woke up until the time he went to bed. He was into something, doing something. Nothing slowed him down. So they were very professional. They knew that they had a challenge ahead of them and they took it on. It worked out, obviously.

It started to work out when Philip Anselmo, an eighteen-year-old kid from New Orleans who was fronting his own dolled-up band, Razor White, called Pantera up in late 1986 and changed everything. They'd heard of Razor White before; every time they rolled through Shreveport, someone was telling them to check out the group—mainly its singer. They brought Anselmo to Texas, and just like Rex Brown, he left his initial meeting with the band as a member of Pantera.

"I picked him up from the airport in this drug dealer's '77 Corvette," Brown remembered in 2007, during an interview with *Decibel* magazine. "He was fresh out of high school, a real cool dude. Anyway, I took him over to Vinnie and Dime's house, where we smoked and took slugs off a bottle of tequila. The rest is history, as they say."[10]

The new version of the band played its first show in January 1987. "The chemistry clicked like a vice grip," Anselmo wrote on his Web site in January 2005. "We hit it off like four bad motherfuckers could. Perfection. Dime, Vince, and Rex could play fucking anything. You pick the style, they could pull it off. So in reality, we had to find out where our musical hearts lay strongest. After short deliberation, our intention was to be the most devastating 'hard-core–heavy-metal' band in the world."[11]

With Anselmo out front, they were well on their way. Pantera released *Power Metal* in 1988, again on Metal Magic, after an abortive deal with Gold Mountain Records. "They wanted to change our style and make us sound like Bon Jovi, which is not quite up our alley," Darrell told *Metal Forces* magazine in a June 1988 interview.[12] Pantera remained signed to Gold Mountain until August 1988 but never officially released anything on the label.

Power Metal only hinted at what was coming next: "On that album, Phil sings more like Rob Halford or something," Warden says. "You've gotta understand, when we first heard Phil sing, we thought we were looking at the next Rob Halford. We didn't know we were looking at the first Phil Anselmo." No one did. Anselmo didn't write any of the lyrics on *Power Metal*, and the band was still shaking off its glam roots. The album even featured a song, "Proud to Be Loud," written by Marc Ferrari of the standard-issue 1980s hair-metal outfit Keel.[13]

But, again, there were definite hints as to where the band was headed. As far as the band was concerned, it wasn't too far away from where it had always been. "Darrell has always been chunking those riffs out from the start," Brown told *Metal Forces*. "I mean, it's not like all of a sudden we've turned around and started riffing out like this. But now with Phil in the band we've got a chance to make those riffs fully happen instead of having some gay singer over the top of them!"[14]

Everyone seemed to like this extracrispy version of Pantera better than the original recipe. Even Glaze, the "gay singer" Anselmo replaced, couldn't deny what Anselmo brought to the band. Plus, he was happy that there was finally someone else out there he could relate to. Someone who knew what it was like to be in that band.

"I met Phil at a guitar show," Glaze says.

He was a skinny little dude, with long hair. And then right after I get out of Lord Tracy, they were on their *Vulgar Display* tour, and I went to the show. I went back. I saw Phil. By this time [almost six years later], he has the shaved head, monster muscles, you know, huge wrestler dude. He walks up to me and puts a hug on me. It was, like, you know, him and me were the only two in that club. The only two singers that totally understood. He was, like, *"Dude,"* and I said, "I know." Phil's a really talented guy. I know he's had a lot of ups and downs, but man, that guy's really talented. Darrell was, you know, the soul of that band. Every one of them, to me, owes everything they have to Darrell. But at the same time, you know, Phil was it.

Warden echoes that sentiment but adds something else. It's something he also said to Darrell not long after Anselmo joined Pantera.

"I will preface this by saying that, one on one, Phil was one cool mug," Warden says. "We'd smoke dope and hang out and chill and just talk about politics. I mean he was a cool guy. He really was. But the problem with Phil was, when you took cool-guy Phil and put him in the established Pantera scene, he became evil-punk Phil. It would drive me nuts. . . . He'd wear his Venom black-metal shirt, you know, and, *rarrrgh,* do the devil sign, that kind of stuff. You're, like, 'Dude, come on, man. We're real, dude. We're just into sex and drugs and, you know, every now and then we'd [get pissed off about] a corrupt politician.'"

"There's no need to have head trips and stuff," Warden continues.

But the thing was, Phil was actually a little ahead of the game, because at that time, it wasn't real popular to be the total evil metal guy. Now, it's totally cool to be the total evil metal guy. I can tell you this: I told Darrell, in Phil's presence—knowing that Phil was hearing, purposely so Phil could hear; it wasn't behind his back, it was in front of his face. I said, "Darrell, even though Phil's going to be your ticket to fame, he's going to be your demise. I mean there's no way that this isn't going to come back on you. Look at him. He's an evil punk, man."

I didn't see it as clearly then as I see it now, but my opinion is, Phil is the epitome of a *Crossroads* experience. You ever seen that movie? Yeah, I think Phil had a meeting [with the Devil] at the crossroads and he signed on the dotted line.

BONUS TRACK:
THE ART OF SHREDDING

The "Dean from Hell"

"Pick me out a winner."

———

ROY HOBBS,
The Natural

Every guitar hero has a signature guitar. Darrell Abbott's was a blue Dean ML illustrated with a stylized lightning storm. It was his prize for finishing first in an Arnold & Morgan music store guitar contest when he was fifteen. Darrell, nearing driving age, had his eye on a different prize: a bright yellow Firebird. He needed six hundred dollars for the car, and as it happened, he had something to sell. His dad had ordered him another Dean model, an ML Standard with a sunburst finish. It arrived just before he won the ML in the contest. One of the guitars was now superfluous, and it wasn't going to be the one his father had scrimped and saved to buy for him.

"Right when he turned sixteen, he was, like, 'Dude, dude, buy my ML. I'll give you a great deal. Man, it's really cool,'" Buddy Blaze says. "Blah blah blah. He thought it was ugly. And it was pretty damn ugly. He wanted that car. I said, 'Darrell, man, that's your trophy. You don't sell your trophies.' I said, 'especially to buy a car. It's a trophy.'"

Blaze refused to buy it, but Darrell found someone who would.

"The singer in my band was also a friend of Darrell's, and Darrell talked him into buying the ML," Blaze continues. "At that time, I had three or four *really* nice guitars. The kid came walking into rehearsal with this case, and I knew it was a Dean case, and I knew *exactly* what was inside of it. He said, 'Wait 'til you see what I got.' And I'm, like, '*Fuck* you.' I said, 'You did *not* buy Darrell's guitar.' And he opened it up, and I go, 'You *fucker.*' I said, 'Any one of my guitars—it's yours. But that guitar doesn't leave this house. That guitar goes to me.'"

Blaze painted over the guitar's original maroon color ("I had a rule that my guitars had to be blue," he says), found someone to finish it out with the realistic-looking electrical storm, and replaced all of the ML's hardware. The result was a guitar that retained its original shape and little else. When Blaze was finished with his work, Darrell wanted his trophy back, or at least a copy of it.

"When I went to Kramer [in 1987], I shut down my shop in Arlington and drove over to Darrell's house," Blaze says.

Because Darrell was begging me for a couple of years to make him a copy of that guitar. I went over to his house and said,

"Why don't you borrow this while I work on the copy?" I didn't need it to duplicate it; I made it, so I knew exactly what it felt like. He was, like, "Dude, dude, I'll scratch it, man. I can't do that." He was, like, shaking. He was all excited and stuff.

I had no intention of *ever* taking the guitar back. He called me at my office in Jersey a couple of weeks later. He said, "Dude, whatever it takes, man, I gotta have this guitar. I can't give it up." On and on, how he had to have that guitar. I said, "Dude, it was always yours. I don't care. You take it."

SIDE TWO
COWBOYS FROM HELL
(1989–1995)

5

BECOMING

Cowboys from Hell,
by Way of Hurricane Hugo

*"God of Rock, thank you for this chance
to kick ass. We are your humble servants.
Please give us the power to blow people's
minds with our high voltage rock."*

DEWEY FINN,
School of Rock

Kerry King met Darrell Abbott in 1989, when his band, Slayer,
came through Texas on tour. They would have been introduced sooner or later; they were too much alike to avoid each other
for long. They both liked to drink and play guitar the same way—
heavily. That more than fit Darrell's requirements for a friendship.

Slayer was in the midst of a creative peak, having teamed up with producer Rick Rubin on 1986's *Reign in Blood* and 1988's *South of Heaven*, and were about to issue *Seasons in the Abyss* in 1990. The trio of albums solidified the band's position at the vanguard of heavy metal, alongside Metallica. Pantera was just starting down the path to its own artistic high. Philip Anselmo was still relatively new to the group, as was the influence of bands like Slayer. For all intents and purposes, Pantera remained a cover band. Only the songs had changed.

That was what first brought the bands—and King and Darrell, eventually—together: a cover. King and singer-bassist Tom Araya turned up at Pantera's May 18, 1989, show at Joe's Garage in Fort Worth. "I don't know how we ended up [there]," King says. "You know, because I didn't know anything about them or anything." Pantera told King they had Slayer's "Raining Blood" in their set.

"I'm, like, 'All right, I'll play,' before I had any idea what I was getting into," King says, laughing.

I played this *crappy* old guitar; I think it was one of their friends' guitars. Who knows what kind of amp I was playing out of. They left out telling me that they didn't play it *exactly* like we did it, so I'm up there looking like a jackass.

Long story short, I got Phil's number. When I used to go out and hang with them, I'd stay with Phil. I didn't stay with Dime, but we'd always hang. As it got later on, Dime was the guy I hung out with and not Phil. . . . Whatever Phil's demons are and whatever he got into, I wasn't into that. Me and Dime, we drank and that's pretty much it.

You know, it's legal, it's somewhat safe, if you keep it down to a low roar. Guitar players, drinkers—we had more in common.

When Pantera finally broke out of Texas, King had a standing invitation—more like a command—to re-create that initial meeting.

If they were coming through town, they'd expect me to go onstage and play "[Fucking] Hostile" with 'em. That was pretty cool, because I did it *so* many times. . . . It was fun to get up there, because Dime was such a great guitar player, and he never had a rhythm guitar player. Or he couldn't do harmony leads. So every time I came, you know, we'd experiment with shit, see what we could come up with.

TWO OTHER events occurred in 1989 that would forever alter the arc of Darrell Abbott's life and career. Without them Darrell might have hung around as a local legend and a regional secret before disappearing from memories altogether. Had those events not happened exactly as they did, he very well could have ended up, at best, as a forgotten footnote, the subject of late-night shoptalk among guitarists who had fared much better than he had. "Should have seen this kid down in Texas," they might have said of the coulda-been, shoulda-been, never-was. "The guy was like a combination of Billy Gibbons and Randy Rhoads. Wonder whatever happened to him?"

One likes to think that talent overcomes all, that Darrell would have made it regardless, maybe not with Pantera, but certainly with some other band, and probably with Vinnie a few feet behind him atop the drum riser. In 1989, that wasn't the case. Darrell had been playing mostly cover tunes for seven years, and though he had a knack for it—could play as good as or better than the real thing—nothing much had changed. He was imitating instead of innovating, still the skinny kid from Arlington who had won all those guitar contests. He even lived in the same room at his mom's house.

Pantera was a dependable draw, a group that could blow touring headliners off the stage. Their club circuit had expanded slightly over the years, spilling over into Louisiana and Oklahoma, picking up a few more steady gigs here and there. For the most part, seven years into their career, it was the same venues and the same fans over and over. That was fine for weekend warriors, guys who moonlighted as musicians as a respite from their day jobs, but it wasn't fine, not at all, for the Abbotts, who always had bigger plans for their band.

Why else play originals? Why else take the time and expense to record and release those songs? Why else send those albums to any label they could find an address for? Why else go to such lengths to ensure that they looked, sounded, and acted like a band that had already made it and then some? Why play every weekend? Why work so hard? Why fully invest their lives and limited resources chasing a goal that was unattainable by all but a select few? If fun was all the Abbotts and Pantera were after, they were going about it the wrong way. They could get that playing a couple nights a month at Savvy's.

Vince sweated over the business end of things and Darrell sweated over little, if anything, apart from his guitar. But that just made them halves of a whole, together heading toward one destination. They didn't consider a different path or a secondary target. They were impervious to any notion that they wouldn't make it on their own.

"Nothing would stop them," Tommy Snellings says. "I would see them where they were just so sick. Darrell with an ear infection, and he couldn't barely function. But when it was time to play, man, that's all there was. I always joked with them. I'd say, 'Man, y'all have got to make it big, because y'all are worthless at anything else.' I mean, they had no other ambitions. They didn't want to do anything. They lived, slept, breathed music. There wasn't anything else in their world except music. I think the only job Darrell or Vince or Rex ever had was Fotomat. I don't think they had any other job that didn't involve music."

In winners, this kind of single-mindedness is seen, at least partially, as the reason for their accomplishments. It proves they had the drive to achieve that maybe others lacked. The lack of another practical skill or sphere of knowledge is a badge of honor in these success stories. The absence of a backup plan is held up as an exhibition of bravery akin to the kind a tightrope walker has who plies his trade without a net.

But if you don't win, if your best wasn't good enough or, at least, not recognized as such, that determination, that focus, that dedication can—rightly, if not fairly—be labeled something else: foolishness, even immaturity. Often, the difference between the two comes down to luck. This is where it gets tricky, discerning exactly where triumph and tragedy diverge. No one can fully control the vagaries of chance. No one can predict the butterfly effect of the countless—and usually innocuous—coin flips that happen every second of every day.

Darrell was talented. Everyone who had ever heard him play agreed on that, and he had, by age twenty-three, enough skins on his wall to convince the doubters. He was also abnormally devoted to his craft. He had enough phlegm on his bedroom wall to attest to that. His combination of genes and gumption seemed to guarantee that he would not fail, even as the years in relative obscurity mounted. And yet he was subject to the whims of fate just like everyone else.

BRIAN SLAGEL started Metal Blade Records in 1982, the same year Pantera formed. As Rick E. Warden mentioned, Metal Blade's first release was a compilation, *The New Heavy Metal Revue Presents Metal Massacre*, notable now because it featured the first recorded appearance of Metallica ("Hit the Lights"). Drummer Lars Ulrich and Slagel were, and are, friends; the band wanted to make its debut recording, the wildly influential *Kill 'Em All*, for Metal Blade, but Slagel didn't have the cash.

Slagel has been called the Forrest Gump of heavy metal. Besides his relationship with Ulrich and Metallica, he's crossed paths with Mötley Crüe (they were supposed to appear on that first *Metal Massacre* compilation album but had released their own record by then and didn't need the help), Slayer (Metal Blade issued the group's first four releases), and Ratt (*Metal Massacre* featured "Tell the World," when the band was still in its New Wave of British Heavy Metal–influenced, pre-"Round and Round" incarnation). That doesn't even include the records he released on Metal Blade by the likes of Diamond Head, Lamb of God, Corrosion of Conformity, Armored Saint, Cannibal Corpse, and even the Goo Goo Dolls.

Suffice to say, Metal Blade's history has been alternately charmed and star-crossed. For much of its existence, the label has served as a springboard to bigger and better. In other words, Slagel signed more than his fair share of quality bands; he just didn't get to keep many of them. He's never had the money to truly compete with major labels. On two occasions, Slagel had a chance to remedy that. But both times, he couldn't afford the buy-in, let alone the game itself.

The first opportunity, of course, came right at the beginning, when Metallica was looking for a home for *Kill 'Em All*. Had he had enough financing to put Metal Blade's logo on the back of that album, Slagel might still be living off the proceeds. (Megaforce Records released *Kill 'Em All* in 1983, and *Ride the Lightning* the following year, before the band signed with Elektra.) In 1989, Slagel had another chance to stake out a spot in metal history when a young band from Arlington, Texas, approached him.

It wasn't the first time Slagel had heard from Pantera. The band had been sending him their albums for years. "They were always trying to get me to sign them when they were doing the more pop sort of stuff," Slagel says. "I was, like, 'Not interested, not interested.'"

This time around, it was different.

Pantera didn't look much changed when *Power Metal* was released in 1988; it's clear from the photo that appears on the album sleeve that the group continued to rack up a sizable hairspray bill. But with Philip Anselmo taking over vocal duties, and the influence of bands like Slayer and Metallica beginning to take root, Pantera certainly sounded far removed from its Terry Glaze–fronted heyday. The distinction was right there in the simple, two-word title of the record: *Power Metal*. It was the first of a string of albums that told listeners exactly what to expect right there on the cover.

Power Metal was more suited to the tenor of Slagel's label. After years of trying, Pantera was almost signed to Metal Blade. Unfortunately for Slagel and Metal Blade, it was the Metallica situation all over.

By the time Pantera contacted Slagel again, the band's prospects were finally starting to brighten. The new direction that was hinted at on *Power Metal* was starting to fully coalesce in the new batch of songs they'd written, the first they'd really worked on together since Anselmo joined the band. Anyone who'd heard the first song to emerge from those writing sessions—"Cowboys from Hell"— knew Pantera was onto something. The combination of Anselmo's words and Darrell's riffs was alchemizing. Based on their track record in Texas and the rough sketches (mostly on video) of what was coming, the group had signed with John Dittmar's fledgling booking agency, Pinnacle, which would go on to handle tours for Kid Rock and Rob Zombie, among others. More important, Walter O'Brien and Andy Gould of Concrete Management, based in New York, had agreed to represent the band.[1] Joining Concrete's ranks was good for Pantera's career, less so for the Abbotts' relationship with their father. The fallout from the decision led to an estrangement between Jerry and his sons that continued until Darrell's death.

Concrete managed some of the other bands on Metal Blade's roster, so Gould reached out to Slagel. "He said, 'Hey, I got this *Cowboys from Hell* album by Pantera. We need seventy-five grand for it. Are you guys interested?'" Slagel remembers. "At the time, it was a huge amount of money for us. I was, like, 'Oh, man, I love those guys but that's way too much money for us.' I turned it down." He laughs at his own rotten luck; he would have gotten his 75K back and then some. "Oops. I had to apologize. But, I mean, hey, those guys had a phenomenal career, so it surely didn't hurt them. But it was really funny. When I first started hanging out with them, I was, like, 'Dude, sorry about that. Man, I kind of fucked up.' They're, like, 'Yeah, it's all right, no worries.'"

Slagel, of course, is right: Losing out on a deal with Metal Blade didn't hurt Pantera at all. In fact, the opposite was true. If Slagel had managed to scrape together enough money to offer Pantera a contract, the Metal Blade version of *Cowboys from Hell* would have, more than likely, done well, but not *as* well: Metal Blade didn't have the muscle to make that happen. While it would have been a good home for Pantera, like many of the bands on the label's roster, it would have been a temporary one.

In retrospect, Darrell and Pantera needed to be right where they were in 1990. Metal Blade would have made them successful, but going with Atco made them powerful. From that vantage point, they were able to withstand the music industry's seemingly wholesale infatuation with Seattle in the early 1990s. From there, they were able to offer heavy metal fans a glimmer of hope at a time when most other metal bands were being phased out of existence or giving up and giving in. (One could argue that Pantera's deal with Atco indirectly set the stage for the rise of Ozzfest later in the decade. Pantera might not have started the fire, but they certainly kept it stoked during a particularly frigid time.) From there, Darrell was eventually able to transcend Pantera and achieve his own level of notoriety.

But that would come later. The late 1980s were a trying time for Darrell and Pantera. They'd seen their former singer, Terry Glaze, and his new band, Lord Tracy, secure a major-label deal before they could do the same. Not only that; they didn't seem to be any closer to reaching that particular goal. They kept sending out tapes, but the best they could hope for was a "no thanks." Rejection was becoming a way of life, at least outside of Texas. Metal Blade was just another "no" in a series of them. With real-deal managers and agents now looking after the group, there was plenty of potential. Without a record contract, potential was all it was. Having a great realtor isn't the same as having a great house.

Meanwhile, the vultures were circling. Megadeth's Dave Mustaine offered Darrell a gig as the lead guitarist in his band, a job that offered him steady pay, health insurance, and all manner of fringe benefits. Vince gave him the OK, but Darrell turned down the offer, insisting that he and his brother were a package deal, and the guitar slot went to Marty Friedman instead.[2]

Then Hurricane Hugo hit North Carolina and everything changed.

THE BAND looked out from the stage at the empty spot where Mark Ross used to be. They had played only four songs. Their audition was apparently already over.

That night wasn't supposed to be an important gig. Quite the opposite, really—just a birthday party at a Mexican disco in Fort

Worth, a low-key show in front of maybe eighty people. It could have been called a glorified practice, except that it wasn't even supposed to be *that* serious. They'd play a few songs, have a few drinks, and have a little fun. Make the birthday girl happy. No big deal.

That plan was scrapped when Ross, who worked in artist development for Atco Records, called to find out if they had a show scheduled that night.

Hurricane Hugo's attack on the East Coast had left Ross stuck in North Texas. He had been headed to North Carolina to see Tangier, a band from Philly that had recently inked a deal with Atco.[3] Since that was now out, he called his boss at Atco, Derek Shulman, to ask if there was anyone in the Dallas–Fort Worth area he should try to see while he was stuck in town.

Shulman told Ross that, actually, yes, there was. "A band from around there called Pantera has been sending me stuff for the last couple of years," he said. "I like them on record, but I've never seen them live. See what you think."

Before making the transition to the business side of music, Shulman had been the front man for a respected but never very commercially successful prog-rock group called Gentle Giant. Pantera had begun mailing Shulman music when he had been an A&R man at Polygram Records. At Polygram, Shulman was responsible for signing Bon Jovi, Cinderella, and Kingdom Come, to name but a few.

Shulman, in short, was exactly the kind of label president Pantera was looking for. Most execs could talk about music, but they couldn't play it. They hadn't been onstage with the lights in their eyes and the kick drum pushing air against their backs. They hadn't been in a van with five other guys, hoping the rhythm of the wheels on the road would finally lull them to sleep. They hadn't been in a studio, trying not to botch a solo or a drum fill because time literally meant money. Shulman had. He was a guy who *got it*.

Pantera might have signed a recording contract earlier, if Shulman hadn't left his gig at Polygram for a better one at Atco. They intrigued him, he says, "because I knew what direction they were going in. . . . At that time, they had big hair, but they were much heavier than the average big hair band, even with *Power Metal*, which was a transition from where they were to what they became." He didn't chase a deal then, because he knew he would be leaving soon "and therefore wouldn't be able to look after their career." Shulman didn't even have enough time left at Polygram to oversee the negotiation process.

Timing remained an obstacle when Shulman arrived at Atco. He had to get up to speed on outstanding business and install his own regime before he actively pursued any new contracts. Fortunately—and surprisingly, to him at least—there was no pressure to get a deal done immediately. Barely anyone else seemed to have noticed Pantera: "I think Roadrunner kind of was putting feelers out, but not really interested," says Shulman.

Shulman was interested, more than he had been when he was at Polygram. Jules Kurz, the band's attorney at the time, had shown him a rough video—featuring a handful of songs that eventually turned up on *Cowboys from Hell*—which only confirmed Shulman's forecast: Lightning was about to strike. "There was just an incredible vibe about the whole thing," he says.

But Darrell and the other members of Pantera didn't know how close they already were to adding "Atco recording artist" in front of their name when Ross called. They only knew that the bad luck of North Carolinian coast dwellers had turned into a potential winning lottery ticket for them. They had just started to check the numbers on that ticket when Ross disappeared.

The members of Pantera were onto Ross as soon as he walked in the door. After years of almosts, the band was very familiar with the appearance of the average record label talent scout. Ross, without trying, made his presence felt at that Mexican disco in Fort Worth. Vinnie spotted him as soon as he walked in the door. Emboldened by the strange sort of arrogance that comes when confidence is mixed with a few years of rejection, he went up to Ross and told him, "We're about to get up and play, and I guaran-damn-tee you, you're gonna shit."

Instead, Ross split after watching Pantera play only a few songs. After watching his back disappear through the front door, the band looked back and forth at each other onstage. With little hesitation, the gig reverted to its original status. For four songs, they had been nervous hopefuls, a quartet of jayvee basketball players trying to make the varsity squad, anxiously peeking at the coach. Now that he was gone, and there was nothing more to prove, it turned into a pickup game in the park. "Fuck it," they decided. "Let's just have some fun."

The audition was over; the birthday party was in full swing. Out came the shots and the cake. Down went the shots, and the cake, too, turning the stage into a Slip 'n Slide covered in icing. They kept playing—Ross might have left, but they still had a roomful of people to entertain. And Pantera never let down a crowd, no matter that the condition of the stage had turned their sneakers into roller skates.

But wait. Ross was back. Shit. Shit, shit, *shit*. What the fuck now? Ah, well, too late to turn back. Pantera finished up its set and left the stage. This time, Ross found Vinnie.

"Man, that's the best damn live band I've ever seen."

"Well, why'd you leave?"

"I went out to the car to call Derek and tell him we're signing you."

A month later, Atco did. On July 23, 1990, it officially introduced the world to Darrell Abbott and *Cowboys from Hell*.

6

A NEW LEVEL

"Metal Gods" and
Other Monsters of Rock

*"Rock and roll is a lifestyle and a way
of thinking . . . and it's not about
money and popularity. Although some
money would be nice. But it's a voice
that says, 'Here I am . . . and fuck you
if you can't understand me.'"*

JEFF BEBE,
Almost Famous

Mark Ross called Derek Shulman at home at 12:30 at night—a bit late for a business call, but then, the music industry never sleeps. He had just walked out on Pantera's set in Fort Worth, and what he had to tell Shulman couldn't wait.

"He said, 'This is the best thing I've ever seen in my life,'" Shulman remembers. "I said, 'I believe you.'"

Shulman went to see the band a few weeks later. His experience mirrored Ross's almost exactly.

"There was about fifty or sixty people in there—very tiny place," he says. "But they were just the most amazing, charismatic, brilliant band I'd ever seen. . . . They were stars right there and then, when I saw them in front of fifty kids from the Dallas area. They just blew me away. It was the real deal. I knew that. So I worked out a deal with their then-lawyer, and we completed it very quickly. It was a no-brainer, as far as I was concerned."

In late 1989, Pantera began recording its debut for Atco, *Cowboys from Hell*. Like on its previous four albums, the band set up shop at Pantego Sound Studio. Unlike on those other albums, producer Terry Date had been hired to supervise the sessions.[4] Except for his studio, Jerry Abbott had been phased out of the operation entirely; he wasn't the band's manager or producer any longer, just Darrell and Vinnie's dad, and even that job title held less responsibility than ever.

Date, fresh off recording Soundgarden's *Louder than Love* and Dream Theater's *When Dream and Day Unite*, was able to get more out of Pantego than Jerry ever had. (In Jerry's defense, the band gave their new producer more to work with.) Still, as much as Date's production style would come to define Pantera's sound, he wasn't the first choice for the job. Max Norman, best known for his work on Ozzy Osbourne's solo albums, was offered the gig but turned it down, deciding to work on Lynch Mob's *Wicked Sensation* instead. While Darrell might have liked the idea of

working with the man who recorded Randy Rhoads's iconic guitar parts, in the end the right man got the job. Date immediately
clicked with the band, and *Cowboys from Hell* was completed in a
few short months.

Once the album was finished, Atco's strategy for Pantera was as
much of a no-brainer as Shulman's decision to sign the group to the
label. They weren't Bon Jovi, or even Cinderella. With their
rough-hewn look and sound,[5] radio and MTV couldn't be counted
on to support the band. The playbook, as Shulman saw it, was right
there in "Cowboys from Hell": "We're taking over this town."

With that in mind, Pantera began its first tour for Atco in
April 1990, almost four months before *Cowboys from Hell* was released. Apart from breaks to write and record new albums, the
band stayed on tour for most of the next decade.

"Forget being in the position of running a company," Shulman says. "I was just a major fan. They just blew me away. And I
knew that they would do that to other people. So my key was for
them to tour and tour and tour, and they did. And they went out
there and they played places they had never even heard of before,
in the States and also in Europe. When thirty people showed up,
they told their friends and their friends and their friends, and
they'd come back four months later and three hundred people
would show up."

Neither Darrell nor the other members of Pantera had to be
coaxed by Shulman into hitting the road to play in front of a few
dozen people. They had busted their asses all over Texas (and
Oklahoma and Louisiana) so they'd be in the position to bust their
asses everywhere else. They couldn't do anything else and didn't
want to. The one job Darrell had held, besides teaching private

guitar lessons, was at a Fotomat (thanks to Tommy Snellings). That had only been good for a laugh at his expense, as friends drove by the tiny Fotomat kiosk just to see Darrell in his uniform, with the hat he had to wear sitting on top of his unruly mop of curls. The rest of the group was of a similar mind-set. Heading out on tour, being in a band full time, worrying about nothing more than playing as hard and loud as they could, onstage and off, that was exactly what they wanted to do with their lives.

Their new schedule wasn't much different from the one they'd maintained since 1982. It was, if anything, better, in that every weekday was like a Saturday night. Living out of a suitcase became the new norm. Christmas shopping at a truck stop off a deserted highway, as Darrell once did, is a telling scenario. They hit twenty-seven of the fifty states (and Washington, D.C.) and Canada, in many cases several times over, sharing bills with Suicidal Tendencies, Exodus, Alice in Chains, and Prong. At every stop, no matter if they were opening or headlining, breaking in a new audience or preaching to the choir, the goal was the same. It always came back to the same five words: "We're taking over this town."

They didn't limit their assault to the club they were playing. As Pantera made its way around the country, the only thing that preceded their onstage reputation was their offstage notoriety. They were just getting started.

"Sat down with some friends, drank some cold ones," Darrell says during a video interview, describing a typical tour stop. His voice is higher and clearer in the clip, revealing little of the twanging, gravelly rumble he would later develop, caused by a decade and change of black tooth grins. "Flipped a coin. Came inside. Hanging out, man. Ran into all sorts of fuckers, man. Drank—7&7's.

Fucking stumbling around. You know that's right." He then tips his bottle to the camera and takes a big swig—before proceeding to fall off his chair and out of the frame, leaving behind only the bottom of his white high-tops.[6]

Not everyone could keep up with them. But everyone was expected to at least try.

"The thing about the band: They were honest and true, but, boy, did they like to live the lifestyle, if you like, of hard, hard partying rockers," Shulman says. "Backstage, before the shows and even after, I had to hang out and do their famous shots. They were standing straight and talking sense. Three or four shots and beers afterwards, I was on my knees."

But that was before and after the show. During, they were a rumbling tank, bent on achieving a different kind of excess.

"That's all that fuckin' matters," Rex Brown would later tell *Metal Edge* magazine. "All of the rest of the bullshit goes away. Twenty-two hours, that's a lot of day to sit around. You sleep half of it, but those two hours onstage are the main focus of what you have to do."[7]

More often than not, they made that time count. "There was no doubting the band's energy or skill," David Surkamp of the *St. Louis Post-Dispatch* noted after Pantera's set at Mississippi Nights, as part of a three-band bill with Suicidal Tendencies and Exodus, on August 31, 1990. "My guess is that these Texas rockers will quickly work their way up the thrash-rockers totem pole."[8]

Two months later, someone gave them a boost.

WHEN PANTERA'S barnstorming brought them to Toronto on November 18, 1990, for a gig at the Diamond Club, it also brought them to the attention of one of their idols: Judas Priest singer Rob Halford, who was in the city prepping for his own band's tour to support its latest album, *Painkiller*.

Halford was watching MuchMusic (the north-of-the-border answer to MTV)[9] in his hotel room and noticed Darrell being interviewed. What actually got his attention was Darrell's black *British Steel* T-shirt. Then he started listening. "From what he was saying and the Pantera video that aired," Halford wrote on his Web site in December 2004, "I knew right away that this man was a guitar god!"[10]

He immediately called MuchMusic and was soon connected with Darrell. They became fast friends. Before he hung up, Halford agreed to drop by the club Pantera was playing that night. By the end of his visit, he was sitting in with the band on a version of *British Steel*'s "Metal Gods," a longtime fixture of Pantera's set while on the cover-band circuit. "From that point on, [Darrell] and the rest of the band became solid friends," Halford wrote. "My gut feeling was that this band would be huge."[11]

That rehearsal would come in handy later. Halford made an oft-bootlegged appearance onstage with the band at Irvine Meadows (now known as the Verizon Wireless Amphitheater) in Irvine, California, on March 14, 1992, performing another *British Steel* track, "Grinder," as well as "Metal Gods." In the video of the show, Darrell—ever the fan—looks as though Santa is at center stage with a sack full of Dean guitars and Crown Royal.[12] It's a wonder he got through either song. (Or how he was able to rein himself in long enough to back Halford, along with the rest of Pantera, on a one-off recording, "Light Comes Out of Black," that landed on that year's soundtrack to *Buffy the Vampire Slayer*.)[13]

By then, Halford had plenty of experience with Darrell and Pantera. After meeting the band in Toronto, Halford trusted his gut and invited Pantera to open the European dates of Judas Priest's *Painkiller* tour in February and March 1991. "Many a night I would stand offstage and watch them tear up city after city, leaving everyone stunned by their intense performances," Halford writes. "It was a thrill to watch and hear Dime invent and advance with his playing."[14]

It was less thrilling for Darrell. Touring with Judas Priest wasn't the problem. Touring with Judas Priest in Europe was. "Europe ain't cool in any of our books," he told *Orange County Register* writer Cary Darling in an interview in advance of Pantera's May 15, 1991, gig at the Bandstand in Anaheim. "They're just a little behind on everything over there."[15]

They weren't behind on Pantera. In fact, European crowds were ahead of the curve.

"I remember them playing their very first gig in London, at the Marquee, when it was still going," Derek Shulman says. "There was a good buzz out there. *Kerrang!* gave them four or five Ks on the *Cowboys from Hell* record. It was the most intense show I had ever seen in my life. I remember it now. The crowd was insane, and the band—they blew it apart. From there, I could see that this was going to be a phenomenon that wouldn't go away. It was going to get bigger. Did I think it was going to be as big? Yes. I did. I just suspected that."

Over time, Darrell would come to appreciate Europe.[16] He got another crack at the continent relatively quickly, when Pantera was invited to take part in the Monsters of Rock Tour that rumbled through Western and Eastern Europe in August and September of 1991, featuring AC/DC, Metallica, and the Black Crowes. The band joined the bill for Monsters of Rock's final date, a free gig at Tushino Air Field in Moscow on September 28 that attracted somewhere between 150,000 and 1 million fans, depending on whose estimate you believe.

As he and the band wandered the streets of Moscow before the show, Darrell seemed to have already started to soften his stance on overseas travel. Russian schoolchildren surrounded him, looking at him in wonder as he looked back with basically the same expression, each side charming the other. "Skin, dude," he says to an angelic blond boy, trying to get him to return a hand slap. The boy finally does, and Darrell musses his hair like a father from a 1950s sitcom. Later, he sits in with a group of street musicians at a sidewalk fair, doing his best to strum a balalaika. "Tune this motherfucker, somebody," he says good-naturedly, before giving up.[17]

Perhaps Darrell's good cheer this time around had a simple source: the bottle of "peppermint whiskey mouthwash" he had brought from home. "Fake seal and all," he says, noting the tape around the top of a bottle of Scope he had emptied and refilled with whiskey. "Gotta love it."

HAVING THE front man of a group they had long loved and emulated on their side was something no one in Pantera, and no one at Atco, could have predicted. Receiving a leg up from a source they had already written off—MTV—was even less foreseeable. But it wasn't an accident. Even better, it happened on Pantera's own terms. It was all there on *Cowboys from Hell*. All they really needed was Darrell.

He would have gone down as one of the all-time great metal guitarists for his work on *Cowboys from Hell* alone. Darrell guaranteed that before the record was half over: the stuttering, snarling pick work on the title track. And the iconic opening riff to "Cemetery Gates," a crunching, squealing beast that sent thousands of suburban kids into their bedrooms to figure out what pinch harmonics were; the pledge of allegiance to Eddie Van Halen buried in the strutting riff of "Psycho Holiday," which also tips its cowboy hat to ZZ Top's Billy Gibbons, and yet doesn't sound like either; the percussive, propulsive lines of "Domination," a jackhammer performance that conjures the sound of Vince's machine-gun double kick drum. Any one of these advanced heavy metal guitar by leaps and bounds. And they were all in the first thirty minutes of Darrell's major-label career.

As for the rest of it, the plan was an organic stroke of marketing genius—selling the band without selling out. By committing to a nomadic existence, the band provided the right kind of demand. By hiring a young video director named Paul Rachman, they took care of the proper supply as well.

Rachman had grown up in the hard-core punk scene and was a filmmaker; he began shooting punk shows in New York City in 1980.[18] In the late 1980s, a few years out of college, Rachman moved to Los Angeles and began directing music videos under the aegis of Propaganda Films, the video production company founded by, among others, *Fight Club* and *Panic Room* director David Fincher.

That's where Rachman was when Mark Ross hired him to work with Pantera, soon after the band signed with Atco. It was a perfect match. "I loved it," Rachman says.

To me, with my background, having really been into hard-core punk and bands like, you know, Black Flag and all that—music was kind of changing in the early nineties. And when I heard Pantera, I was just smitten, because I really *got* it. You know, it kind of, like, ran in my blood the first time I heard *Cowboys from Hell*. At the time, a lot of rock bands in the early nineties were either trying to be alternative or, you know, the kind of tail end of the Sunset hair-metal thing was spinning to an end. You had this kind of new music, like Nirvana and all that fucking crap that ruined the music business in my opinion, Smashing Pumpkins and all that shit. And here came Pantera.

When Rachman met the band that had stirred those old feelings in him, he found he identified with them beyond a musical level.

I worked with Alice in Chains a lot—you know, kind of followed the course of [them] becoming huge and rock stars and relying on managers, and it wasn't the same thing. Vin and Darrell, they were kind of do-it-yourself guys, in a way. There was something very Texan about that. You know, *We're going to do it our way*. And I understand that, too, because my dad, even though he was born in Brooklyn, moved to Lubbock in the early seventies, and he's still there. I used to go to Texas a lot as a kid. So I kind of understood that about them.

Rachman flew to Dallas to spend a week shooting the band. He made the most of his time in the city, leaving with videos for "Cowboys from Hell," "Cemetery Gates," and "Psycho Holiday."

Much of his trip was spent at the Basement. Back then, it would have been unusual for Rachman to film the band anywhere else.

As the 1980s wound down and the 1990s began, metal bands basically had two venues to choose from in Dallas: the Basement and Dallas City Limits. Given the dearth of clubs, most groups performed at both, though where a band played the most determined its place in the local heavy metal community. Dallas City Limits was for the pretty boys, the ones for whom music was a means to an end, the guys who lived life as if it were a Poison song, who cared more about what being a band offers than actually *being* a band. Dallas City Limits was more about making the scene than making a sound. The Basement, on the other hand, had a faux-rock interior that belied the all-rock attitude of its patrons. The bands and fans that haunted the Basement were there for the music. (More or less: When the Basement closed in 1995 and was replaced by an Eckerd's pharmacy, the running joke was one drugstore had replaced another.) As is so often the case with metal clubs, the crowd was predominantly male.

"It was definitely the full-on black T-shirt, no-poseurs, get-your-ass-kicked, serious-moshing type of crowd," says Dale Brock, who booked the bands for the Basement and later served as manager. "Stage diving was just *insane* at that point. It was more or less allowed, before however many people died or got paralyzed for life, as the case may be." By the time of *Cowboys from Hell*'s release, Pantera, which had started out as more of a Dallas City Limits-type band, was the Basement's top draw. "They were turning away people at the door," Brock says.

Pantera performed at the club often—at least until the size of the audience necessitated an upgrade to a larger venue—but they *played* there even more. Darrell and Vinnie were the welcome wagon for every hard-rock or metal band that swung through town on tour, and they usually took it upon themselves to bring every hard-rock or metal band to the Basement. No one ever knew who would show up with them. Maybe Marilyn Manson or Trent Reznor. Maybe Kerry King and Slayer. Only two things were for sure when the Abbott brothers came by the Basement: Everyone was going to drink and no one was going home anytime soon.

"Man, when those guys would roll into the club, at first it was cool," Brock says. "After awhile, it was like, 'Oh no, here comes Vinnie and Dime. We're gonna be here until five.'" He laughs. "Employees would groan. It was always going to be late. It was going to be after hours. No telling who they were going to bring. . . . Vinnie kind of had the rock star persona a little bit more. Dime was just always Dime. Loved everybody. 'C'mon, let's throw down,' you know? The scummiest guys in the bar, who we hardly paid attention to, he'd come in and just be, 'Hey, brother!' He was just always that kind of guy."

Whenever the Abbotts visited the Basement, the end result for all present was the same: a massive hangover. What happened before that was unpredictable, as it usually was when Darrell was around, and always is when alcohol is involved. And alcohol was always involved.

"Darrell would come in the Basement just shit-faced, and he was the bartender's nightmare, because he'd get behind the bar, start slinging drinks, pouring shots into people's mouths. Just, you know, whatever the hell he wanted. Completely illegal," Brocks, says, laughing. "[Texas Alcoholic Beverage Commission] or anybody would have freaked. Just come in, throwing beers at everybody, pouring shots. I tell you, the only time I have drank whiskey in the last twenty years was with those guys. You just had no fucking choice. There was not an option. This is going down your throat if we have to hold you down. You'd just never hear the end of it. That was all there was to it. Throw it down and hope it stays down."

That policy led to plenty of good times, with the occasional off night thrown in for good measure. "Me and Rita got into a huge fight, and I was glad that Dime never really held it against me," Brock says. His wife (another former Basement employee) and Darrell's longtime girlfriend are still close friends. "She was shit-face drunk one night. I couldn't even tell you what it was about. She was doing something in the club that she absolutely shouldn't have been doing, whatever it was. And she just *freaked out* screaming at me, 'I'll get you fired!' That whole bit and everything. And of course, Dime just kind of laughed it off when it came time."

Darrell wasn't really in a position to judge anyone's behavior at the Basement. "One time, Darrell was so drunk he peed in the ice machine," Brock continues, laughing. "Literally, walked in, dick out, peeing in the ice machine. It was, like, *Aw, man!*" He laughs again. "Needless to say, that thing had to be cleaned out. But there were probably a few disgusting drinks served that night. That was definitely one of the highlights."

There were plenty of other highlights that happened in and around the Basement during the period when Pantera was using the bar as a makeshift clubhouse, and they didn't (all) concern Darrell putting his dick in the ice machine. The most memorable, or at least the most important to Pantera's career, happened a couple of years later, when MTV came calling. *Head-bangers Ball* wanted to film an episode with the band after *Vulgar Display of Power* was released; the shoot took place at the Basement. Like they would do for any touring band, Darrell and the band showed the crew from MTV a good time at the club. Which meant drinking and strippers, both in abundance.

"We went to the Basement, and all I remember is that there were just so . . . many . . . *girls*," *Headbangers Ball* host Riki Rachtman says. "That was the one [episode] in my life that I will always remember because there were just so many fucking girls. It was at your disposal. It was like you got to pick and choose. And my friend went with me—he was just, like, this big, fat Mexican guy—and *he* got to pick and choose! It was, like, for everybody! Every silly rock cliché you can think of? That was what that place was like."

Viewers of the channel already had a good idea what the Basement was like, thanks to the videos Rachman shot there. They were like updated versions of *Mutual of Omaha's Wild Kingdom*, as Rachman shot the lions in their natural habitat.

"Back then, in the early nineties, the whole thing about a *live show* [video] from bands like Metallica and everything, it was, like, big lights, big stage, you know?" Rachman says. "Live shows were like stadium things that people spent hundreds and hundreds of thousands of dollars on. When I look at 'Psycho Holiday' and 'Cowboys from Hell' today, just as a filmmaker, there's so much more energy on that stage in those videos than any of those other bands could have *dreamed* of having."

To capture that energy, Rachman filmed the band during its last local gig before Atco released *Cowboys from Hell*. He got into the show as much as the band and its fans did. "Those guys wanted a really raw, live, energy thing," he says. "I shot it very much in the style like I did hard-core videos. Like, I was onstage with a camera." But not for long: To properly capture the fury and passion in the room, Rachman repeatedly dove into the packed crowd with his little hand-cranked 16-mm Bolex camera.

The resulting trio of videos shoveled dirt on top of the coffin *Cowboys from Hell* built for the band's spandex-and-hairspray days. They were as stark and visceral as wartime photography, and unlike anything on MTV at the time. They translated the experience of seeing Pantera live better than anything Atco could have dreamed up, and better than everything the band did after, including its 1997 album *Official Live: 101 Proof.* The videos also helped turn Anselmo into a star, spotlighting the muscular charisma he had developed, a stage presence that would bring to bear massive change in the archetype of the heavy metal front man.

More than a decade and a half later, Rachman still believes those videos, most notably "Psycho Holiday," hold up as well as or better than anything he ever did in his stint as a video director. (After helming clips for the likes of Alice in Chains, the Replacements, Sepultura, and Roger Waters, he quit in the late 1990s to focus on a big-screen career.) But Rachman—who would work with the band again on the stylistically different video for "Mouth for War," off *Vulgar Display of Power*—remembers the collaboration more than the product.

"Those guys were great to work with," he says.

They were very different. Phil's attitude was all about the energy and keeping it real and just being, like, as truthful as you can be to the audience. Vinnie, as the producer, was really into the technicality of the music. A certain integrity was important to him. And Darrell was actually the most fun to work with. Because he had the true kind of rock-and-roll spirit. I don't want to call it "rock star spirit," but he had a glow about him. Where it was this balance between being, you know, a great guitar player and really caring about your band and your music and your *fans* having a good time. Kind of balancing all of those things. It was really an art.

He didn't have to try to be a rock star, because he was one. You know what I mean? He was a natural. With all the bands I worked with, not so many people were naturals like that. I'm trying to think back, like who was a natural—gosh—it's, like— you know, Roger Waters.

In the early nineties, there were a lot of opportunities for rock. Labels were signing a lot of bands. Everybody was looking for the jackpot. Everybody was kind of, like, worried about becoming a rock star. Darrell didn't worry about that.

PAUL RACHMAN also had a hand in another part of Pantera lore: *Cowboys from Hell: The Videos*. Released on April 2, 1991, it collected Rachman's videos, along with professional and amateur footage of the band onstage and off. Rachman served as director for the project, but it was really Darrell's baby. Darrell filmed anything and everything, a habit that he began in the early days of the band and never shook. Not that anyone wanted him to. Atco, in fact, gave him a camera when it sent Pantera out on the road.

"I remember working with Darrell a lot on that, talking to him a lot on the phone," Rachman says. "Darrell actually was the one in the band who really was handling the video camera a lot. This is kind of the early days of bands taking Hi-8 cameras on the road with them. Darrell was the one shooting a lot. He was the one who logged everything. They sent me hundreds of hours of tapes."

Darrell didn't merely document the usual scenes of the band hanging out backstage, drinking and goofing off with friends and fellow bands, although he did do plenty of that. Much of what ended up on tape could have been a prototype for MTV's *Jackass*, a full decade before anyone had heard of such a thing. There were don't-try-this-at-home-kids stunts, pranks and practical jokes, dick and fart jokes, fireworks assaults on anyone who happened to be around, and, naturally, copious amounts of alcohol.

One of the best sequences in *Cowboys from Hell: The Videos* is a playful confrontation with Swedish guitarist Yngwie Malmsteen outside a hotel on tour. Darrell serves as both cinematographer and director of the scene, prodding one of the members of the crew into attempting to give Malmsteen a bag of Dunkin' Donuts.

"Go, go!" he hurriedly whispers when he sees the masturbatory guitar hero lingering outside the door.

"Get the fucking thing out of my fucking way!" Malmsteen yells at the camera, as he makes his way into the hotel. "No! I don't eat donuts. I don't fucking eat donuts!"

"Pure hostility," Darrell notes, after the elevator closes and takes Malmsteen away. Then he turns the camera on the security guard, holding the bag Malmsteen couldn't be bothered with. "*He* likes donuts, though."

The brief scene was typical of Darrell's take on life: Nothing was to be taken too seriously, and nothing was to be taken for granted. Never act like royalty, but treat everyone else like they are. While someone like Malmsteen wasn't fond of anyone deflating his air of superiority, whenever anyone tried to put that same kind of atmosphere around Darrell he was the first to wave it away.

"He loved taking the piss out of rock stars," Buddy Blaze says. "Where he's picking on Yngwie about the donuts—that was Darrell. That was Darrell all the time. Before he was famous he was like that. He didn't change after he got famous. The only thing that changed was how many cars and how big the house got and things like that. But that should. He earned it."

The prefame Darrell on display in *Cowboys from Hell: The Videos* utterly lacks pretense. He is clearly thrilled to be getting paid to do what he would have paid to do. He even seems to revel in the mundane duties of a touring musician. When the band visits J.J.'s Ear Candy in Carson City, Nevada, for an autograph signing, Darrell doesn't look like he's suffering with a smile as he greets fans like long-lost friends. Nor does that appear to be the case when they drop by the studios of a Reno radio station—Z-Rock, KZAK-FM (100.1)—later that day to chat with a portly DJ in a Cosby sweater and a mustache that even a veteran 1970s porn actor might roll his eyes at. As Z-Rock plays "Cowboys from Hell," Darrell sings along and air-guitars as fiercely and happily as he would onstage.

Darrell wasn't just doing his job. He was having the time of his life.

7

RISE

From Skid Row to
Spacewalking with Ace Frehley

*"You know, I'm just a regular guy who
grew up with the posters of these guys on
my wall . . . and now I'm one of them!"*

CHRIS "IZZY" COLE,
Rock Star

Sebastian Bach first heard of Darrell and Pantera in the mid-1980s when the band he was in at the time, Madam X, played a gig at Savvy's in Fort Worth. The members of Pantera were there, but they weren't on the bill. They were in the audience, sitting at a table in front of the stage. Their presence was a big deal to Madam X, conferring on it a measure of respect. This was, after all, Pantera's territory, long since conquered. Pantera's arena-level approach to the club circuit had started to extend the borders of its legend. While the group had not made it outside of its Texas-Louisiana-Oklahoma orbit, word of what it was doing there had. Pantera wasn't a big band yet. In the eyes of a struggling group from Detroit, it was.

A few years later, the roles reversed. By then, Madam X was long gone, and Bach was fronting Skid Row. The band's self-titled 1989 debut record had spawned three hit singles—"Youth Gone Wild," "18 and Life," and "I Remember You"—and a headlining arena tour. Though Skid Row had a harder edge than most of its pop-metal contemporaries, the success of power ballads like "18 and Life" and "I Remember You" tended to obscure that side of the group. The band aimed to change that perception, both with its follow-up, *Slave to the Grind*, and the accompanying tour. To complete its transformation, Skid Row needed to find the right opening act for its shows, to set the tone. "We wanted to take out the heaviest, coolest band on the road that we could find," Bach remembered, in a eulogy posted to his Web site in late December 2004.[19]

The search ended when guitarist Scott Hill pulled out a copy of *Cowboys from Hell*. Bach hadn't thought of Pantera much since Madam X played at Savvy's. "I couldn't believe my ears," Bach wrote. "As the opening guitar riff to 'Cowboys From Hell' came out of the speakers, I knew we had found the band we were looking for to come on tour with us. This was like a new kind of Judas Priest meets ZZ Top meets Van Halen divided by Slayer equals its own kind of thing. I remember cranking the album and smiling to myself, 'I cannot wait to help introduce this fucking band to North America!' I knew they were gonna blow up huge as soon as the public at large got a chance to feel their power."

The Skid Row–Pantera tour kicked off on New Year's Eve 1991 in New Orleans. When it ended six months later, it was difficult to decide what was the most memorable moment.

Maybe it was the show on March 14 at Irvine Meadows[20] in California, when Pantera (in full makeup) joined Bach and his bandmates onstage for a cover of KISS's "Cold Gin." Darrell had taken the extra step of fashioning an ad hoc Ace Frehley costume out of empty twelve-pack boxes of Coors Light, wrapping them around his arms, legs, and chest. Or maybe it was earlier that night, when Judas Priest's Rob Halford joined Pantera for blistering versions of "Grinder" and "Metal Gods."

Maybe it was when Skid Row guitarist Dave "Snake" Sabo and Darrell got both bands permanently banned from a Philadelphia hotel. Which is generally the course of action a hotel takes when two men drop acid, and one of them (Darrell) slices up a fancy leather couch in the lobby with a knife. Or maybe it was the nights when they didn't get kicked out of the hotel, and Bach and Darrell would stay up drinking and screwing around with Darrell's four-track recorder. "Even at 7–8 A.M. with twelve hours of drinking in us, Dime was ready to do what he did best—create rock 'n' roll music like you never heard before," Bach wrote.

Maybe it was the off-day softball game between the bands and their respective crews. (Bach claims the cinematic version of the game—which wound up on 1993's *Vulgar Video*, claiming a thirty-three-to-three victory for Pantera—was the result of "some major Dimebag digital editing magic": "Skid Row completely destroyed

Pantera on the baseball field, by at least twenty runs, which wasn't hard because they were all sporting the black tooth grin by early afternoon!") Or maybe it was the outdoor gig in Missouri that felt like nothing more than a day off, since Darrell and Pantera hosted a barbecue in the sand in front of the stage during Skid Row's set. "There I am singing '18 and Life' as Dimebag squirts ketchup and mustard all over his beef frank," Bach wrote. "As I get into the song, I look out at Dime looking straight into my eyes, offering me a hot dog, mouthing the words, 'Duuuuuuuude! You want a bite of this delicious wiener, bro, c'mon!'"

Maybe it was the night Bach's wife, Maria, and Darrell got into a drinking contest, knocking back thirty-three shots of tequila—thirty-three between them, according to Bach; thirty-three *apiece* according to Maria. "I think this is physically impossible," Bach wrote, "but this was over the course of a full evening, and our tolerance was way up back then, so while I hope I am right and Maria is wrong about this, I must admit that if anyone could do this it would have to be Dimebag Darrell!"

Or maybe it was the day before the show in Vancouver. Just prior to that, the *Seattle Post-Intelligencer* had noted that Skid Row was "already looking over its shoulder at opening act Pantera."[21] Pantera's new record, *Vulgar Display of Power*, debuted in *Billboard*'s album charts at No. 42, and Bach's prophecy had come true: Pantera had, indeed, blown up huge.

PANTERA PLAYED almost two hundred shows supporting *Cowboys from Hell*, staying on the road for close to two full years. The only significant break from touring they had wasn't a break at all. In the summer of 1991, just before leaving for Moscow and their

Monsters of Rock debut, they spent two months at Pantego Sound writing and recording *Vulgar Display of Power*, again with Terry Date producing. The band was so tight at the time, personally and musically, they might have been able to do it in two weeks. As it stands, its construction was practically effortless.

Upon reflection, this record may have been the group's pinnacle. Released on February 25, 1992, *Vulgar Display of Power* is by far the group's best album and easily the most influential. (Korn's Jonathan Davis credits *Vulgar* with turning him onto heavy music, and he's not alone.) The disc's cover—a fist violently connecting with a man's jaw—was the perfect visual representation of the music.

Vulgar Display of Power opens with "Mouth for War," one of Darrell's finest amalgams of the techniques he learned sitting on the floor of his father's studio, the 1970s heavy metal and hard rock that both started and stoked his fire, and the underground thrash records that completed his education as a guitarist. Though its genesis was a melody hummed by Anselmo, and though it's equal parts Billy Gibbons and James Hetfield, it nonetheless mostly sounds like Darrell. Once again, he had simply dicked around and come up with a new lick. "It's just a weird off-time riff," Machine Head's Robert Flynn told MTV.com, speaking for many others, "and the first time I heard it, my jaw dropped to the floor."[22]

From there, *Vulgar* further expands upon the dynamic that was set in motion when Darrell and Vince had begun jamming together a decade before, while perfecting the element that was introduced when Philip Anselmo joined the band. As photographer Ross Halfin puts it, "It was sort of like Anselmo wanted to be Henry Rollins and the others wanted to be Van Halen." That idea was never more in evidence than on *Vulgar Display of Power*, with its inclusion of the atomic-punk metal of "Fucking Hostile," perhaps Pantera's signature song, and "Walk." As such, if you take Anselmo out of the equation, it's not wildly different from what Pantera did in its Terry Glaze–led incarnation.

"The music sounds almost the same; it's just you took a girl singing [and replaced her with] a caveman singing," Glaze says, with a laugh at his expense. "You listen to *Vulgar Display*—that's my favorite record—and even though it's got that real heavy sound, to me it's still Van Halen. And that's what all of us grew up liking the most. *Van Halen III* and *IV*. Those were the ones. And so when I listen to [*Vulgar*], I hear the influence of Metallica, but it just sounds like bad-ass Van Halen to me. And that's what I always wanted to do."

Atco had mostly left Pantera alone during the sessions for *Cowboys from Hell*, since no one was expecting any radio or video airplay anyway. The fact that it received both, however, changed the label's attitude. During the recording of *Vulgar Display of Power*, Atco used a slightly broader definition of *mostly*. Upon hearing the album, the label sent someone to ask the band where its "'Mr. Sandman' track" was—meaning: Pantera's answer to Metallica's breakthrough hit, "Enter Sandman." Atco likely wouldn't have gotten its way regardless, but swinging and missing on the song title certainly didn't help. After that, no one offered any other suggestions.

As it turned out, the label needn't have worried. While *Vulgar Display of Power* did not, in fact, contain anything that would break quite as big as "Enter Sandman" had, it did have two songs ("Walk" and "This Love") that came close enough, with a third ("Mouth for War") not too far behind. And if the album wasn't as successful as Metallica's had been, it would at least become as significant, if not more significant: Charles M. Young complimented the album, somewhat backhandedly, in the July 2000 issue of *Playboy*, saying that it "set the standard for Nineties metal to come: Limp Bizkit, Korn, Tool, and all the others who dispense almost entirely with melody."[23]

That backhanded compliment would have been better applied to the band's next album, the far-less-tuneful *Far Beyond Driven*. But if you disregard the last ten words of Young's sentence, it still rings true. *Vulgar Display of Power* built a bridge of hard rock between everything that had come before and most of what would come next. The buzz that started with Pantera turned into a blare in 1994, which turned into a boon for metal in the late 1990s.

THOUGH DARRELL'S influence on hard rock and heavy metal would be writ large at the end of the 1990s, he was inspiring guitar players before he even really left the Dallas–Fort Worth area. Take Scott Minyard, for instance. To Minyard, Darrell Abbott was already a star, shining every bit as brightly as Randy Rhoads and Eddie Van Halen. But to the aspiring guitarist, Darrell was even better, because he was *right there*. He wasn't remote or untouchable; he was from Arlington, and so was Minyard. They shopped at the same guitar stores, went to the same clubs, saw the same bands, probably drank from the same bottles of booze. Darrell was a lot like Minyard, except he was a better guitarist. But he didn't act like it.

Minyard felt comfortable enough to strike up a conversation with Darrell after a gig at Dallas City Limits in the late 1980s. He could have brushed Minyard off, and most people in his situation would have. He was on his way, after all. Local stardom had spread all across the Lone Star State. National fame, even international—it was next. Everyone was sure of it.

But Darrell talked to Minyard that night. In fact, he went one better. He *always* went one better, as Minyard and hundreds of other fans found out over the years. He pulled Minyard into his world. Soon enough, Scott Minyard was a member of the extended inner circle, the recipient of phone calls, party invites, and as many shots of whiskey as he could stomach—and some that he couldn't.

What Minyard always wanted to do, from the first time he met Darrell after that show at Dallas City Limits, was to see his mentor at work in a recording studio. It wasn't idle idol worship; Minyard was in a band, too, and wanted to get familiar with those surroundings. He hadn't had the privilege, like Darrell and Vince, of spending his formative years in a studio. Minyard finally told Darrell about his wish not long before he told him something else, seemingly unrelated. During an impromptu house party at Minyard's place, he rhapsodized over one of his favorite records at the time, Soundgarden's *Badmotorfinger*. Specifically, Minyard was a fan of "the sound quality, the mixing, the production," he says. "It had sort of a classic recording sound; it's not overpolished. And the producer was Terry Date."

Minyard had already received a rough version of *Vulgar Display of Power* and fallen hard for it. So he was thrilled when, a week later, Darrell invited him to come over while he and the album's producer worked on mixing a song from the disc.

"They mixed the whole CD backward; the very first song is the last one [they did]," Minyard says.

They had a certain order and they decided to try it backward. You're getting real good at that point, at the very end. . . . So they're mixing the last one, and Darrell calls and says come on down at midnight. We went down at midnight, and he introduces me to the engineer. He goes, "Yeah, this is T." He called him T—guy in a hat and glasses. "Hey, nice to meet you," and everything. I had no idea who this guy was. Just one week ago I'm telling him how I like this guy's engineering so much. He didn't ever tell me that was Terry Date. He let me figure out myself. That's the kind of jokes he played. So I got to sit with Darrell and Terry Date, listen to them mix "Mouth for War."

Since Darrell could rarely sit still for long, mixing sessions were a chore for him. Bring up this track here. Move this one down there. So Minyard and Darrell—along with Bobby Tongs, a member of the crew who was almost always around—loaded up in Pantera's tour van and set off into the early morning, leaving Date alone to finish the mix.

"We're driving around, and he goes to Dalworthington Gardens—this is not when they lived there—and it was trash night," Minyard says. "We're blaring the *Vulgar Display of Power* stuff, and I'm just tripping out on everything. We're driving around, and he's pulling over and Tongs and him are getting out and getting trash. 'You wouldn't believe the stuff these people throw away,' he says. 'It's unbelievable what they'll throw away.' He's getting all of their stuff, like an old beat-up chair or whatever it was. He loved that stuff."

That kind of occurrence wasn't rare if you happened to be along for the ride with Darrell—literally and figuratively. It wasn't easy to detect what, exactly, would flip his switch, just that something invariably would.

"They called that 'Dime Time,'" Minyard says.

Everybody wants Dime Time. He was just plain fun to be around. He loved garage sales. When [he and Rita] first moved into this house over there in Dalworthington Gardens, this guy was helping him fix it up or whatever to get it ready. Painting and whatnot. Darrell was driving his Escalade with him in the car.

They see this garage sale and he backs up to the garage sale. He gets out and walks to the lady having the garage sale and he goes, "How much?" She says, "Well, for what?" And he goes, "All of it. I want all of it." And she wouldn't sell it to him.

She didn't want to sell all of it to him. She was having fun having her garage sale or something.

DARRELL WAS already becoming well known for his type of fun.

Circa *Vulgar Display of Power*, he had transformed into the Dimebag character he would be known as the rest of his life, physically and otherwise. He had the long pink goatee; the razorblade pendant on a chain around his neck (a riff on the cover of Judas Priest's *British Steel*); the dissolute-skater-kid wardrobe; the whole deal.

Darrell's aversion to marijuana—at least in public—was well behind him. He could finally stop worrying about derailing his career. He had made it through a close call, relatively unscathed. On January 21, 1991, on tour supporting *Cowboys from Hell*, he was arrested in Santa Rosa County in Florida and charged with possession of marijuana, a first-degree misdemeanor, exactly the situation he'd once feared. But it turned out to be no big deal: He pleaded no contest to the charge on May 22, after he'd returned home from Europe, and it more-or-less went away. Unabashed, he took to sparking up onstage. There was always an opportunity to do so, since fans regularly tossed joints (not lit, usually) at the band. He could call himself Dimebag and not worry about painting a giant target on his back. He could blow up giant papier-mâché pot leaves with fireworks if he wanted to. (He did.) In general, though, life on the road was fueled by something else: "A vulgar display of fucking liquor," as Darrell said.

In three years, Pantera had taken Darrell all over the world, from Canada to Denmark to Berlin to Akron to Barcelona to Santa Monica to New York to Italy to Atlanta to Washington, D.C., to Moscow to a few dozen other places. It was a heady time for Pantera, and for Darrell personally. For one thing, the boy who had pretended to be Ace Frehley in his bedroom mirror finally got a chance to meet his idol.

When Darrell appeared on the cover of the August 1993 issue of *Guitar World*, that should have been a big deal on its own. But that was nothing. What mattered was that on the cover with him were Skid Row guitarist Snake Sabo—and Ace Frehley. The photo shoot is documented on *Vulgar Videos*, and it's interesting enough, as far as photo shoots go. Which is to say, it isn't, really. What is particularly revealing is the moment when Darrell is introduced to Frehley. There is no sense of entitlement on his part, no trace of a mind-set that says, "Of *course*, I should be hanging out with Ace Frehley. In fact, he should be lucky to hang out with *me*." Instead, he shyly asks Frehley to sign the photo he brought with him, a tattered shot of him as a kid in his full Frehley getup, blown up to almost poster size. "Now it's fully set," he says after Frehley autographs it. He later goes a step further and has the KISS guitarist sign his name on his chest as well; he immediately had the signature tattooed over for posterity.

That was just about the only time Darrell would come off as shy. You were more likely to find him shooting bottle rockets off the V-shaped headstock of his guitar, as if they were specifically built for that purpose. *Vulgar Display of Power* had sold more than five hundred thousand copies, giving the band its first gold album, and the tours were getting bigger and bigger. Darrell had a little bit of fuck-you money now. He could do whatever he wanted, and often he did, rumbling through life like Peter Pan at the wheel of a monster truck.

Though Darrell was just getting started having fun with his newfound wealth and success, at least in one respect, the party was over. Jerry Abbott sold Pantego Sound Studio as soon as the recording of *Vulgar Display of Power* wrapped, and he moved to Nashville, where he set up a new studio, Abtrax, and tried to make a go of it as a country songwriter.

"Really, from the day I met Jerry, he really wanted to be in Nashville," says his former engineer, Jerry Hudson. "I guess a little bit of Pantera's success helped him to finally be able to go up there. As soon as they finished *Vulgar*, he hauled ass. He was packing stuff up as they were finishing the album. And literally, as soon as they said they were done, he put stuff in a truck and he left."

After their father left Pantego behind, the Abbotts returned a few times, once to deliver a gold album to Hudson after *Vulgar*

Display of Power received its certification from the Recording Industry Association of America on February 9, 1993. ("We won't go into the story of why I don't have that anymore," Hudson says.) The last time they came by they left behind something far less valuable.

"They brought this old yellow Ryder truck that was all *done*, I mean, just worn the fuck out, and parked it in front of the studio," Hudson remembers. "They had a bunch of old speaker cabinets, most of them with the shit robbed out of them, and said, 'Hey, man, if you can sell any of this stuff, fine'—and then I never saw them [there] again. I think the police came and hauled off the truck eventually." And with that, Pantego Sound Studio's role in the Pantera story was over, and so, for the most part, was Hudson's. He would see the brothers one more time when he went to Nashville to visit Jerry Abbott's new studio—a trip that, no one should be surprised, took a detour through some of Music City's strip clubs.

But even that—not to mention their rising stature in the music business—didn't change how Hudson saw the brothers. To Hudson they were and always would be the same kids drawing KISS logos on the walls of the control room. There was some truth to that.

8

DOMINATION

The Heaviest Album to Hit No. 1 on the Charts

"Gee, I wish we had one of them doomsday machines."

GENERAL "BUCK" TURGIDSON,
Dr. Strangelove

Every Pantera album, from *Metal Magic* to *Vulgar Display of Power*, had been recorded at Pantego Sound Studio. But that was gone now. While Jerry set up a new studio there in time for the band to start work on *Far Beyond Driven*, again with Terry Date producing, it wasn't the same.

Recording at Pantego Sound had been a painless process. They could continue what passed for normal lives: sleep at home, eat and drink at the same dives they always did, hang out with friends when they wanted to escape the soundproof booths. After more than a decade of sessions at Pantego Sound, it was part of their routine, no different than a trip to the supermarket or Sunday church.

In Nashville, they couldn't rely on old routines. They couldn't rely on much of anything. Only, as the song inspired by their time in Tennessee says, "Good Friends and a Bottle of Pills."

"We were fuckin' flying there for three weeks at a time, writing songs and cutting them," Darrell said a couple of months after the album's release, in an interview with *Guitar Player*. "On the past records we were able to go to the studio and work until we were sick of the place. Then I'd call up a close friend and go out, look at some tits, and drink beer. You need to get a breath away from the band so you can forget about the whole situation and come back freshened. In Nashville, all we had was each other. We'd go to each other's hotel rooms, fuckin' sit around and listen to more music, fuckin' pop pills, drink beer, and smoke dope. We weren't able to completely escape the joint."

That bunker mentality helped the band arrive at a strategy for how best to use the overwhelming force at its disposal. The songs that predated the trips to Nashville fell right in line with their new ethos. Darrell, working on a tour-long hangover that foreshadowed his mental and physical state during the Nashville sessions, hit upon the menacing slow-burn guitar figure at the center of "I'm Broken" during sound check before one of the *Vulgar* shows. Vinnie and Rex joined in behind him, and that was pretty much that; the song would go on to be *Far Beyond Driven*'s lead single and representative of the band's simpler, surlier approach.

"We wanted the songs to have the most impact, period," Darrell said later in the *Guitar Player* interview.[24] "Everything we do is for the band as a whole. It's not like we've got a spotlight lead guitar player in the band. You're going to hear me, Rex, Vinnie, Phil, everybody. 'Slaughtered' used to have this dynamic lead section. Everybody was hatin' it, but not saying nothing, thinking it might come around. We fucked with it for maybe ten minutes, and finally Phil said, 'Man, for the sake of the song—' and I went, 'No shit.' We all looked at each other and went, 'Fuck that shit.' Fuck, the whole song's a solo anyway."

It's interesting to note that, even after all the guitar contest victories, the endorsement deals, after the success of Pantera's first two major-label albums, Darrell would still say things like "It's not like we've got a spotlight lead guitar player in the band," even though he was one of the few in the early 1990s who could claim that distinction. To Darrell, playing guitar was much like what playing golf is to some, a game you can get good at, but never quite master.

"I've known this for years but I still have trouble, battling with this thought in my head, thinking that others are gonna know what little crack or crevice makes you cringe," Darrell admitted once, in one of his many videotaped "confessionals," filmed while looking at himself in his bathroom mirror, aping the arrangement that had set him on this course to begin with.[25] "Well, little do we realize . . . It's hard to realize that what may sound like a squeaky, out-of-tune, fucking irritating violin to someone sounds like the most serene beautiful tone of a fucking saxophone beautifully in tune in the moonlight. You know, so sassy it can sway you and really make you feel fucking great. So what's a little imperfection to the man who made it might be the fucking one little thing that's always pointed out by one of my close friends [as the thing they love the most], . . . 'Nah, that's the coolest thing.'"

While he was confident in his skill as a guitar player and only grew more so as the years ticked by, thanks to those little cracks or crevices he was unwilling to elevate himself to the level of the guitarists (like Eddie Van Halen) he had grown up worshiping, or the newer breed (like Zakk Wylde) he admired. When he'd talk about the dearth of potential guitar heroes in the metal community, guys who could, as he said, deliver "the full-meal deal," he would never suggest that no one out there could play like him. Just that fewer people could play like the guitarists of his youth.

But few people *could* play like him, and that had been the case practically since that first show at the Ritz. "He was extremely influential—*before* they did their first national release, major release or whatever," Scott Minyard says. Before Pantera was anything, Darrell Abbott was already somebody. When people saw Darrell with his guitar, they *knew*. Even if he was onstage playing a Loverboy cover. Even if he was onstage by himself. Especially if he was onstage by himself. It was one of those things in life that just *was*. Grass is green. The sky is blue. Darrell could play guitar.

Darrell knew this, too, knew that was the reason he was put on the earth. When he learned how to play "Smoke on the Water," the world had opened up to him, and his future cleared up like a shaken Polaroid. School wouldn't take him where he needed—was destined, really—to go, so he stayed at home with his guitar, picking and grinning until he found his sound, his style, his signature, stopping only to add to the loogie wall, the disgusting monument to his focus. That combination of natural talent and unnatural dedication made Darrell a winner. He won so many guitar contests the organizers stopped letting him enter; he became a judge before he was out of his teens. He won readers' polls in every extant guitar-related magazine and the unofficial title of "World's Most Dangerous Guitarist" (according to *Guitar World*'s April 1994 cover). He won the admiration of his heroes and contemporaries.

And yet, while Darrell could have rightly said he was better than most and could build a strong case to that effect, he had the disposition of a pauper rather than a prince. When he would hop onstage with anyone to play KISS songs, it wasn't to show off or draw attention his way; he just liked playing KISS songs. When people called him the Idol or King Dime, he laughed it off; he wasn't anyone's king or idol or whatever else. Fuck that, he'd scoff. He constantly extolled the virtues of other guitar players like a starstruck fan, as though he hadn't already reached or surpassed their level.

"Darrell would call me up and tell me about these guys, and I'd be, like, 'Don't you *know?* Don't you *see?*'" Buddy Blaze says. Blaze toured with Steve Vai and built guitars for Eddie Van Halen. He had seen and heard most of the greats and had worked with many of them. He knew guitar heroes, and he knew Darrell not only belonged in their company but also was one of the best.

But it was obvious even to those who weren't in the guitar business like Blaze. "The guy really was a genius," Dale Brock says. "I mean he was one of the few guitar players out there that had a signature sound, like a vocalist's signature voice. You could hear a Dime lead on anything and go, 'That's Dime.' He just had an amazing style that took some elements of Van Halen and what have you and made it his own. Just fucking amazing. When I saw him I was seventeen and he was a little kid in a cover band; it was just, like—I mean he was obviously a prodigy, like, 'Oh my God, this is the best guitar player I've ever seen in a club.' He was *it*."

"Jimmy Page told me this," says rock photographer Ross Halfin. "I once watched a guitarist and I finally said, 'How can you tell if they're good?' He said you can tell if someone's good whether they play one or fifty chords because you can instantly know it's them by the sound. And you instantly knew it was Dimebag by his guitar sound. And that's the sign of a good guitar player. Where someone like, say, Richie Sambora could be anyone. Someone in Megadeth could be anyone. In the sense that Kirk Hammett sounds like a lot of other people, Dimebag Darrell sounded like Dimebag."

Darrell's ability was even more obvious to people who were in the guitar business. "He was up there with everyone," says David Karon, who works in artist relations at Randall Amplifiers and Washburn Guitars, two of Darrell's one-time endorsers. "I mean, to me, regardless of what he meant to me, when you'd just sit in a room with him playing guitar, I don't know if people realized what a versatile player he was, but it was just like—I've been around a lot of great guitar players, and I still have never heard someone play like *that*. Just in a room by himself, kind of fucking around. He was insane. Probably the memory that will always go there is the first time I was at his house, just watching him play. Just checking shit out. So, to me, he will definitely go down in history as one of the greats."

"I think he was just the Natural," Slayer's Kerry King says. "'Course, he worked hard at what he did, but he was like [Dave]

Lombardo in our band—Dave, he's a natural. Motherfucker, Dave doesn't even warm up to this day. He just walks onstage and we'll jump into 'Disciple,' where I've already warmed up for an hour just so I can play that song." He laughs. "That's how I think Dime was. That talent, he just had it."

The talent made Darrell a first-class guitar player. But it was something else that made others think of him as a first-class man, flaws and all. At heart Darrell was modest and empathetic, more eager to champion the accomplishments of others than crow about his own. Remember: "It's not like we've got a spotlight lead-guitar player in the band."

"I played in a punk rock band for a while called Battery Club," says former *Headbangers Ball* host Riki Rachtman. "We ended up doing five shows in Texas. And when we played in Texas, Darrell and Vinnie came by to see us play [without being asked to]. I mean, it wasn't a big thing, because I never put my name in the band, because I just didn't want to. They ended up going and buying a demo and buying a T-shirt—and obviously, you know, we would have given it to them."

Darrell, being Darrell, took it a step further.

They said, "Hey, you know, we're in the studio mixing some tracks [for *Far Beyond Driven*]. Do you guys wanna come down?" So my whole band came down, and these were guys that were just in all these different punk rock bands at the time. So we all went down to the studio and hung out with them, and without a doubt, that was the night that was almost a disaster, because everybody in my band got *so* drunk with those guys that they were fighting with each other. One guy said that he wanted to stay and that he'd meet us later. Everybody was just partying with those guys, and everybody just got so fucked up. But the whole time that you were partying with those guys, it was like high school. It wasn't "Oh, rock stars doing coke in the backstage." It was like fucking hanging out at a kegger. It was just a blast.

A brief exchange captured in the final Pantera video collection, *3: Watch It Go*, more succinctly explains why people loved Darrell, and not just his ability to play guitar. As the band relaxes backstage before a show, Darrell rushes in with a copy of the August 1994 issue of *Modern Drummer*, which marked his brother's first appearance on the cover. It is unquestionably a big deal for Vinnie. But if you turned the sound down, obscured the cover of the magazine, and tried to guess who was on it just by watching the people in the scene, you would more than likely guess wrong. Because Darrell is enjoying the moment more than anyone else.

PANTERA WAS a sleeper cell, quietly (so to speak) going about its business, never imagining that four not terribly attractive or trendy guys from Texas might actually be the Next Big Thing. With few exceptions, metal was supposed to be dead, or dying, annexed by the new alternative nation headquartered in Seattle.

Darrell and Pantera did not waver. They were a heavy metal band, and that was it. Their stubbornness was bolstered by success. *Cowboys from Hell* was more than a moderate hit, and *Vulgar Display of Power* fared even better. But none of that prepared anyone for what happened when *Far Beyond Driven* was released on March 15, 1994. One could argue that was the moment when the rock-and-roll administration began a transfer of power, ushering in the blizzard of Ozzfest. *Far Beyond Driven* sold 186,000 copies in its first week and debuted at No. 1 on the *Billboard* charts, easily the heaviest album to do so, at least up to then.

It was clear that the work Pantera had put into promoting *Vulgar Display of Power*—a continuation of the work ethic forged during the Metal Magic years, only now backed by corporate muscle—had spilled over onto the release of *Far Beyond Driven*. It was also clear that the band had not been seduced, but emboldened, by the sales figures of *Vulgar Display of Power*. Other groups, when placed in a similar position, might chase after hits, soften their sound, smooth over at least some of their rough edges for easier mass consumption. They might play the game, tailoring their image and music to appease radio and video programmers.

Take Metallica, the band that once drove Darrell to make his own music heavier and heavier. Metallica helped validate and galvanize the heavy metal underground with a string of vicious, ambitious albums in the 1980s: 1983's *Kill 'Em All*, 1986's *Master of Puppets*, and 1988's . . . *And Justice for All*. But after . . . *And Justice for All* landed in *Billboard*'s Top 10 without the benefit of radio airplay and only minimal assistance from MTV, Metallica altered its plan of attack. The band's self-titled *Black Album* followed in 1991 and, with its shorter, simpler songs, seemed designed to capitalize on the commercial potential . . . *And Justice for All* had happened upon organically.

The disc's massive success (No. 1 on the charts; more than seven million copies sold by 1993) only took the band further away from its roots. When *Load* hit stores in 1996, Metallica had adopted a look more in line with the alternative rock scene (which helped prepare the band to headline the sixth installment of the Lollapalooza package tour), along with a sound that recalled, at times, 1970s arena rock (which didn't). They appeared in arty Anton Corbijn photos that wouldn't have looked out of place on a U2 album. Metallica made more new fans but lost more of their original ones.

Pantera, on the other hand, went in the opposite direction, removing even the slightest suggestion of compromise. The success of *Cowboys from Hell* and *Vulgar Display of Power* encouraged not only the band to stick to its guns, but the staff at EastWest, Pantera's newish label[26] as well. There was no one pressuring the group for a "'Mr. Sandman' track" this time around. "Given their track record, it would be completely inappropriate for us to try and tell Pantera what to do," Steve Kleinberg, vice president of marketing at the label, told *Billboard* a month before *Far Beyond Driven*'s release. "You've got to trust them to know what their fans want. The fact is that they have tremendous credibility and integrity out there. We do not want to get in the way of that."[27]

It was evident from the album's art that no one would be getting in Pantera's way, and God help whoever did. *Vulgar Display of Power*'s cover featured a visceral photo of a fist colliding with a face; *Far Beyond Driven* went a step further, with a stylized depiction of a drill bit twisting into a man's skull. The difference in cover art worked well enough as a shorthand description of the difference between the two albums. If *Vulgar Display of Power* was the musical equivalent of a fistfight, then *Far Beyond Driven* was the sound of bare fists giving way to heavy artillery.

That escalation of firepower was the point, wasn't it? At least it had been since Anselmo joined the band, and since Darrell and

Vince started trying to ride the lightning themselves. See how far you can take it, then take it further.

"We're into topping ourselves," Darrell told *Guitar Player* in May 1994. "Most bands come out with a heavy record, then it gets lighter and lighter. You're stuck listening to the first record, wishing and dreaming. That ain't what we're about, though."[28]

There was nothing light about *Far Beyond Driven*. Except, perhaps, for the live-action cartoon character at the center of it all.

BY THE time Bugs Henderson arrived in Spain for his first tour of the country, he hadn't seen much of Darrell since finishing the recording of *Still Flyin'* at Pantego Sound Studio with Jerry Abbott back in 1981. A few years after those sessions, he had been asked by a Dallas radio station—"probably the Zoo or 102, whatever was happening back then," he says—to judge a guitar contest at the Palladium, a long-gone club on Northwest Highway. Darrell was one of the contestants.

"Each kid would get up and play for three or four minutes, some little solo thing by theirselves," Henderson says. "And he blew everybody away. It was no contest. He was so far ahead of everybody else that was playing. It was obvious, you know?"

After that contest, Henderson lost track of Darrell and his burgeoning career as a guitarist. Darrell was making a name for himself, but Henderson wasn't around enough to notice. His own band kept him busy on the road, and his family kept him busy at home.

Years later, when he finally caught up with Darrell (or, more accurately, when Darrell caught up with him) and he, at long last, started hearing about Pantera, it took a little while for Henderson to make the connection. It was difficult for him to associate the kid who had sat on the floor of the studio, watching the older guitarist's fingers, quietly asking questions, with the bombastic entity Pantera had become. When he saw Darrell at the NAMM[29] show in Anaheim, or when his publicist would hand him another magazine in which Darrell mentioned the impact Henderson's playing had had on him growing up, he had even more trouble reconciling the two wildly divergent ideas of who Darrell Abbott was.

"He always came over and talked and was real nice," Henderson says, remembering the times when he crossed paths with Darrell at the NAMM shows. "The guy I knew was so opposite from that image. My kids were into his music and they'd been to the shows and they would tell me how crazy it was and all of the shit that was going on. And I was like, 'Really? Darrell? That's just weird.'"

It got weirder for Henderson when he arrived in Spain.

"They had huge posters of [*Far Beyond Driven*]," he says. "I remember it was real—it was like some giant tool going into a chick's ass or something. I mean you wouldn't have seen them over here.[30] And they were right next to our posters; it was real bizarre. Because ours were just, like, me making the standard I'm-passing-a-stone face that all guitar players make. And right next to it was this giant ass with this drill going in it or something that said 'Pantera.' That's when I started getting an idea of the kind of thing they were doing and the wildness of it all. Which was great with me. I mean I understand showbiz."

But Henderson never met *that* Darrell Abbott; he never saw Dime. "Every conversation I ever had with him, he was just like the same kid," Henderson says. "He never came up to me and was that guy that he was onstage at all. He was just Darrell, and supernice."

Nothing would change the idea of Darrell that Henderson kept in his head. Not even that poster in Spain. But for many others, the opposite was the case: They only saw Dime. They only saw a lowlife living the highlife, the so-called World's Most Dangerous Guitarist. They never saw Darrell.

Granted, Darrell, and the rest of Pantera, made it as tough as possible.

WHEN THE Abbotts went back out on the road in the summer of 1994 on Pantera's biggest headlining tour yet, with Biohazard and Sepultura supporting, it was readily apparent just how far the brothers had progressed from the years of touring every weekend and watching every penny, not to mention how far removed they were from the time when they'd tag along with their dad to Pantego Sound and Darrell would stare at the guitarists' fingers.

Pantera had come a long way in just the previous couple of months. After *Far Beyond Driven* was released in March, they set out on a club tour, which included a sold-out, two-night stand at New York City's thirty-five-hundred-capacity Roseland Ballroom. "Its fans crave the wallop," *New York Times* critic Jon Pareles observed after the first of those NYC gigs.[31] Exactly how true that was would be proved on the band's next tour.

Flush with success, Pantera was booked in venues like the World Music Theatre[32] in Tinley Park, Illinois, a suburb of Chicago, which held upwards of twenty-five thousand people. It wasn't only the crowds that were bigger. Everything was. The shows were now massive affairs that took the better part of a day to erect and disassemble. The hour and a half the band spent on-stage was the simplest part of the entire process.

Pantera, its crew, and its gear traveled from city to city in four tour buses—the days of the beat-up RV they'd used on the *Cowboys from Hell* tour were long gone—and a trio of tractor trailers. Besides enough amplifiers to fashion a decent-sized dam with, those trucks were loaded with four colossal lighting rigs, each holding up to twenty spotlights and each weighing in at a hefty six thousand pounds. These rigs also held the band's computer-controlled Vari-Lites, swiveling devices that projected various designs around the stage and the arena, including the Pantera logo. A dozen or so Vari-Lites would be in service every night of the tour; each one had set the band back a cool thirty-five hundred dollars. Clearly, Pantera had come a long way from the days of air-force-issue light shows and "Ken-gineered" pyrotechnic displays.

The difference manifested itself in other ways that the general public wasn't privy to. Back in the day, the members of Pantera couldn't afford to break anything they didn't already own—and, really, they couldn't afford to harm their own property either. But they knew that real rockers tore up hotel rooms, so they went through the motions, knocking the lampshades askew, jumping on the beds, making sure none of the pictures on the wall were level. If someone accidentally did some real damage, it meant they'd be sneaking out of the parking lot before they could get stuck with the bill.

Now? They had a No. 1 record and were selling out amphitheaters. If they didn't leave the dressing room in exactly the same condition in which they found it, who cared? Send the bill to their tour manager, and fuck 'em if they couldn't take a joke. In the cover-band era, they had had to sell one of their amps to a kindhearted fan in Gainesville after breaking a door at their hotel. Now they would go out of their way to systematically disintegrate a hotel room door, taking turns punching and stomping it until it was little more than splinters and a knob.

Money was no object. It was just something they used to pass the time, or to pay for the other ways they chose to pass the time. No one found more ways to give away money than Darrell; his adolescent high jinks now had a budget. He could buy fireworks by the case and shots by the tray. He could shoot out hotel lamps with a pellet gun, unless he felt like taking them down via hand-to-hand combat. He could (and did) give someone three hundred dollars to chug an entire bottle of Lea & Perrins Worcestershire sauce. He could (and did) offer a crew member a thousand dollars to eat an entire birthday cake. Upping the ante for no particular reason, he could (and did) offer security chief Val Bichekas over four grand to finish that same cake when the first contestant had to bow out. "That's the fun I have," he'd say.

An ever-increasing number of people got to share in that fun. When Pantera returned home for a sold-out show with Type O Negative at Dallas's Fair Park Coliseum on February 5, 1995, the backstage guest list was 680 names long. The band was a long way away from the Basement days. The members were now to the point where they could invite enough people to fill up a club like the Basement to hang out backstage at an arena show.

"It got to the point where they had a *huge* backstage area for all these people," says Dale Brock, former manager of the Basement. "They'd have their own little dressing room tucked away, or they'd have their bus and wouldn't let everybody on. But, I mean, they'd just have it catered to the hilt, all kinds of booze. In-town concerts were a huge party for all their friends and everybody. Personally, I liked to see them out of town. That was the best time, just going on the road with them and hanging out with them—out of town, where they didn't personally know, you know, eight hundred people."

That was the problem with Darrell's generosity—with his time, with his alcohol, with himself: Eventually, there wasn't enough to go around. He picked up strays like a kindly old cat lady. Over the years, his inner circle expanded to the point where it surrounded everyone he met. It had a circumference so vast no one could see the edges of it.

By the time Pantera was playing bigger venues, even if Darrell had gotten his hands on a fresh batch of fireworks or a few bottles of Lea & Perrins, and even if the guest list was the size of a novella, it was probably safer backstage. The fans out front were matching the band's increasing intensity, calling every raise. At the Fair Park Coliseum gig, the crowd ripped up a handful of huge plywood planks that covered the ice the venue used for Dallas Freeze minor-league hockey games, using some as ad hoc surfboards, lighting others on fire. The previous Pantera gig in Dallas, a July 29, 1994, show that marked its first headlining appearance at the Starplex Amphitheatre, had proceeded in a similar fashion. "The only difference between a riot and a Pantera concert is that cops don't ride horses at a Pantera show," the *Dallas Morning News*'s Michael Corcoran said. He described the fourteen-thousand-strong crowd as "the wildest, scariest, most pumped-up audience I've ever been a part of. I half expected to see vendors going through the crowd yelling, 'Raw meat! Getcher raw meat!'"[33]

Corcoran was exaggerating, but only slightly. In time, even his wry comment about mounted police would prove false. Pantera canceled a January 31, 1995, gig at Shreveport's Hirsch Coliseum at the last minute, due to a recently adopted Louisiana state code forbidding open-floor seating at concerts. The band wasn't willing to find out what metal folding chairs plus metal fans added up to and backed out of the show. The twenty-nine hundred fans waiting outside—the concert was called off at 7 P.M.—weren't particularly happy that someone was looking out for their safety. According to the New Orleans *Times-Picayune*, in the ensuing melee four people were arrested on charges including "battery, inciting a riot, and cruelty to an animal after an angry patron punched a police horse in the neck."[34]

Dale Brock happened to be tagging along with the band that night. "They said people are going to get killed if these folding chairs are here," Brock remembers.

Which they would have. Metal folding chairs? They would have folded them up and thrown them around and people would have got killed. So, man, was it mayhem when they called the show. I mean, from our side, it was a pretty fun night, because we had a coliseum to ourselves. I mean, nobody inside. And we're behind the glass doors looking out as they make this announcement. There's cops on horseback, and ten thousand people[35] essentially rioting. You know, "We've got our tickets, we're coming to the Pantera show." These are diehard Pantera fans and, you know no fucking show. Doors aren't opening. Go away. That was ugly. Yeah. It was cops on horseback, you know, beating people, people throwing shit. I think somebody actually threw something through the front door. I think that's about the time we retreated.

But that turned into just a big huge party in the dressing room all night long. . . . Then we took the entire tour bus over to Isle of Capri casino, where Dime proceeded to throw down *huge* amounts of money in blackjack, make stupid goofy calls, probably just because he could.

Lost tons of money. But that was a fun experience, pulling up to a casino in the tour bus.

AFTER THE commercial success of *Cowboys from Hell*, *Vulgar Display of Power*, and *Far Beyond Driven*, not to mention the lucrative tours to support them, Darrell Abbott could have completely abandoned his hometown, said good-bye without so much as a glimpse in the rearview mirror. He could have opted for a mansion in a ritzy area of Dallas or Fort Worth, or maybe a nice spread out in the country. Something that was a symbol of his having made it. Most would.

Darrell did, in fact, technically move away from Arlington. But he didn't go far. Instead of Dallas or Fort Worth, he and his longtime girlfriend, Rita Haney, opted for a relatively modest house (according to county appraisal records, it's worth $361,500 today) in Dalworthington Gardens, not so much a suburb of Arlington as it is an emancipated neighborhood of the city. By then, Darrell and Rita were essentially married, though they'd never made it official and never would. "We didn't believe in the marriage thing—why fix something that ain't broke?" Rita said in

July 2006, during an interview with *Metal Edge* magazine. "Why have someone you don't know tell you it's OK to be with someone you do know? We didn't need the middleman! We had a one-on-one with the man upstairs ourselves."[36]

The couple bought the house in June 1995. Like Darrell, it accumulated various nicknames over the years, including Camp Strapped and the Fortress. "Instead of spending all my money on beer and tattoos," he told *Guitar World* in a June 1996 cover story, "I thought I'd buy something that's worth a shit for once."[37] It's just a short drive from Pantego Sound Studio and is so close to Arlington that you wouldn't know it wasn't actually a part of the city if a sign didn't instruct you otherwise.

Nothing about the house sets it apart from the others on the block. In fact, if you had been told a famous musician had a home in Dalworthington Gardens, there are plenty of other homes in the area that are more likely candidates based solely on curb appeal. Well, OK, there was *one* thing about the exterior of the house that might have tipped off people on pilgrimages to worship at the feet of King Dime.

"Dime had a goat," Dale Brock says. "He had a goat that he owned that ran around his property. Something was wrong with the goat, if you can imagine that. And the goat had his beard dyed purple just like Dime. He loved that goat. And this goat was mean and obnoxious. The goat would jump up on people's cars and kick in their hoods and kick in their windows. You'd be trying to leave and the goat would jump on your hood. It was just nuts. I can imagine what the neighbors thought, in Dalworthington Gardens, that has its own police force and everything. Wow. The insane, purple-bearded, Dimebag goat."

Inside was a different story. One didn't need to keep an eye out for a goat with a dyed-purple beard to know who lived there. "His house is kind of like a funhouse," Scott Minyard says. "I'm sure he spent a lot of money at Spencer's throughout his life," referring to the novelty gift store that used to be a shopping-mall staple. Beyond cheap gag knickknacks, Darrell's house was a celebration of his life in rock and roll; photos of him with the various rock stars and famous people he'd met hung next to his gold and platinum plaques. Also hung on his wall were the twisted remains of a stop sign he and Zakk Wylde had forcibly uprooted in December 2002, after binge-drinking with a couple of writers from *Guitar World*. His house was like a scrapbook, the slightly more grown-up version of the room he had when he was fifteen years old and skipping school.

Now that he could afford it, Darrell had his own studio built on the property, just down the driveway from the main house, in a converted RV garage. Pantera and Damageplan would eventually record albums there, but that wasn't the point at the time. It was for him, not the band. He never wanted to be far from a guitar or a tape machine when inspiration struck. Before he built his home studio, he had accomplished this by always carrying a four-track recorder with him. "When the urge would hit him, he'd be, like, 'Let's go record!'" Brock says. "Frigging mediocre musicians would be around, 'Let's go record!' He didn't fucking care. He'd go rip it up. Hell, *I* got to jam with him on a couple of songs."

His guitars weren't confined to the studio. They were part of the home's interior decoration, strewn throughout the house, including a nylon-string acoustic model in his bathroom. "Yeah, nothing feels better than knowing I can put a guitar in my hands at any time and rip—even when I'm taking a crap," he joked. "I guess you could just call me a shithouse poet!" The bathroom was something of an office to him. "He would wake up in the middle of the night to use the restroom and have something in his head; he had notes tacked on the wall in front of you where the toilet is," Minyard says. "He's got little notes and stuff, whether it would be a new shape or kind of a modification on one of the guitars that he's working with for Dean, or anything." To this day, two pages of notes, his playbook for the next Damageplan album, are stapled to the wall.

The center of most activity in the house was—no surprise—the front party room. Its walls painted blood red, the room was—and is, since Rita Haney still lives there—outfitted with a pool table, Darrell's collection of KISS pinball machines, and a jukebox. The latter is loaded with Van Halen, Judas Priest, Iron Maiden, and KISS records, but there are a few surprises on there, such as *Spilt Milk*, the 1993 album by LA power-pop band Jellyfish. (He was also a fan of Simply Red's "Holding Back the Years.")

The house was, in many ways, an outward representation of Darrell himself. Just as everyone wanted to be around Darrell, everyone wanted to be at his house, too. (Maybe not in the downstairs bathroom. It was dubbed "the Slaytanic bathroom"— painted dark with heads coming out of the walls.) Minyard tells a story that's typical of what a day at home was like for Darrell. It happened on the Fourth of July, but it's doubtful he needed an excuse to have a good time. Minyard says:

He had some Black Velvet, and I go, "I don't want none of that." He goes, "You can't tell the difference." And I said,

"Yeah, we're doing the Pepsi challenge, but we're doing the whiskey challenge." He was making black tooths with Black Velvet and Crown, and I immediately knew what it was.

So we were doing that, and then we were outside throwing cheap beers at this old truck. He had plans on giving it to a friend; it was an old, beat-up, red, rusty truck. But he wanted to dent it up as bad as possible and *then* give it to the guy. Even more, you know? So we're sitting there throwing beer cans. Everybody's hurling full beers at this truck, really hard. He noticed this car going back and forth out in front of the house. They have, like, a wall around his house, so you can't really see real good, but you could see this car. It ended up being some young kids—sixteen, eighteen, seventeen, something. He goes out there and pulls 'em in, and next thing you know, he's got these young kids on the pool table, and he's signing posters for them and everything. He knew what they were doing and wanted to do 'em one better and give them some posters and CDs, stuff like that. Send them on their way with more than just driving by the house.

Kids driving by the house often had a better time of it than people Darrell had actually invited to come over, at least once they fell asleep. This was never a good idea, unless Darrell was already out for the count, and his guests were confident they could beat him out of bed in the morning—or afternoon. If there were fireworks around, and there usually were, it was best not to sleep at all.

Years later, Damageplan bassist Bob "Zilla" Kakaha learned that rule as he was trying to outrun a whistle chaser that was very much living up to the second part of its name. "This thing, I swear everywhere he went to get away from it, it just chased him in a full circle," Darrell said on a 2004 episode of *Headbangers Ball.* "He had this beanbag running from it. And it was just *on him.*"[38]

Over time, most visitors to Darrell's house learned to keep their wits about them. But some didn't have the advantage of knowing what was in store. Someone who had the misfortune to deliver a pizza to that address might find himself surrounded by Darrell and his friends, all of whom could appear rough-looking without trying very hard, and all of whom didn't mind using that detail to their advantage. On these occasions, Darrell often elected to have some fun and roll tape while he interrogated the nervous pizza deliveryman, wondering how, exactly, he had screwed up the order so badly and who he thought would be paying for such a disgrace. A tense moment or two would ensue before Darrell broke character and into a wide grin: "Ah, man, I'm just fucking with you." One usually had to learn that the hard way.

BONUS TRACK:
BY DEMONS BE DRIVEN

Devil's Night, Dime's Night

*"We've got all kinds of
beer and shit in here."*

———

REX,
Airheads

As one might expect from a man who so idolized Ace Frehley and KISS that he had the guitarist's autograph tattooed on his chest, Darrell Abbott treated Halloween like Christmas. It was the biggest holiday of his year. When he and Vince still lived with their mother, they'd turn the garage into a haunted house for the neighborhood kids. As Darrell and Pantera got more successful, the parties grew bigger and more elaborate, and the guest list, more star-studded. But at heart, every party remained the same, because Darrell was at the heart of every party, fueling each with the same sense of humor and mischief that never managed to age past sixteen years old.

"It was his big, giant party of the year," Dale Brock says. "He'd totally deck the house up like a haunted house. The house was crazy: It had, like, hidden cameras in places, and he had a hidden control room, where he could watch what was going on in different rooms. As part of his Halloween decorations—just as a stupid little aside—he had a table with all these cans of potted meats, just like the worst, awful things you could think of, because it was *scary*. The scariest frigging canned meat you could think of, he'd have little displays of it setting out. People would be, like, 'Jesus, that's scary!'" He laughs. "It kind of took a minute to catch on. And the parties were always all night long."

The rules were simple: If he invited you, you had to show up. And you had to show up in costume—"no ifs, ands, or buts on that," says Scott Minyard. Darrell had a thing for costumes going way back. From his time spent in front of the mirror done up like Frehley and on through the early days of Pantera running around motel parking lots dressed like a low-rent gladiator, he always seemed to be in a costume of some sort, including when dressed as Darrell Abbott. But on Halloween, Darrell, of course, always went one step further; his costumes had costumes.

"It was almost like a kid going through a Halloween aisle and just grabbing a little bit of everything, sometimes," Minyard says. "You couldn't tell what it was. It was just something whacked out. As much garb as you can get on. He's gone as pimps—but he'll have a razorblade stuck in his head, you know? Just, like, 'Oh, I like that, too. I'm gonna use that on the pimp outfit'—even though it doesn't go. Just as much stuff as you can throw together. His stuff was pretty wacky."

The Halloween parties were never actually on Halloween, nor did they ever happen at a time that most normal people would set aside for revelry. For an extra element of surprise, partygoers would typically find out about the shindigs the night before. Maybe later than that. It never mattered. The parties were always packed, and everyone came properly attired. No one would consider missing an Abbott Halloween party. Darrell was hard to turn down when it came to Halloween.

Minyard knows this as well as anyone. He was at Vinnie's house the night before the 2002 get-together—though at the time, he didn't know it was the night before. Not knowing they had to save themselves for the next night, Minyard and his group stayed up drinking until dawn, finishing up by admiring the sunrise from the house's balcony. That's the last thing Minyard remembers about the morning; as it turned out, he tripped by the pool and knocked himself out. When he finally came to, it was 6:30—at night.

"I get home and I am *done* for the night," Minyard says. "I didn't want to do *anything*. I had a headache from not only the hangover, but also the bump on my head from falling over and knocking myself out. I get this phone call. Guess who? Dime. He's, like, 'I heard you had a little mishap over at the house last night.' And I go, 'Yeah, I'm feeling it, man.' And he goes, 'Well, guess what? Get 'er thrown on, and I'll see you about ten. Halloween party tonight.' And I'm going, 'Nooooo,' and he goes, 'Yeah, you gotta make it.' So I was there, in my old Charles Manson outfit. I had to throw it together at the last minute."

Minyard remembers another last-minute invite, another occasion on which he futilely tried to beg out of attending. This time, his excuse wasn't as good: He couldn't come up with a concept for his costume. Darrell, ever the Halloween pro, counseled him that some of the best costumes come from last-minute ideas, and furthermore, he was headed to Home Depot to pick up the rest of his own outfit. Meaning, "I'll see you there, brother." Darrell was right; inspiration struck. Minyard, thinking about all the cheap beer they drank, specifically Milwaukee's Best (known more colloquially as "The Beast"), went to Wal-Mart and bought eighty bucks' worth of Milwaukee's Best along with the other accessories for his getup.

"So I get over there, and I'm walking in, and him and Rita are walking by the front," Minyard says. "Inside, as soon as the door opens, he stops. I had this 'fro on, but I had the eighteen-pack box on as a hat. I had these Elvis shades on. I had this black plastic trash bag, and I put a hole in the bottom, and wore it like a gown. I had a cape on the back, and it was, like, random empty beer cans duct-taped on me. A walking piece of trash is what I looked like. It was pretty good, though. But he stopped and looked, and he figured it out: 'Now that's what I'm talking about.'" Minyard still seems touched by the memory of his friend and mentor approving of his last-minute idea.

SIDE THREE
THIRTEEN
STEPS TO NOWHERE
(1996–2000)

9

YESTERDAY
DON'T MEAN SHIT

The Highs and Lows of Rock and Roll

*"Success is having to worry about every
damn thing in the world, except money."*

JOHNNY CASH

Ulrich Wild had no idea what he was signing up for when he agreed to come to Texas to help Terry Date, Pantera's longtime producer, record the band's eighth album, *The Great Southern Trendkill*. Wild had previously worked with Date on recordings by White Zombie and Deftones. None of that prepared him for sessions with Pantera, given the fact the band had decided to record the bulk of *Trendkill* at Darrell's home studio, just a few miles away from the group's original home base at Pantego. The studio had been built as nothing more than a place for Darrell to jam, but after some demos for the disc were recorded there, the sound—deemed "fuckin' lethal" by Darrell—was too good to ignore. Plus, recording at home appealed to everyone, particularly Darrell, since, after all, it was his home.

"It's pretty damned difficult to keep your dick hard on a song when you have to drive forty-five minutes to some alienating recording facility before you can start jamming on it with your band," Darrell later explained to *Guitar World*'s Nick Bowcott.

And when you get there, you have to chill out and wait for everybody else to roll up. Then, of course, somebody's bound to be hungry so you leave the studio to go eat. This leaves you feeling like shit when you get back, and you end up slamming some beers and lying around watching a TV show you're not even interested in because your flame's not hot. And all the time you're waiting around to get inspired, you're shelling out big bucks for the place. To hell with that, man! We can do all time-wasting stuff at my hut and it doesn't cost us a dime. We've got a keg going, 50 bottles of whiskey, a pool table, a big-screen TV—inspiration can and does strike at any moment, and it's easy to keep the fire going when all you've gotta do is walk to the bottom of the goddamned garden![1]

Given all the time wasting that actually happened at Darrell's hut—or, to be more accurate, local strip clubs—it was probably better and certainly more cost-efficient for the band to record at its own studio. Wild arrived in town a few weeks before Thanksgiving in 1995. Apart from holidays, he stayed there until mid-March, before everyone decamped for Larrabee Sound Studios in West Hollywood to mix the disc.

"We could have probably recorded that entire record in a month," Wild says, "but there were so many distractions."

Why did it take so long? Look at Wild's explanation of his schedule—and we are using the loosest possible definition of the word—when Date left him alone with the band for a little over a week, so he could record vocals with Anselmo, who had returned full time to Louisiana, at Trent Reznor's studio in New Orleans:

Like, Dime, he wouldn't even get up until 3 P.M., usually, and that would be the early time he was waking up. Usually it would be kind of between three and six. Because Terry was out of town, Dime took liberties with the schedule a little bit. We got kind of turned around, and Dime wouldn't actually wake up until midnight.

He'd wake up at midnight, roll out of bed, drag everybody down to—what was it?—Babydolls, the strip joint, for last call, basically, for breakfast. Whoever remained there, at like 2 A.M., went over to Dime's house until about five, six in the morning to party. And that's when we actually finally ended up starting to work. So we finally started recording at, like, six in the morning until about eleven.

And then we decided—we meaning Dime; I was able to just say yes and go on with it—that we would go down to Babydolls for first call, for a nightcap.

We'd stay there until, like, one or so, and we'd come back and they would start fucking around—you know, he'd get these prototype guitars from Washburn, and he would customize them by just drilling holes into 'em, and spray-painting 'em, and, you know, chiseling 'em out, and just making some cute little drunken designs on there.

I would kind of skip out on that and start going to sleep. Because I'd have to wake up at, like three, four to at least make some phone calls and take care of some stuff—like buy tape or what have you—that we needed. You know, while the stores were still open. I didn't have the leisure of getting up at midnight, like Dime did.

The sessions were rarely more structured when Date was in town, riding herd on the band as much as he could. Playing guitar and just playing, period, went hand in hand for Darrell, and that was part of the deal if you were recording, or doing pretty much anything else, with him. He didn't pick up a guitar so he could have a job for the rest of his life. He didn't keep regular hours, he didn't have normal days, and that's the way it had been since he was fifteen years old. Even when he was in high school—a period of time in one's life dominated by routine—it had been that way.

The most dependable thing in Darrell's life was his guitar, and even that didn't dictate the course of any given day. Darrell could be almost bookish about guitar playing and guitars in general, and he spent plenty of quality time with his guitar almost every day, whether he was recording an album or recording on his four-track. When that actually happened, though, was anyone's guess, was hard to predict, and tended to happen when it happened. Wild and Date had to be prepared to roll with everything else, and to roll tape when he was ready.

When Darrell was ready, Wild learned something else about working with him that was unexpected: King Dime, the Idol, the man with the signature, dirty guitar tone, was still searching, still toying with his sound. Dozens and hundreds of guitar players tried to perfect their imitations of him. Darrell was trying to do it, too.

"The reason they put this studio together in the RV garage was that they could record on their own and keep a take from demo recordings if they were good and they wanted to keep 'em," Wild says.

It's hard to chase demo performances, you know? They'd record these demos and everything, and we'd listen to 'em and want to improve 'em and redo most if not all of it. Then it comes time to get the guitars down, and we've got the good gear now; Terry's stuff is in. Dime says, "It's not sounding the same." "Well, what's different?" It's, like, we're using the same heads, same guitars, same pedals, same everything. "Well, it must be the mikes." No, it's the same mikes. "Well, it must be the preamps." Well, yeah, that's the only thing that's changed. So, we go from, like, the Focus Right pres and the API pres and whatever else good stuff back to the Mackie, because that's what he used in the demo. So you plug it into the big Mackie board, like the 32-amp one that they were using for monitoring. And "It's just not sounding the same. It's just not sounding the same." I was, like, "Well, you said you used the Mackie—which one did you use?" "Well, this little four-channel Mackie." So we plug his guitar rig back into that, and use the Mackie preamps, the cheapest ones you could possibly find, and that was the guitar sound. It was far from worked out. . . . I don't think you ever have anything really figured out forever, because you change. Your taste changes, your touring [rig] changes, your endorsers change.

One thing never changed: no one could tell Darrell what to do or not do. By this point in his life and career, he'd earned at least that much. Though he constantly worked to make himself a better guitar player and, beyond that, could hero-worship with the best of them, there were very few people who could tell him anything about what to do with a guitar in hand that he didn't already know. After half a life spent in various bars and clubs, smiling his way through an endless stream of black tooth grins, giving his liver a pounding rarely seen outside of a mixed-martial-arts octagon, no one could tell him what to do with a shot glass in his hand either. He knew his body, his skills, his limits, his wants and needs (musically and otherwise) better than anyone. So he kept his own counsel on most things. He'd get the results he wanted, even if his methods were unorthodox. Banging out riffs and pounding shots were part of who he was. To get the former, you sometimes had to deal with the aggravation the latter all but ensured. It was usually worth the hassle.

"It was amazing what he was like with that thing strapped around him," Wild says.

He takes [his guitar] very serious, and the visions that he had of what he wanted to accomplish with it. That was always very important. But it was also very important to him to have a good time doing it. He wasn't really losing sight of it, per se, but it was frustrating at times to get him to work, because he was really living it up, you know? He bought a new Caddy—you know, it was just stuff like that. Terry got a phone call: "I need you to go into this room and fax me the insurance papers to this number." It was, like, "Uh oh. What's that all about?" Two or three hours later, he shows up with a Cadillac, right? And it's customized already—it's got the longhorns on it, the Coors cans wrapped around in the center. He found the button for traction control, to release it, and so he could do wheelies with his Caddy. So we're not going to get anything done because it's joyride time. He's having a good time, but then he's going to be happy and recording well for a few hours after that, so you know, what are you gonna do? For starters, you can't catch him. He's in a car and you're on foot.

He always liked to live it up, and drinking was definitely a part of that. During the recording, everybody was always drinking, unless you were in AA. If it was known you were not drinking, that was the only reason you weren't drinking. You know, there are all the drinking rules, like drinking out of turn. And the answer to everything was always "Have a shot." You know, "I'm cold." "Have a shot." "I'm hot." "Have a shot." "I'm hungry." "Have a shot."

That atmosphere led to an interesting souvenir for Wild. He had shown up in Dalworthington Gardens with long ringlets, a hairstyle that mimicked Darrell's to a degree, though it was a bit shorter. Being the new guy, Wild was promised an initiation into the fold, and one look at his head made it clear what that would be. Every day, Darrell would growl at him, "Yer hair's coming off." Wild fought them off by playing it cool, acting as though not only did he not care, but he actually welcomed the impromptu haircut. "That kind of took the wind out of their sails," Wild says. "It wasn't quite as much fun."

But after another heavy night (and early morning) of drinking at Babydolls, Darrell and the band decided to finally go through with it. They sat Wild down in Darrell's kitchen, turned on the video camera, and went to work.

"They started shaving a bald spot in the back," Wild remembers.

And they started shaving up from the front a little bit. But they didn't have the big clippers. They had, like, little beard clippers. It took *forever*. They started just chopping stuff off left and right, mostly in the back. They made two horns in the front with whatever was left and they spray-painted it pink, with that, you know, punk hairspray stuff. Then they made one big horn in the front out of the two horns, like a unicorn-type thing. And they singed that—that was pretty smelly. Eventually, they just laughed the whole thing off and gave up on the shaving of the head, because they didn't have clippers and it was too much labor. They kind of left me looking like some really bad, awful version of Billie Joe from

Green Day, with pink hair instead of green. And then they left for three days.

I was there trying to sober up for three days. Those were probably the only three days I didn't drink, mind you, in that whole thing. Basically, I went down to Texas with them and I was drunk for—what?—four, five months.

Wild didn't really stay in touch with Darrell and the band after *Trendkill* was finished. He'd see the group in LA when it was on tour, but mostly they'd send word back and forth through other bands. One of the groups Wild was recording would get a Pantera tour, and he'd tell them to say hello for him to Darrell and the guys. Someone else would come off tour with Pantera and head into the studio with Wild, bringing back Darrell's regards. Though he didn't see Darrell much after his Texan adventure, Wild always had a reminder of those months together.

"At some point, we were doing guitar overdubs," Wild explains.

Dime was sitting there, listening, kind of chilling out. There was a pair of scissors lying on the [guitar] rack. He saw them, and was starting a sentence, and as he was saying what I was about to do, I was doing it: I just grabbed the scissors and then snipped off the top of his beard. Or the bottom of it, actually—the pink part. He was in the middle of a sentence: "I can't believe you haven't picked up these scissors and cut off my beard yet," or something like that. It was such a weird thing, because we were thinking exactly the same thing: Cut off his beard. He was, like, "Can't even be mad at the dude—I took his whole wig off."

Darrell's beard now sits in his studio, in a Ziploc bag. Tons of people have done shots with Darrell, and even more have personal little stories involving him. Ulrich Wild is one of the few, if not the only one, who can say he literally has a piece of him.

More than a few guitarists have approached Wild during recording sessions thinking he has something else: The secret. The formula. The right mixture of gear and studio wizardry to achieve Dime's sound. "You worked with him," they say. "What did Dime do?"

"The answer is always 'If you were to take Dime and put him on your rig, he would still sound like Dime,'" Wild says. "'And if I take you and put you on Dime's rig, you would sound like you.' You can't sound like Dime, because it's in the fingers and it's in the heart. It's in the soul of the playing, not just the gear. People neglect their right hand for picking so much and it's so sloppy so often. It could very often use a lot of improvement. And a lot of the sound actually comes from the right hand, from how you pick and attack the strings and attack the instrument. Some people don't want to hear that at all. Some people are very enlightened by it."

THE GREAT Southern Trendkill wasn't exactly a concept album, but there was definitely a concept behind it. "There was a huge resentment for the alternative scene that came up," Dale Brock says.

> That's right when alternative had peaked and metal had died from the airwaves. That was, like, their retaliation: *The Great Southern Trendkill*. Thinking that they were going to change things back. . . . So many of the metal bands tried to change their sound, tried to be more alternative at that time, even

Metallica. Pantera thought the world of Metallica, then they came out with a much softer, radio-driven album at that time, and they just totally called them pussies. Called them pussies onstage, called them pussies on the radio, just completely became enemies with those guys. But I've got to hand it to them: They didn't change their sound. They stayed as aggressive as they always were, if not more, and they were completely on their own there for a while. They were one of the only bands doing it.

Other than a resolve not to change with the times, there wasn't a unifying thread to the album. It was a much more eclectic effort than *Far Beyond Driven*, though it continued on the same downward spiral in terms of tone. If there was any thematic presence beyond the title, it was that *The Great Southern Trendkill*, in a way, acted as a survey of Pantera's career up to that point. Darrell described it as being "almost like a best-of." This was partly because he had resurrected some riffs that first surfaced during the making of *Cowboys from Hell* and *Vulgar Display of Power*, as well as others that had been born even earlier. Though their presence on the album seems to indicate otherwise, it would be wrong to suggest that he had run out of ideas. As long as he kept getting new guitars, he could keep figuring out new things to do with them.

"Every different type of guitar I pick up—electric, acoustic, twelve-string—brings something different out of me," he said at the time. "That's how [*The Great Southern Trendkill*'s] 'Suicide Note Pt. 1' was written. Washburn sent me a twelve-string acoustic and all of a sudden there it was—another influence and another piece of inspiration. I wrote that riff the very first time I pulled the twelve-string out of its case."

In Darrell's view, he was only then coming into his own as a lead guitar player. That might have struck some observers as an odd way of thinking, since his guitar tone and his trademark techniques (like pinch harmonics, the squealing sound he picked up from listening to ZZ Top's Billy Gibbons and perfected even further) had long been lionized. But there is more than a little truth there.

When he was younger, Darrell's approach to his guitar was much like that of any kid with a new toy: He wanted to see everything it could do. That he idolized players like Eddie Van Halen and regularly squared off in top-*this* challenges with other guitarists only reinforced this approach. As he got older, there was a shift. He had matured, if only with a guitar slung over his shoulder. Darrell learned that sometimes the best thing a guitar player could do was *not* play. "Jerking off all over the neck," as he said, was fine for winning contests and impressing colleagues. But it didn't always serve the song, which meant it didn't serve the fans, which meant it didn't belong.

"I think it's the subtleties that really add to the depth of our material," he said, "much more so than having some outrageous lead guitar jack-off in every damned song!" It's difficult to imagine, given his indulgent nature, but Darrell had discovered the value of restraint.

Unfortunately, not everyone in the band rated self-control as highly. On July 13, 1996, after a triumphant homecoming gig at Dallas's Starplex Amphitheatre, as part of Pantera's co-headlining summer tour with White Zombie, Anselmo overdosed on heroin, an accidental by-product of his attempts to numb the crippling back pain that had resulted from years of intense live performances. The singer would later claim to have been dead for "four or five minutes." "There were no lights, no beautiful music, just nothing," he said in a statement issued shortly thereafter—yet he recovered quickly enough to perform at the band's gig in San Antonio two days later. But things weren't the same after that.

Things hadn't been the same in the Pantera camp for a while, in fact. Behind the scenes, Anselmo had been distancing himself from the rest of the band, another by-product of his secret dalliance with heroin. Onstage, Darrell, Vinnie, and Rex found they were distancing themselves from Anselmo's between-song vitriol, ad hominem attacks on whatever came to mind. The distance was quite literal during *Trendkill*'s creation, when Anselmo stayed home in New Orleans to record his vocal tracks. It was becoming increasingly difficult to lure Anselmo away from his hometown. He had even started another band, Down, with a few of his fellow New Orleans residents: Corrosion of Conformity guitarist Pepper Keenan and Crowbar's rhythm section, drummer Jimmy Bower and bassist Todd Strange. The group released its debut, *NOLA*, in 1995, supported by a brief, thirteen-date tour.

None of this bothered the other members of the band too much then—"Phil's a musical guy and he likes to stay busy," Darrell explained—but Anselmo's wandering eye would eventually tear the house asunder and involve Pantera's legacy in an ugly custody battle. At the time, his drug use was the bigger problem. Though he successfully kicked his habit, the damage had already been done. He had built a wall around himself, one that was never fully demolished. Anselmo had done more than alter his own chemistry; he had changed that of the band as well. That Pantera retained its drawing power spoke more to the strength of its fan base than the strength of the group. It's the kind of situation that makes people wonder what might have been.

"When all the trouble started with Phil and the band, I think they were still trying to reach an even higher level of potential," says their former boss, Derek Shulman.

> Because they were always constantly changing and looking to do new things and being more extreme, more heavier, and different. They were just brilliant players, too. That was the other thing. Apart from everything else, their musicianship was unbelievable. Dimebag was an unbelievable player. And Vinnie— I've never seen a double-kick played so rapidly in my life. It was almost like a machine gun. And Phil was an extraordinary star, with charisma from hell. And Rex was a solid bass player. It was one of those dynamics you see in these classic acts like The Who and all that stuff.

IT'S A bit difficult to consider an album that debuts at No. 4 on the *Billboard* 200, rises as high as No. 2, and sells almost five hundred thousand copies in its first six months in stores as a disappointment, but that's what *The Great Southern Trendkill* was, at least commercially.

When it was released on May 7, 1996, EastWest had merged again, this time being subsumed by the Elektra Entertainment Group, which brought together four labels (EastWest, Elektra, Asylum, and Sire) under the same umbrella. Since *Far Beyond Driven* had debuted at No. 1 and had sold close to a million copies, the new conglomerate had high expectations for *The Great Southern Trendkill*.

Label chief Sylvia Rhone held out hope, even after the album fell out of the Top 200 altogether. "The marketplace changed a little bit on them," Rhone told *Billboard* in its November 9, 1996, issue. "But they're the kind of group that will come back. Over time, [the album] will sell over a million units."[2]

It did. On August 17, 2004.

By the time Pantera played its first gig together (seen here) at a now-defunct club in Dallas called The Ritz in 1982, Darrell was already beating grown men in guitar contests.

CREDIT: COURTESY OF TOMMY SNELLINGS

The original incarnation of Pantera (pictured here in its first promotional photo) included singer-guitarist Terry Glaze (left).

Darrell was the unquestioned star of Pantera's early club days, thanks to his ability to master an instrument that was almost as big as he was.

CREDIT: COURTESY OF TOMMY SNELLINGS

As you can see in this flier for Pantera's first album, *Metal Magic*, the Abbotts' father, Jerry, was practically a member of the band in the early days.

Any road trip was an excuse to find new costumes. Whether it was for the stage or the motel parking lot rarely mattered.
CREDIT: COURTESY OF TOMMY SNELLINGS

Pantera would play anywhere, including on the shore of Eagle Mountain Lake at Twin Points Resort, where it was so hot they had to ditch the spandex and play in shorts.

Darrell had fun anywhere he could, whether it was at the venue (above) or the motel (below), where he behaved as he thought a "real rocker" should: knocking the paintings on the wall askew and making sure the lampshade was crooked.

CREDIT: COURTESY OF TOMMY SNELLINGS

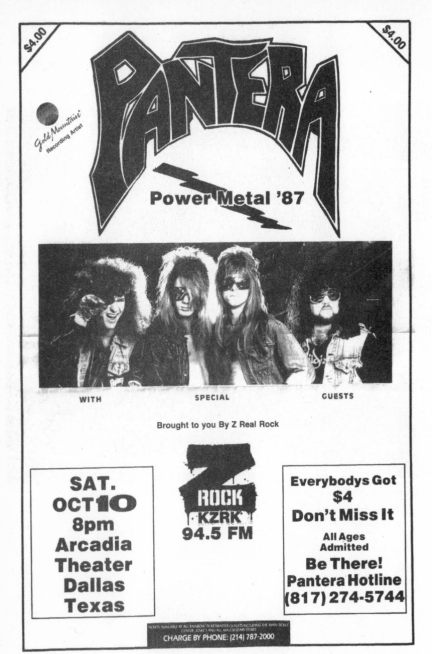

Pantera changed when Phil Anselmo joined the band . . . but not overnight.

CREDIT: COURTESY OF TOMMY SNELLINGS

Darrell and Pantera celebrated the 1990 release of *Cowboys from Hell* by signing autographs at an Arlington Sound Warehouse.

CREDIT: MICHAEL INSUASTE

Phil Anselmo and Darrell onstage during a July 13, 1996 concert at Dallas'
Starplex Amphitheatre, a triumphant homecoming show that was part of the
band's co-headlining tour with White Zombie. Later that night, Anselmo would
overdose on heroin, forever changing the band.

Darrell never forgot the guitar heroes he was raised on, including Point Blank's Rusty Burns.

CREDIT: COURTESY OF CHUCK FLORES

Darrell never missed a chance for a good costume. A Rob Zombie concert at the Smirnoff Centre in Dallas, only weeks from Halloween (October 13, 1998), certainly qualified.

Darrell with one of his signature Washburn guitars on the *Reinventing the Steel* tour. He didn't know that it would be his last jaunt on the road as a member of Pantera.

Darrell arrives by limousine to Damageplan's October 25, 2003 show at the Smirnoff Centre, its last gig in Dallas (above). Later that night, he acted as a billboard for his newest endorsers (next page, bottom).

CREDIT: MICHAEL INSUASTE

Back in the saddle again: Signing copies of Damageplan's debut album, *New Found Power*, at Tower Records in Dallas.

The "Dean from Hell" appears onstage one final time (above), at Darrell's public memorial service at the Arlington Convention Center, where two of his heroes, Zakk Wylde (left) and Eddie Van Halen, eulogized him (below).

10

PLANET CARAVAN

Endorsements, Existentialism, and Endless Nights

"One cannot become a saint when one works sixteen hours a day."

JEAN-PAUL SARTRE

It's evident from the marker covering Darrell Abbott's grave at Moore Memorial Gardens in Arlington that, even in death, Darrell is doing right by one endorser. Darrell is depicted wearing a baseball cap emblazoned with Dean Guitars' eagle-wings logo, with two Dean models crossed over his chest.[3] These include his signature axe, the so-called Dean from Hell, a Dean ML he won in an Arnold & Morgan contest as a teenager that Buddy Blaze later painted blue and customized with a stylized lightning storm.

Thanks to that guitar—and now, thanks to his grave as well—Darrell will always be closely associated with Dean Guitars, the same way Eddie Van Halen is known for his tape-striped home-made axe and Zakk Wylde is identified with his bull's-eye Les Paul Custom. But the truth is, Darrell spent more time (1996–2004) on the Washburn Guitars roster. Dean went out of business, so Darrell entered into a lucrative and creative partnership with Larry English, his liaison with the company, around the time of *The Great Southern Trendkill*. "He and I designed the guitars for that tour together," English says, "and it just kept going from there."

In fact, most of the guitars Darrell is known for, aside from (obviously) the "Dean from Hell," were the result of his work with English and Washburn.

"He had *great* ideas on how he wanted things to look," English says.

He certainly knew how he wanted things to sound, and play. We did some interesting things together, like his rattlesnake guitar and the Southern cross guitar and dozens of—you know, the metal-top guitar, you know, the diamond plate? All the wild inlay issues. It was so much fun, I can't begin to tell you. It was like a designer's paradise. All he wanted was for me to be creative with him. He wanted me to be able to read him, to understand what he was saying, and then be able to translate that into an inanimate object. So that was the challenge. And it was more fun than most people could deal with getting there.

DARRELL HAD a habit of collecting brothers. Even though he was born with an older brother, and even though he always got along well with Vinnie, Darrell was in a unique position because his brother was also his bandmate and had been since he was in his early teens. Add to that the fact his father was Pantera's manager for much of the band's first decade of existence, and it's not terribly difficult to understand why Darrell was always looking for someone else to help fill the role, someone outside the Abbott family. There were certain things Darrell might not have always been able to talk to Vinnie about. They were in a band together, which meant they were in business together. Given that both of their lives were so deeply connected to band business, it would be impossible to get a fresh opinion if one of them had a problem involving Pantera. It would be tough sometimes to even talk about matters outside Pantera because, inevitably, one of them would wonder how the issue at hand affected the band.

Darrell was tight with his brother, but he also craved straight answers. So he collected a group of friends and mentors whom he could call on at any time and count on to give those answers to him. Not surprisingly, most of them knew a thing or two about guitars.

There was Buddy Blaze, who taught him everything about guitars except for how to play them and later helped him navigate the choppy waters of endorsement deals. There was Zakk Wylde, his partner in crime, his mirror twin onstage and off, his soul mate, musical and otherwise. There was Nick Bowcott, the former Grim Reaper guitarist who worked with him both on his *Guitar World* column and toward the ruination of their livers. And there was Larry English, his artist relations guy at Washburn Guitars. Their relationship began solely as a business partnership; they designed guitars and amps together. But out of that partnership was born a mutual respect that grew into a tight friendship.

"I think he thought I was emotionally connected to an extent, but not so much of an extent where I would not give him the straight response that he always really needed to have," English says.

> Our relationship was one where pandering was unacceptable and straight talk was essential. He had a lot of relationships where, basically, you know, he was the star. Everybody basically just kissed his ass and that was the relationship. I think that's very typical of any star. You know, he was a star. He was a music star. I think that's true of anyone who is a public person. So, inside of that understanding, every one of those personalities hopes to find somebody in their lives who, for some reason, they trusted or respected or felt that they could get straight answers from, maybe confide a bit, be able to talk about stuff. I think I kind of filled a little bit of a void for him.

It was a different role than English was used to. With most of his other clients, like KISS's Paul Stanley, English maintained a businesslike presence in their lives. He was their man at Washburn, and that was it. They talked facts and figures, contracts and deadlines. But Darrell was too emotional for something like that. Very few people had a strictly business relationship with him. If he trusted you enough to work for him or with him, then he trusted you enough for anything and everything else. Simple as that. Besides, it's tough to comport yourself in a purely professional way when you're on your fifth shot in two hours. Or when the phone rings in the middle of the night, and Darrell's on the other end of the line, just to talk. Nothing was purely professional in Darrell Abbott's world.

"He would call me at 2:30 in the morning, 3 in the morning, with no particular reason," English says.

Something had come to mind. He'd think about something. It might have to do with guitar stuff. It might have to do with something going on in his life. I'm fifty-nine, and so he always kind of looked at me as a friend, but kind of an older friend. I always tried very hard to give him good input and good guidance whenever I was called on to do it, which was a pleasure. Spent a lot of nights out drinking and doing the thing with him, which, of course, you have to. Had a lot of crazy dinners with a lot of crazy people and a lot of crazy things going on. Throughout everything, the ups and the downs, he was always Dime. He was always kind of a beautiful person, in that he had a lot of great, positive energy, which he liked to spread around.

But I think simultaneously inside of him, he was still a human being and, like all of us, had his own share of concerns and frustrations. He could be temperamental to the extreme, in some cases. He could be loving and giving to the extreme, in most cases. You know, I would see him do some great things. When we'd call on him to come and work with us somewhere and ask him to sign guitars or autographs for people, he would make sure that nobody left empty-handed, no matter what it took, how long it took.

English never left empty-handed from one of his encounters with Darrell either. Though they differed in age and background, English and Darrell connected on a level neither one of them necessarily understood. All they knew was that they'd each found someone they could talk to. Really talk to, the kind of conversations that aren't always readily available. The kind of conversations you tend to take for granted, until you can't have them anymore.

During the eight years they shared a business and personal relationship, the setup for these talks rarely varied. English would be in town for a visit, bunking at Darrell's home in Dalworthington Gardens. After they recovered from the previous night's carousing with a late breakfast and maybe a pick-me-up cocktail or two, they'd end up on the couch, "talking existentially," as English puts it.

"Talking about life and people's places in it, what philosophies I or he had or shared," English explains. "Actually, these were very, very deep conversations. Most people I don't think have the opportunity to meet somebody they can share all of those thoughts and feelings we just never seem to have an opportunity in life to explore. I mean, who do you do it with? Those times that we shared together, those were the times that meant *the most*, I think, to both of us, in terms of our relationship."

THOUGH THEIR respective conversational skills were important to Darrell and English's connection, there was also another thing in play, something that had been a part of Darrell's life longer than he could remember: KISS. Darrell had never stopped being a fan. Now that he had a man on the inside, Darrell could fully indulge his KISS fandom, peppering English with questions, lapping up every detail, every tossed-off anecdote. He could be fifteen again, except this time, with better access and more souvenirs.

"Oh, he would eat up anything about them," English says. "He just totally enjoyed them. What an incredible KISS fan. They have millions of fans, but I mean Dime—his house had KISS blankets on top of chairs. He had KISS stuff everywhere." He laughs. "Anything that we would do that was KISS-related, I always made sure he got whatever we were doing. Because he loved it so much. Hell, I loved giving it to him, because it was like seeing a kid at Christmastime."

One of the most important KISS nuggets English passed on to Darrell wasn't another trinket in a long line of band-branded merchandise. It was something far more tangible, allowing the wannabe Frehley to get a step closer to the real thing. Years after he had stood in front of a mirror in his bedroom, face painted, *Alive!* cranked up, he finally got his hands on something that would help him capture that sound.

"I turned him onto one of these boxes—it's called an isolation box," English explains.

I built him some for his use. With an isolation box, you could play from your guitar into this box, and then from the box to your PA system. And what it did was it cut out all the ambient noise, everything around it. It's really cool. It's a trick I had learned from KISS. They already knew about this trick and they had been using it for a while. Since I worked with them, I was backstage once and saw how their rig was put together, and I was absolutely astonished. Each guitar and bass had this one little isolation box and had a speaker in it. And each one of those tied back to the sound system and the board. Then you could mix with the board. You had this really pure, crystalline sound that was incredible live. It was kind of part of the KISS mystique. I talked to Dime about this and showed it to him and he used it ever after. He loved it.

Of course, had English told Darrell that the members of KISS prepared for gigs by soaking their hands in fox urine, he probably would have tried that, too. When he found out he'd been snowed, he would have laughed harder than anyone.

11

PSYCHO HOLIDAY

Rebel Meets Rebel, Hockey Players, and Strippers

"Where is the rebel base?"

GRAND MOFF TARKIN,
Star Wars: A New Hope

When Pantera released *Reinventing the Steel* on March 14, 2000, it ended the longest period between Pantera studio albums, a gap that was slightly offset by the appearance of the band's first live disc, 1997's *Official Live: 101 Proof*, culled from recordings during the *Trendkill* tour. Not that the band hadn't stayed busy in the interim. They had fulfilled boyhood dreams by touring with KISS (South America, 1997) and Black Sabbath (North America, 1999) and had sandwiched in two stints with

Ozzfest in between. All that was in addition to a few tours Pantera headlined itself. On one of those, they were also able to repay an old favor.

In 1998, Sebastian Bach was on his first solo tour of the country. At the time, he was solo in just about every way possible. He didn't have a record in stores, or a label to get it there. But after Bach's gig in Pittsburgh, at a club called Graffiti's, he had all the support he needed: a three-week stint in the opening slot for Pantera's U.S. arena tour.

"Vinnie told me that he told Dimebag about seeing us in Pittsburgh," Bach wrote on his Web site in the wake of Darrell's murder, "and Dime said, 'Let's bring that fucker out!' as a kind of 'thanks' for us bringing them out in 1992. I will never, ever forget this act of generosity on the part of Pantera. For a band to ignore the industry to the point that Pantera did is something that I doubt we will ever see again. To put me onstage in front of 20,000 people a night in 1998, like I did for them in 1992, is one of the highlights of my life."[4]

Beyond settling old debts and sharing stages with some of their heroes, the Abbott brothers also stayed busy with three intriguing detours during the four-year gap between albums, two musical and one only vaguely.

The latter was the Clubhouse, an all-nude strip bar in northwest Dallas. The Abbotts, along with a handful of investors (including Rex Brown), opened the club in 1996. The idea came from Vinnie, whose original vision was of a rock-and-roll golf course, with "a strip club at the nineteenth hole." Building an entire course proved too expensive. Building that nineteenth-hole bar—that they could do.

Though it isn't located anywhere near an actual golf course, the Clubhouse has a links-based motif. Its logo is a silhouette of a naked female golfer using a flagstick as a stripper pole. The platforms on which the women dance are fashioned to look like putting greens. The walls are filled with paintings and photos of renowned courses and famous golfers. It sounds like an odd concept, but it worked immediately. Even without the benefit of alcohol sales—Texas Alcohol and Beverage Commission rules state that all-nude clubs cannot have a liquor or beer license—the Clubhouse quickly became one of Dallas's most profitable adult-oriented businesses. Which is saying something, since Dallas has more than its fair share.

Considering how much time the Abbotts already spent at various topless (and more) establishments in the Dallas–Fort Worth area, and around the country, it was a bit like a hard-core drug addict taking a job with a pharmaceutical sales company. But in other ways it was a smart decision for everyone involved. While the Clubhouse may not have had a liquor license, with its celebrity owners it had something almost as powerful. Vinnie and Darrell continued the act they began at the Basement, escorting every hard-rock and heavy metal touring act that hit town through the doors at the Clubhouse. A visit to the club became a part of many bands' itinerary. It wasn't just musicians, either: NASCAR drivers, members of the local sports teams (and their traveling counterparts), and—appropriately—pro golfers also made the scene. The famous names brought normal ones with them, since on any given night there was a chance to see anyone from a movie star to a Dallas Star. The worst-case scenario was a room filled with naked women.

Visitors could (generally) expect to at least find the Abbotts at the Clubhouse. They didn't really run the day-to-day operations, but when they were in town, they could have. They were certainly there enough. Beyond investing in the business, and rustling up some prominent clients, their role at the Clubhouse was the same one they played to much acclaim everywhere else: having a good time. Around Halloween, they'd host a top-of-the-line haunted house upstairs, and on New Year's Eve, the Abbotts would play there with Gasoline, their classic-rock "good time band" (as Vinnie referred to it), which mixed in self-explanatory originals like "Get Drunk Now" and "This Ain't a Beer Belly, It's a Gas Tank for My Love Machine" alongside Pat Travers and Ted Nugent covers. When one of their new records hit stores, no one had to ask where the release party would be held. That said, they never needed a reason to party or to do so at the Clubhouse. Most nights, they'd come in late and set up shop in a corner booth to the side of the main stage, where they had a view of all of the action and enough room to accommodate the empty trays of shots.

Besides for postconcert soirees or Pantera-related shindigs, the Clubhouse's biggest turnouts happened after local sporting events, specifically Dallas Stars hockey games. It makes sense, as a Venn diagram depicting the relationship between hockey fans and metalheads would have a huge overlap. The Abbotts were right there in the middle, big supporters of the team, and close friends with many of the players. In 1999, the brothers—and their band—would become more formally involved.

Once again golf provided the inspiration. Vinnie was playing a round of golf with Stars defenseman Craig Ludwig when he asked what he could do to help the team, apart from providing the players with a place to relax after games. The answer, it turned out, was obvious: The Stars were missing a kick-ass theme song, something that would get them, and their fans, fired up at games. Since most of the team were already fans of the group, Pantera was the clear choice to provide one.

The result was a short (but not too sweet) sample of the band's trademark "power groove," an instrumental save for its chanted chorus: "*Dal-las—Stars! Dal-las—Stars!*" The song quickly became an integral part of Stars games; the team played it over the PA system before every period at home games, beginning with the playoffs that year. As the Stars stayed alive in series after series, the song started getting airplay on local radio stations. The team took a copy of it with them on the road, playing it in the locker room prior to road games, except when Ludwig left it behind during a trip to St. Louis, where the team was playing game six of the Western Conference semifinals. The disc was airmailed to the arena, and it arrived as the Stars were leaving their locker room to begin overtime. Refusing to take the ice until they listened to the song, *their* song, the team went out and won the game on a Mike Modano goal. The Stars were on their way to winning the Stanley Cup, and Pantera's place in Stars history was secured.

If there was any doubt of that fact, the Abbotts demolished it during a party at Vinnie's house over the summer, which featured a number of players, a few dancers from the Clubhouse, and a special appearance by the Stanley Cup itself. There's no telling how many black tooth grins were consumed out of Lord Stanley's cup that day, but judging by the fact that it ended up dented at the bottom of the pool, the smart guess would be "quite a few."

As for the song, it's still a fixture at Stars games. "It was just the right song at the right time," Ludwig told the *Dallas Morning News* in 2004. "I know every Stars fan knows and loves that song, and they'll remember it for the rest of their lives."[5]

The pairing of the Stars and the Abbotts was natural, but their partnership with country outlaw David Allan Coe was inevitable. It should have happened sooner, though they were separated by genre, since both sides were blessed with hands that contained nothing but middle fingers, which they regularly flashed to the music industry. Darrell and Vince grew up with Coe's music in the house, since their parents were both fans. Over time, they became converts as well, using Coe's "Jack Daniels If You Please" to warm up the audience before Pantera went onstage. Still, they had never met the man until Coe played a gig at Fort Worth's Billy Bob's Texas in 1999.

After the show, Darrell patiently waited in the autograph line for almost half an hour. That sentence alone sums up the disconnect between who Darrell was and who he acted like. He could very easily have had one of his flunkies send word to Coe's road manager and skipped the line altogether. He probably could have watched the show from backstage. But Darrell didn't really have flunkies and he didn't mind waiting. He thought Coe would have no idea who he was.

He was right. Coe figured the long-haired guy with the pink beard was *somebody*; he just didn't happen to know who or why. When Darrell finally reached the head of the line, Coe asked him what he did. He usually didn't make much small talk at these postshow signings, but this was different for some reason he couldn't quite grasp. Darrell told him about his "little band" and how they had used one of Coe's songs as intro music at their shows. He left behind copies of Pantera's home video collections and his phone number. Coe was dumbstruck by the brief encounter. He couldn't believe a guy like Darrell had heard of *him*, much less be a fan of his music. There wasn't much metal about Coe's act, save for his eccentric, beaded-beard appearance and his history of hard living.

After watching the videos, Coe wasn't puzzled anymore—he was embarrassed. How could he not know who Pantera was? There were thousands of kids screaming the name in city after city. He asked around and found out he actually knew Jerry Abbott. He used the number Darrell gave him and called to apologize for making him wait in line. While they talked, they realized they had more in common than just a fondness for Coe's music. Darrell invited Coe to come and hang out at his house.

The first part of that initial visit was spent doing what most first-time (or second-time, or third-time, or fourth—) visitors did there: drink. One of Coe's crew got so drunk he fell into the pool with his cell phone in his pocket, and Coe's oldest son, Tyler, puked on Darrell's couch. In other words, it was business as usual. Eventually they made their way to the studio out back. By the time Coe said his good-byes, they'd written and recorded a song ("Nothin' to Lose"). It was the start of what would become *Rebel Meets Rebel*, a full-length collaboration between Coe and three-fourths of Pantera (the brothers drafted Rex Brown to play bass). Recording would continue in fits and starts between 1999 and 2003, whenever Coe's and Pantera's schedules coincided.

After Pantera's demise, the plan was to release the album after Damageplan issued its follow-up to *New Found Power*. Since

there never would be a second Damageplan album, Vinnie released it on his own label, Big Vin Records, in 2006. Unlike most
posthumous releases, it was completely finished long before Darrell's death. *Rebel Meets Rebel* is by no means essential listening,
and the pairing of Coe and Pantera (more or less) sounds less like
collaboration and more like coexistence. But much like many of
Darrell's Halloween costumes, it doesn't quite make sense and
yet still, somehow, it works.

12

GODDAMN ELECTRIC

Don't Call It a Comeback

*"If you think you got what it takes,
shove it out, run it up the flagpole,
and see who salutes it."*

LEMMY,
*The Decline of Western Civilization,
Part II: The Metal Years*

Riders—a band's list of wants and needs given to a concert promoter before the show—have been around so long they have become fodder for jokes and the stuff of legend. Surely, by now, everyone has heard the story of Van Halen and its "no brown M&Ms" demand, a request that neatly falls into both categories. The Smoking Gun Web site (www.thesmokinggun.com) even has a section dedicated to concert riders, a peek behind the curtain that is as entertaining as it is maddening. (For some reason, during Metallica's 2004 arena tour, it was "very important that bacon be available at every meal and during day."[6] Also, the band and crew required seventeen dozen clean white towels at every tour stop, a number that is both seemingly random and exceedingly specific.)

There are no Pantera or Damageplan riders on the site. But Darrell Abbott did enter the pantheon of great riders in 1999 when he delivered one—for a magazine interview.

Pantera was set to release its final album, 2000's *Reinventing the Steel*, and Jon Wiederhorn, a writer and editor at *Guitar* magazine, was trying to set up a sit-down with Darrell for a planned cover story.

"We got a call from the publicist saying that, well, Dime has agreed to do the interview," Wiederhorn says, "but he'll only do it if you provide him with, I believe it was, a fifth of JB or Crown Royal—I'm not sure exactly the brand; I think he drank Crown. And two six-packs of beer—I don't know if it was Coors specifically. I don't want to fuck it up, but I can't remember. And then there was a long pause, and he says, 'And they have to be cold, or he walks.' It was pretty funny. I kind of wondered in the back of my mind, well, what happens if we come in with warm beers, or only one six-pack? But I didn't want to take the chance of blowing the interview just in case he was serious."

Wiederhorn had interviewed Pantera before, but Philip Anselmo—as he did onstage, and in most interactions with the press—took the lead. The rest of the band had quietly chimed in whenever necessary. Without much to go on, and given Darrell's reputation as well as his preinterview stipulations, Wiederhorn wasn't sure what to expect.

I was just wondering, before we went in, you know, if he'd be intimidating, if it would be a "How metal are you?" kind of game, or it would turn into a drinkathon. But, no, he was just a fun, free-spirited dude who came in and was, like, "Yeah, let's rock this thing. Let's have a good time."

What struck me most, you know, was that he wasn't really an angry guy. The music he played was so brutal and so vicious and so ahead of its time, but it didn't stem from a rage or a difficult upbringing or frustrations. It really was just an all-out celebration, a real explosion of life. He played it like he lived it. He was all about having a good time and partying and making people laugh and being crazy. You know, he didn't fit in with the mainstream society. He was certainly iconoclastic. But it wasn't a resentful iconoclasticism—if that's a word. It wasn't a "Yeah, well, I'm different, so fuck you!" kind of thing. It was "Hey, take me or leave me, but this is what I'm all about. If you want to join the party, great, we'd love to have you."

SINCE SLAYER'S Kerry King met Darrell and Pantera in 1989, he'd maintained a close friendship with the band, one that often spilled onstage, where he'd join Darrell on guitar for a blistering version of "Fucking Hostile." While Pantera was recording *Reinventing the Steel*, King had a chance to commemorate his relationship with the band for posterity. Darrell called and asked if he would record a guitar lead for the band's valentine to heavy metal, "Goddamn Electric." He got his chance to do so when Slayer came to Dallas on the 1999 Ozzfest tour.

"I had a pretty tight schedule," King says. "I played with Slayer and then I'd go onstage with [White] Zombie every night and play 'Thunderkiss.' I was flying out that night, to make things tougher. Pantera had a dressing room—even though they weren't on tour, they had their own dressing room there—and set up a little digital studio in their bathroom. Had a half stack pointing at the couch that Dime was sitting on. He showed me where I had to play, and I'm, like, 'Right here?' 'Yeah.' So we just did a try at it, and Dime almost fell off the couch, screaming, '*Don't let him do it again!*'" He laughs. "Because he dug it. I *did* try it again, just in case, but we stayed with the first one."

King would get a chance to try it again and again when Pantera began touring behind the album. Since Slayer was also on the bill—along with Morbid Angel, Static-X, and Skrape (the tour was appropriately titled Extreme Steel)—King's former standing invitation became a scheduled part of the act. Except now, it was expanded into a two-song cameo that saw him take the stage for "Fucking Hostile" and "Goddamn Electric."

"THE HIGHS and lows of rock and roll": Nothing summed up Darrell's saying about the music business more than the recording sessions for *Reinventing the Steel*. After a disjointed few years that broke the long cycle of studio-tour-repeat, Pantera was recording again. But when they reconvened at Darrell's home studio to lay down tracks for their ninth studio album, for the first time since *Cowboys from Hell* the forecast for Pantera was cloudy. While *The Great Southern Trendkill* did well enough by most bands' standards, it was the group's least successful album, in terms of both sales and fan reaction. Away from prying eyes, dysfunction had sprouted. The recording sessions for *Trendkill* and the touring behind it had started to slowly tear the band apart, with Anselmo becoming progressively more remote, in every possible way. Where once his mercurial personality had been one of Pantera's prime assets, it was now arguably its biggest liability. Problematic, too, was the fact that, despite heavy music's renewed luster, the strain of metal Pantera had perfected had mutated and metastasized. Many of the band's students had now, in some instances, become the masters, or at least they were considered such by the black-clad recruits that had signed up for the Ozzfest army. The racks that housed *Trendkill* were increasingly crowded and foreign.

Though the marketplace had shifted in the years since *Trendkill*'s release, the band members were, as ever, free from self-doubt and stubborn to a fault. Every record they'd released since *Cowboys from Hell* was released into a climate observers felt was unsuitable, yet Pantera had always prevailed. This time would be no different. Every negative was a plus. *Trendkill* hadn't done as well as hoped? That only meant they had something to prove; they did better with a chip on their collective shoulder anyway. The masses had moved on to something new? That gave Pantera the advantage of surprise. The people wouldn't know what hit them.

Instead, it was Darrell and Vinnie who were caught unawares. In early August, not long after one of the highlights of the *Reinventing* sessions—Kerry King's one-take solo in an Ozzfest dressing room—came the lowest of the lows: Their mother, Carolyn Abbott, was diagnosed with lung cancer. Six weeks later, on September 12, 1999, she was dead.

The effect on the brothers was impossible to calculate. Their father, Jerry, had had a more active role in their careers, giving them a genetic head start, then providing them access to everything he had learned from a life spent in and around the music business. He had toured with Pantera during those early trips on the cover-band circuit, giving up his weekends to help the boys further their dreams. But it was Carolyn who had allowed them to have those dreams in the first place; she had given them the freedom to find their way. After the world took them away from her, she became a lighthouse in the chaotic storm of the road, a welcoming presence to guide them home. In a life that had been unpredictable since they were teenagers, Carolyn was one of the few sources of stability and comfort.

The Abbotts, though shell-shocked, managed to finish work on *Reinventing the Steel* without much interruption in the wake of Carolyn's sudden death. Yet it was a wound that remained open long after. Friends say Darrell and Vinnie were unable, or unwilling, to really talk about her passing for years. In a way, that was practical. Dwelling too long in that place was antithetical to what they needed to do as bandmates rather than as brothers and sons. But it wasn't healthy. Darrell, especially, had become unmoored by Carolyn's death. The next few years, and what they would bring, certainly wouldn't help change that status.

Darrell and Vinnie didn't know that their band was dying, too. They were blinded by their desire to make a new album, then blindsided by their mother's death. Like Carolyn, the symptoms went unnoticed until it was too late.

"It was like pulling teeth to get [Phil] down to the studio," Vinnie said a few years later, in an interview with KNAC.com. "He didn't like any of the material, and it was always just like this head-butting contest. It wasn't like it was when we were just starting out, when it was all for one and one for all."[7]

BROTHERS BUDDY Blaze and Ken "Pyro" Webster both saw Darrell for the last time the same night: May 23, 2000. It was at a Nine Inch Nails show at Dallas's Starplex Amphitheatre, now known as the Smirnoff Music Centre.

Buddy was working with Nine Inch Nails front man Trent Reznor at the time, and he arranged for Ken and his fourteen-year-old son (who was attending his first concert), to come backstage. Darrell and Vinnie had their own pass, courtesy of Reznor. They had always taken care of Reznor when he came to town, making sure he got a hero's welcome at the Basement and, later, the Clubhouse. Now Reznor was returning the favor.

"I never told Trent that Darrell and I were really close friends or anything like that," Blaze says. "But Trent threw down. He sent limos out for them and stocked them all up and all that shit. He made the green room a Pantera room after dinner was done. They catered it just for Pantera. . . . I grabbed Darrell and took him back to see Trent. Trent, like, pissed his pants when I walked in with Darrell. He was, like, 'You know this guy?' Darrell goes, 'Fuck yeah! Fucking known him all my fucking life, man!'" He laughs.

The Abbotts were happy to see Reznor again, but above all, they were thrilled to find that their old friend Pyro was there, with his son. "Darrell made sure my son got good treatment," Ken says. "He was just such a gracious person. And Vince, too, you know? Vince was telling my son, 'Your dad used to build our lights out of B-52 lights.' And my son thought that was pretty cool."

It was the first time both sets of brothers had been in the same room in years, since Buddy left Arlington and Pantera followed suit a few years later, breaking free from the constraints of the Texas cover-band circuit. It was not an entirely joyous re-union. The Websters hadn't seen the Abbotts since their mother had died.

Buddy, who had remained the closest to the family, was on tour in Europe with Nine Inch Nails when it happened. Ken had long since passed out of the Abbotts' lives. He lived in Pantego, not far from Darrell's new home in Dalworthington Gardens, so he'd run into Darrell and Rita every now and again. But their en-counters were more the result of coincidental trips to Costco than actual planning. Carolyn and Kitty Webster, once best friends and "Pantera mamas," had drifted apart over the years, as Carolyn's life had gone in a different direction once her boys could provide for her, instead of the other way around.

None of the Websters knew about Carolyn until it was too late. "My mom called me up one day and she said, 'Buddy, Car-olyn Abbott died,'" Blaze says. "And I go, 'Oh—my—God.' I was kind of pissed, because she died of cancer, and I'm, like, 'How could Carolyn have cancer and not call my mom?' Because we were kind of like family. But the thing is, [with] Pantera and Nine Inch Nails and whatever else I was doing, our schedules weren't always the same. I might see those guys five times in a year, and then I might not see them for two or three years. That's kind of how it worked out. We did a lot of drinking that night. We shed some tears over Carolyn privately; then we had fun."

That night provided Buddy Blaze his last opportunity to talk to Darrell on the phone, too. Earlier, during Nine Inch Nails' set, Reznor had, as Blaze puts it, "supersmashed a guitar." As soon as he saw the guitar splinter apart, Blaze knew what had to happen.

"I just went to Trent and I said, 'We've got to give that one to Darrell,'" he says. It was in many ways the perfect gift for Darrell, a man who appreciated the beauty in broken things more than most and who had remained more-or-less the same teenaged rock-and-roll fan throughout his life, despite everything he had accomplished. "And he said, 'Yeah, I agree.' So I said, 'Go sign it up for Darrell and I'll go ship it out to him.' That was the last time I talked to Darrell, when I sent that guitar to him. Because I didn't tell him I was going to do it and it really, really freaked him out. 'Dude, that's going on my fucking wall! That's the baddest motherfucking thing I've ever seen in my whole fucking life! Oh my God!'"

CONTRARY TO its title, *Reinventing the Steel* wasn't so much a reinvention of Pantera's sound as it was a rediscovery. "We wanted to get back to the raw, ass-kicking basics of it all," Darrell said while on tour with Ozzfest in 2000. "We had time off between *Trendkill* and *Reinventing*, and we gave ourselves an overview and noticed that the *Trendkill* stuff wasn't coming across as powerfully onstage as *Vulgar* or *Cowboys*. On *Reinventing*, we wanted to grab the youth of *Cowboys* and the groove of *Vulgar*, but also the unstoppable extremities of *Far Beyond Driven*, adding just a bit of the layered sound of *Trendkill*. . . . We made everybody happy for a change."

But could they make everyone happy? Since so much time had passed between Pantera albums, and since their last release, *The Great Southern Trendkill*, had been something of a letdown, there were legitimate questions to answer. A different style of metal, with bands like Korn and Limp Bizkit at the forefront, was in vogue. "Can [Pantera] reclaim their old territory in a new millennium when they sing 'Yesterday Don't Mean Shit?'" *Playboy*'s Charles M. Young wondered. "I predict they can. It's good shit, particularly in the production, where they nail the details."[8]

It was an accurate prediction. No matter who was ruling the charts, Pantera's fan base proved to be stronger than all. *Reinventing the Steel*, like *The Great Southern Trendkill*, debuted at No. 4 on the *Billboard* charts, and the band continued to be booked in the biggest venues. Pantera remained a success. They had weathered Anselmo's drug problems and the personality conflicts among the band. They had withstood plenty of pretenders to the throne. They had done it all their way, never bowing to trends or compromising their approach to fit in with someone else's marketing plan. They were one of the last true metal bands, and proud of it.

"We still play lead guitar, we have a drummer who can play every tom, and a singer who really sings," Darrell said.

Bands hardly ever play lead guitar anymore. Dude, back in the seventies, if you couldn't play the guitar or sing, you were nobody. Now music is so easy—all you've got to do is tune your guitar to an open chord and jump around. That's what sets us apart. And we're not afraid to carry around a heavy metal moniker. It's who we are and what we do. A lot of bands have shied away from that—they've said, "Don't call us metal," and tried to change their styles. We don't bend, man. We do what's really in our souls, what our fans want, and what we're really good at, as opposed to trying to be something else. "I want to fit in with the times and the trends"—fuck all that shit! It ain't gonna happen, brother. I'd be bored, for one. And our fans would throw us the bird finger.

They didn't have to worry about that. Their record sales may have dropped off some after the commercial high of *Far Beyond Driven*, but they were still one of the most dependable bands at the box office. After a decade atop the metal world, there didn't appear to be an end in sight.

"This is a band that can only stop itself," the *Indianapolis Star*'s David Lindquist foreshadowed after the band's March 18, 2001, gig at the city's Pepsi Coliseum. "In 10 years, Pantera won't be subjected to the type of comeback in which it plays embarrassing mop-up dates in 1,000-seat nightclubs."[9]

BONUS TRACK:
THIS LOVE

Good Friends and a Tray of Shots

"Once it hits your lips, it's so good!"

———

FRANK THE TANK,
Old School

Most people's first encounter with Darrell Abbott mirrored David Karon's, not long after Karon started working for Randall Amplifiers, one of Darrell's sponsors. The setting might be different, the cast might change slightly, but the plot and script were remarkably consistent. The following things generally featured prominently: a sizable quantity of alcohol, a smattering of cursing, and a level of generosity that bordered on complete disdain for finance. In Karon's version, he was at the NAMM show in 2001.

"It was a very interesting meeting," Karon says. He's now director of artist relations for Randall Amplifiers and Washburn Guitars. "He was on one of his long tears. He was in rare form.

I remember one of the first things that he did. He's, like, 'Go get me some shots.' Gives me a *wad* of cash. And I'm, like, 'Well, all right.' So I go get him his shots and I bring them back and I'm, like, 'Here's your change, man.' He goes, 'I don't want that shit.' I said, 'I'm not taking your money.' It was, like, two hundred bucks. 'I'm not keeping your dough,' and I shoved it in his pocket. It was just one of those typical things. I'm, like, 'Ah, that's the introduction you get.'"

Most people's relationship with Darrell mirrored Karon's as well. If you worked with Darrell, or for him, the dealings rarely remained confined to business. Darrell put too much of his heart into everything else that he did to leave it out just because his head had got involved. Those two organs didn't often work independently of one another, except when a third (his liver) applied peer pressure.

That combination of head and heart was so palpable, Karon could feel it even when he and Darrell weren't in the same room, which was often the case; his and Darrell's partnership played out mostly on the phone. They spoke often, and during those frequent conversations, Karon found that Darrell was even more up-front when separated by a long-distance connection than he was in person.

"I remember one time when I was hanging out and something happened, and he [called and] was, like, 'What are you doing?'" Karon says. "I'm, like, 'Uh, walking my dogs.' He's like, 'Well, if you don't get this shit straightened out I'm gonna fuckin' shoot your dogs.'" He laughs.

"You know, he was a really smart guy," Karon continues.

Great business guy, great business sense. But I think a lot of the time, yeah, he used his heart before anything else. Whenever he'd deal with people, it was first through his heart and then it was through his head, and then through his hands. So, I think people could see how genuine he was as a person. I mean, you can tell when someone's bullshitting, and he was never one to bullshit. If he wasn't happy, he'd tell you straight up he wasn't happy. If he was happy, he'd tell you straight up when he was happy. Usually metal people don't show their emotions, and he was one that would show his emotions. Not afraid of them. Regardless of if there was good things or bad things or whatever, he always showed you how much he cared about you. Not every artist is that way. He made sure he told you what you mean to him. Not everyone else that you work with does that. He made sure of it.

Darrell didn't just let Karon know how much he and Randall meant to him during those regular phone calls. His show of support was public and prolific and had little to do with his endorsement contracts. "Every time you saw him in a photo or on TV or anything, he was always wearing either a Randall or a Washburn shirt or hat or something," Karon says. "Or, you know, BLS [Black Label Society]. He always backed his friends and his family."

Darrell usually went well beyond wearing a T-shirt or hat when it came to showing how he felt about someone. No one ever had to ask, but when people did ask for something, he gave it to them and then some. It didn't matter if he'd known them for years or minutes. More often than not, it didn't matter if he knew them at all.

"When I was playing in Slow Roosevelt, the guy that was helping me out, my guitar tech live, he was a real big guitar fan and really loved Darrell's playing," Scott Minyard says.

I called Darrell one time around Christmas, and asked him if there was a way that he'd have time to sign me a poster. This is what I wanted to give this guy, because this guy gave me a lot of stuff, and I wanted to give him something, something he couldn't pay for—because he made pretty good money and everything. I wanted to do him up right one year and get him a poster signed by Dime, and I was going to get it and put it in a frame and everything for him the right way. Darrell says that he's going out to this club over in Fort Worth and to meet him out there. So I go out there to get the poster, and he's got two posters signed; he's got a shirt signed; he's got a bag full of picks with his name on them that have been unopened. He saw what I was doing. He *loved* stuff like that.

When one of Darrell's endorsers flew him in for an event, he made sure no one left without getting a piece of him. Because he never lost the mind-set of a fan, it was easy for him to put himself back in that place. Darrell knew what he would have wanted if he were in that line, and so he gave it. Sometimes it was an autograph or a photo. Sometimes it was a guitar pick. Sometimes it was a guitar.

At Darrell's public memorial service at the Arlington Convention Center, his longtime friend and collaborator Nick Bowcott told a story that shed even more light on Darrell's random acts of kindness. A kid showed up with his father at one of Darrell's autograph signings. Darrell asked the kid if he played, and he told Darrell that he wanted to, but he couldn't afford a guitar. Darrell said he knew what that was like and gave the kid his John Hancock. When the boy and his father were out of earshot, he told one of the members of his crew to make sure they didn't leave. They waited around while the line emptied, and Darrell had them come into the back of the store. Waiting there was a new guitar. He would have given it to the boy earlier, but he didn't want to embarrass the father by doing it in front of the crowd. "When I come back, you better be able to rip!" he said.

SIDE FOUR
NEW FOUND POWER
(2001–2004)

13

SHATTERED

The End of Pantera

"All things end badly, or else they wouldn't end."

DOUG COUGHLIN,
Cocktail

Though the actual end of Pantera is a bit hazy—for several years, there was an ellipsis at the end of the sentence rather than a period—the beginning of the end is an easy date to remember: September 11, 2001.

Late the night before, the band flew out of New York's John F. Kennedy Airport, en route to Ireland to begin the European stretch of its Tattoo the Earth Tour with Slayer, Biohazard, Vision of Disorder, and Static-X. After landing in Ireland and learning of the events that had taken place during their flight, they decided to cancel the tour dates and return to Texas. Given the climate of fear at the time, when no one was sure if there would be another terrorist attack, or where, the choice was simple. What they didn't know, however, was that it would be one of the last decisions the members of Pantera would ever make as a band.

Between the uncertainty of air travel and their presence in a foreign country, the group was stranded in Ireland for almost two weeks. When they finally made it home to Texas, still recovering from the shell shock of the events of the previous days and with no shows to perform, the members of the band decided to shut it all down for a while. It was supposed to be a brief hiatus, a short break to recalibrate their respective compasses. They would come back together with clear heads, ready to refocus on Pantera. The plan was to take some time off and then reconvene six or eight months down the line.

"We needed it," Rex Brown told *Metal Edge* magazine in 2007. "I mean, dude, 20 years on the road with each other, sleeping together, shitting and eating [together], dude, in a way it was a dysfunctional marriage."[1]

It wasn't the kind of situation that required a press release to explain. It wasn't even a situation, as far as the Abbotts were concerned. It was the same thing they had done after they finished touring behind *Far Beyond Driven*, and again after *The Great Southern Trendkill*. This time the break never ended.

During one of Pantera's previous time-outs, in 1995, Anselmo had recorded an album with his side project, Down, and then he returned to Pantera. After Pantera released a live album in 1997, *Official Live: 101 Proof*, Anselmo took on a different type of downtime venture, setting up the House of Shock, a haunted house in Jefferson, Louisiana. He also stayed busy musically during the late 1990s, playing guitar (under the name Anton Crowley) with singer Killjoy in various death-and-black-metal outfits, including Necrophagia and Viking Crown (along with his wife, Stephanie). But Pantera had always remained his main gig.

As Pantera's brief hiatus grew ever longer, it was difficult to say that Anselmo was still committed with any certainty. In March 2002, Down released a second disc, *Down II: A Bustle in Your Hedgerow*, which also featured Rex Brown on bass. Two months later, yet another one of Anselmo's bands, Superjoint Ritual, released its debut, *Use Once and Destroy*. Since Anselmo fronted both bands, and since both albums were on prominent labels (Elektra for Down; Sanctuary for Superjoint Ritual), and since Brown was a member of one of them, the Abbotts couldn't help but wonder: Were they the only ones still in Pantera?

With Anselmo in Louisiana—and, according to the Abbotts, not of a mind to return their phone calls—the brothers could only answer that question themselves. They sat around on each other's couches, wondering what they had done wrong, trying to figure out how they had driven everyone away. Anselmo's quotes to the media didn't help clarify the matter—and would only become more problematic over time. In 2002, he proffered hope for the future with one hand and ambivalence with the other.

"Before we do anything else new, we need to really take a look at the climate out there, which has not been a problem for us in the past," Anselmo told the New Orleans *Times-Picayune* in May 2002. "We've always done well no matter what's popular at the time. Magazines push all these other bands, but every time we go to Detroit there's 12,000 people. As many times as I've felt we've done all we can do, somehow it works out for us. All my nerves dissipate after the first two or three shows. It's like, 'Damn! They're still coming to see us.' Pantera's audience is very diehard, now more than ever. But I don't want to go on with Pantera and become boring to the audience or past our time. If we're going to do anything, we're going to have some fresh ideas."[2]

Later in the *Times-Picayune* story, he mentioned that, on Pantera's last tour, he and Brown had discussed not recording another Pantera album until 2003, at the earliest. "I was like, 'Really? Fine.' That gives me a chance to give the fans an opportunity to hear a broader spectrum of what Philip Anselmo is capable of."[3]

Comments like that painted the picture of a man in no particular rush to hurry back. But back in Arlington, the Abbotts still believed Pantera would regroup in 2003, once Anselmo finished supporting the Down and Superjoint Ritual albums. Instead, Anselmo recorded a second Superjoint Ritual disc, *A Lethal Dose of American Hatred*, and made it clear the band was his sole focus.

"The last record that we did [*Reinventing the Steel*] was everything that I wanted the Pantera record to be, the tour [in support of the album] turned out beautiful, and we ended up with Morbid Angel and Slayer, and to me, it's, like, how can you beat that?" Anselmo said during a May 20, 2003, appearance on Don Kaye's *Hard Attack* show on SIRIUS Radio. "I was thinking, you know, [if we were to put] out a new record, who the hell am I gonna go on tour with? . . . Last year was a bit of a screw-up with Down and Superjoint [Ritual] coming out at the same time, and people were confused, and this and that, and this and that. I wanted to put all of that on the side and concentrate on one band, as I should, and that band is Superjoint Ritual right now. It feels extremely important to do this band, and that's what I'm doing right now—no other band."

Around the same time, according to the Abbotts, Darrell received a phone call from Rex. He was "completely lambasting everything I did for Pantera, everything Dime did for Pantera, and everything we did as a band," Vinnie later told KNAC.com. "Where the fuck did this come from? He got the biggest free ride of anyone in this motherfucker."[4]

The closest Pantera came to a reunion was a meeting set up by the Abbotts in New York, which was hard enough to pull off on its own. But Anselmo and Brown never showed.

The Abbotts gave up waiting for Anselmo to return, and Brown, too. Pantera was over. Its tombstone was erected on September 23, 2003, when Rhino Records released *The Best of Pantera: Far Beyond the Great Southern Cowboys' Vulgar Hits!* a sixteen-track overview of the band's major-label career. By then, it had racked up three platinum albums (*Cowboys from Hell, Vulgar Display of Power,* and *Far Beyond Driven*) and three gold albums (*The Great Southern Trendkill, Official Live: 101 Proof,* and *Reinventing the Steel*). And *3: Watch It Go* and *Vulgar Videos* had both been certified platinum, and *Cowboys from Hell: The Videos* had reached gold status. They had been nominated for four Grammys in the Best Metal Performance category: for "I'm Broken" off *Far Beyond Driven* in 1995; for "Suicide Note Pt. 1" from *The Great Southern Trendkill* in 1997; for the live version of "Cemetery Gates" on *Official Live: 101 Proof* in 1998; and for *Reinventing the Steel*'s "Revolution Is My Name" in 2001.

For his part, during Pantera's reign Darrell had been named, in various readers' polls: Best Breakthrough Guitarist in *Guitar for the Practicing Musician* in 1992; Best Metal Guitarist (*Guitar Player*) in 1995, and again in 1996; Most Valuable Player by *Guitar World* and Best Metal Guitarist by *Guitar* magazine in 1997; and Best Heavy Metal Guitarist (*Guitar World*) every year from 1995 to 1998, and again in 2001.

That stacks up pretty well against just about every other metal band out there. Not too bad for a "little band" from Arlington, Texas.

14

HOLLOW

"Dr. Dime" Starts Over

*"We had a band powerful enough to
turn goat piss into gasoline."*

DONALD "DUCK" DUNN,
The Blues Brothers

When it became apparent that Pantera's break was, in fact, a breakup, years of mostly hidden dysfunction began spewing out in the heavy metal press, each nugget chronicled by Blabbermouth.net, the so-called CNN of heavy metal and hard rock news. Pantera didn't dissolve immediately, cleanly, or at all amicably. Accusations from both sides filled the heavy metal press for some time. The band's fan base was forced to choose sides and every account could be spun to fit each side's needs—and often was, in intense debates that filled page after page of Internet message boards. It was never clear who was right and who was wrong, only that Anselmo and the Abbott brothers were both angry.

"They won't talk to me," Anselmo told *Revolver* in its September 2003 issue. "I speak to Vinnie maybe once every blue moon. But I think Dimebag and I have had a falling out that's going to be a little tough to reconcile. I'm not even sure what the hell it's about."

Pressed for details on what had happened between him and Darrell, Anselmo added, "He's got a lot of resentment in his heart, and I don't really know where it's coming from. I'm not sure he's mad at me at all, you know? He's got a lot of personal issues in his life that he has to face, and once he does, I really, truly hope he becomes a better person—the beautiful person that I came to know and love."

Though the interview had a largely conciliatory tone, when discussion turned to the potential for another Pantera record Anselmo's answer didn't do him any favors.

"It's not the right time. One thing you've gotta understand is, with Pantera, I've *always* been the one to question things. I've always been the one to say, 'Are you sure you wanna do this?' 'Are you sure this is right?' And they listen to me, they hear me out. And by no means am I saying that I'm the brains behind the entire thing. But I am saying that when it comes to music, due to my knowledge and very natural connection to what the underground scene is, I had to enlighten them several times over. Without me, it'll be real interesting to hear what they come up with."[5]

It snowballed from there.

In *Revolver*'s February 2004 issue, Vinnie said of Anselmo, "One night he would walk in and be a fucking animal. The next night, I'd walk backstage and he'd be lying in the corner and he'd say he was tired. I will never take anything away from that dude from when he was at the top of his game, but where he's at right now, I think he's much less than sub par at what he does. I have a hard time watching him when I see him on MTV talking about Superdope Ritual, or whatever they're called, and he can't keep his fucking eyes open."[6]

Responding to the statement via SMNnews.com, Anselmo said:

I just hear a big and sad yellowbelly crybaby fuckin' knowing that his meal ticket is in a different fuckin' band, and [long pause] you would have to know those fellows to really understand where I was coming from—they're scared of their own fuckin' shadow. And, all that said, I wish them the best of fuckin' luck. I still love 'em.

For Vinnie Paul's information and anybody else who would like to know, I've been fuckin' stone-cold sober for fuckin' two years—I feel like a fuckin' boy scout, for God's sake. And fuckin', you know—I can have a couple of beers, let's get it straight.

Then Anselmo turned his attention to Darrell:

There was another thing brought up in that interview where Vinnie Paul said that he knows how to stop drinking, you know, and they can control themselves. And magically Diamond Darrell didn't answer a fuckin' thing. You know why that is? Because his fuckin' friends have to carry him fuckin' home every goddamn night—every night on tour, he gets carried to the fuckin' bus. Now, you tell me—me fucking up one time in my life compared to his fuckin' three thousand and seven. Give me a fuckin' break, man![7]

Darrell counterattacked in a *Guitar World* interview:

If you look at the home videos, you can see that I'm the same dude in *3: Watch It Go* that I was in the first video shot some eight years earlier. And I still am today. I still have the same love for life in my heart, and my drive is still there for the same reason— the love of music, the love of playing guitar and the love of jamming for people and interacting with the fans. And my brother's the same way.

Anyone who's heard Phil's recent radio interview, which is all over the Internet, or seen him hosting on MTV speaking three octaves down, hardly able to talk or keep his eyes open, knows what his real problem is. For some time now, he's obviously been around people that accept that, as opposed to being around me and Vinnie, who have a different standard level. I tried to get through to him and help, because I truly love the dude, but it's impossible to connect with someone in that state, and that's when I became the enemy in his mind.

Some people like to compare hard drugs to people who like to party on alcohol. But look, man—one's legal and one's illegal, and there's a reason for that. Sure, I've been a drinker since day one, and I ain't perfect, but I've never missed a show and

I've never played a half-assed one because of it. For the record, I've never, ever snorted cocaine, I've never, ever done crank, I've never, ever smoked crack, and I've never, ever done heroin. It just plain grosses me out. I've seen too many motherfuckers go down in flames because of that shit.[8]

Darrell and Pantera didn't go down in flames because of drugs, necessarily, but they went down all the same. The war of words was a long way from over. The battle to keep Pantera alive wasn't.

AS DIFFICULT as it had been at times—with Anselmo off in New Orleans, devoting his attention to an ever-increasing assortment of bands—Darrell never wanted Pantera to end. He had enough money to let it go, but money wasn't the point. It never was and never had been. The point was the music, being in a studio, on a stage, playing his guitar and making people happy, including himself. He wanted to do that with Pantera. Just like he always had. He'd spent most of his life in that band. As far as he was concerned, he'd spend the rest of his life there. He and Vinnie often talked about being the Rolling Stones of heavy metal.

But it wasn't going to happen. Pantera played its last gig on August 25, 2001, at Beastfest in Tokyo.

It would be wrong to say that Darrell drank more during this period, because he *always* drank more. The presence of alcohol in his life had long since elevated beyond the status of a regular visitor; by then, it was so closely involved in his day-to-day routine that it was more like his Siamese twin. But if the attendance and the amount of alcohol remained the same, the effect of the alcohol had changed. Friends noticed a growing darkness. The happy-go-lucky Darrell they knew wasn't always so happy anymore. With Pantera's future nonexistent, and his own future as a musician less than clear, he wasn't feeling very lucky either. It put a strain on his relationship with Rita. Most of his other relationships, too.

"The move, the shift in and out of Pantera, certainly took its toll on him, and it certainly changed him to some degree," says Larry English. He worked with Darrell for almost a decade at Washburn Guitars, but their relationship transcended business. "He had an anger in him that a lot of people would never have seen otherwise. That change promoted that part of him. He was already a big drinker, but there was a certain moroseness that seemed to take over at some point, that began to bleed through the initial phases of the drinking contests. Later on into the drink, there was a bit of moroseness there which wasn't there before."

No one could hold those moods against him. After all, Darrell had spent more than two-thirds of his life with "Pantera guitarist" in front of his name. He had spent half that time as a certified star, a bold-faced name, a somebody. The general public might not have recognized him as such, but the people that really mattered to him, the heavy metal community, did. He was King Dime to them, whether or not he had an album on the charts. Besides an adoring fan base, Pantera had given him platinum plaques, shiny toys, a big house on a nice street, and more. He had made Pantera, but Pantera had also made him. But that was Pantera guitarist Darrell Abbott. Would ex-Pantera guitarist Darrell Abbott fare as well?

"It was like watching your life floating away in front of you," English says.

Pantera was him. It was his life. He was watching the end of his life. He was watching the end of his friendships. These were guys who spent a hell of a lot more time with him than I did. Not only was it ending, but also Phil was talking smack about him—to the press, never mind to lots of people. It was painful. I liken it to a real bad divorce. We know that a bad divorce is a tragic family matter. It's tragic. And usually what happens is there are people who are hurt by that action who never get over it for their whole life. Now we all know that and we all understand that. This is the case with Dime. It was an ugly, bitter divorce.

That period of time was very, very difficult for him. You know, he was a guy who certainly had his share of doubts, remorse, incredible levels of frustration. Sometimes he was hurt, sometimes he was mad. When he was mad, to me that was way better than being hurt. It was kind of like getting over it. He also needed a lot of assurance and reassurance that the road he was going down was going to be the right road.

Yet even with all of that doubt and anger and frustration swirling around him, threatening to envelop him, cover him in black like a Pantera concert T-shirt, Darrell was still, for the most part, Darrell. Even if it was just a front, a face he put on in public, he could still be the guy who did the cheering up, not the other way around. That said, he could never get too far away from his problems, because everyone else's concerns, in some way, reflected back on his own.

"I was going through a lot of stuff three years ago in the summer, over a bad breakup thing," says Scott Minyard.

I was kind of lost . . . and he spotted it. Everybody else was passing out except for me and him. He and I went on the porch. He goes, "What's wrong?" He goes, "Something's wrong, dude. I can tell something's wrong. Tell me about it." We started talking. He was telling me about how he needed something musical going again. We talked for quite a while on the back porch. He just really lifted me up. He was talking about how bad the Pantera breakup hurt him. It was just horrible. He was really touched by that. He goes, "No disrespect to you—because, I mean, you did great with your band and everything—but imagine being where I was and having that ripped out from under you." They were on top of the freaking world, the metal world.

I called him the next day and left a message about bringing me up. I said, "Thanks, Dr. Dime"—I called him Dr. Dime. He had a way of making you laugh and bringing your spirits up.

IT WASN'T the first time Darrell had found himself at a crossroads in his career. He had faced a period of anxiety after Terry Glaze had left the band and before they had hired Anselmo to replace him, and again when Pantera was trying to make the jump to a major label. Nothing, however, compared to this. He'd always had the confidence in himself and his band that things would eventually work out for the better, and he was right; they always had. Anselmo turned out to be a much better fit for Pantera than Glaze had been, allowing the band to explore its heavy nature in full. Whether by luck or design, the right label had come along and exploited the chemistry between the Abbott brothers and Anselmo and Brown to the hilt, laying the groundwork for Pantera to be the heaviest metal band to top the *Billboard* charts. It always seemed to work out perfectly for Darrell.

But that was when he had a band, a gang, someone to back him up against all comers. What he was up against now, then, wasn't merely another bump in the road. It was more like the road was gone. The past had been rendered meaningless, the present had been turned upside down, and the future he'd imagined might never arrive. Darrell was nearing forty, and he was going to have to start over, more-or-less from scratch.

Or maybe not.

English had a vested interest in Darrell's future, both as a friend and as a businessman. Darrell was his little brother and a big client. So for many reasons, he wanted to see him succeed again, to get back onstage again, to be happy and satisfied again, to sell records and, yes, guitars again. To that end, he asked Darrell to consider this: Was Pantera really done? Or had the band merely lost its lead singer?

"We spent a lot of time reviewing the issues surrounding this," English says.

I basically took the position that he really needed to consider what it would take to own the name Pantera, and what that meant from a legal standpoint, from an investment standpoint—my position always was Pantera is a brand, is a franchise, and if what you're talking about is starting a new brand, that's a tough road, that's a long road, that's an expensive road. I really kind of counseled him to put in some time and a couple of bucks into really figuring out that aspect of this change. To make the wisest possible financial decisions for himself. Because he was concerned about finances like everybody else, and he needed to be. It's like being fired. You no longer have a company named Pantera that you work for, even though you did it your whole life. These were some of the issues that were weighing on him heavily, and we talked about them almost daily.

Had Pantera continued without Phil Anselmo, it wouldn't have been the first band to carry on with a new front man. A number of Darrell's favorites—Van Halen, Black Sabbath, Judas Priest—had kept going after losing their singers. Had Pantera continued without Anselmo, it wouldn't have even been the first time Pantera had carried on with a new front man either. Sure, the band had got exponentially more successful since Terry Glaze left back in 1986. Yet, while Anselmo was pivotal in that run of prosperity, Darrell's guitar playing was just as much of an attraction. More than he even knew.

"I remember a story that Aaron Barnes was telling me once," says Chris Paluska, who was part of Darrell and Vinnie's last management team. "That was their lifelong sound guy. You know, he had to point out to Dime way, way, *way* late in Pantera's career . . . he was, like, 'Dude, you are the *star* of this thing.' Not that the story is important, but just the fact that it almost had to be pointed out to Dime that he was a really big draw and a really big deal to this band so late in their career. That's his mind-set: 'All for one, one for all. We're Pantera and that's all there is to it.'"

Even after Pantera was over, Darrell had trouble seriously referring to himself in the same terms that almost everyone who followed guitar players used to describe him.

"I think those days are done, man," he said when Juliya Chernetsky from Fuse's *Uranium* show asked him about the qualifications to be a guitar god. "Yeah, man, you just gotta be able to rip, man. You know? You gotta be signature, you know? All the great guitar players that I look up to, I think of Edward Van Halen, I see his guitar in my mind, I see the stripes on the guitar. I think of Zakk [Wylde], I see the bull's-eye. You think of the Idol"—yet another one of his nicknames—"you see the fucking guitar shooting out, shapes and shit coming at ya, pink goatee going on. Just kidding. Ya'll know I'm jacking you off about this Idol thing. Get that straight real quick, you know? . . . It's a fucking joke."

Whether he knew it, or admitted it, Pantera was arguably more Darrell's band than anyone else's—including his brother's—at least in a spiritual sense. In a legal sense, one can never rely on the whims of the courts. But even in that arena, the Abbotts had a pretty clear case of ownership, since they predated Anselmo's arrival in the group by almost five years and three albums. Why not keep the name?

If Darrell and Vinnie had not been stuck on the sidelines for so long while Anselmo's silence kept them in perpetual limbo, they might have moved ahead under the Pantera banner. Doing so, however, would likely have resulted in a court battle. Since there was so much acrimony on both sides, it would have been a protracted and costly one. Darrell and Vinnie would have remained trapped in their quiet hell, while Anselmo continued to tour and record.

Starting a new band—or a new brand, as English says—probably cost them more in the long run than a lawsuit would have. Keeping Pantera going might have kept them in arenas and theaters instead of landing them back on the club circuit they had graduated from more than a decade earlier. It might have meant a few hundred thousand more in record sales.

It might have kept Darrell Abbott alive.

But saying good-bye got them back in the game. At the time, that was good enough.

15

REBORN

The Abbott Brothers
Concoct a Damageplan

"Metal Up Your Ass"

—original title of Metallica's *Kill 'Em All*

"You know, everybody's got a crystal ball when it comes to stuff like this, and mine is no better than yours," Larry English says.

All I can say is Pantera was a "made" group. They were made guys. The new guys in the Abbotts' new band were good guys and certainly talented guys, but I can't say that the world was going to accept the new lead singer and the new bass player and go on as normal. I think that's a real stretch. A lot of their fans are tough. All fans are tough. They love you, but they're very tough inside of that love. My crystal ball does not automatically say that they would have ended up in the same place. In fact, I think not. They were older guys. It's like starting all over. I mean Darrell started it in his twenties. Now he's going to start it all over in his forties? Pretty tough.

English's crystal ball wasn't alone. Very few people expected Darrell and Vinnie to again approach the heights they had reached with Pantera. Some, like rock photographer Ross Halfin, don't even qualify it as much as English does. "Not a chance," Halfin says of the idea. "It was very unique with Anselmo. Whether they liked each other or not, it worked. Whether they liked Anselmo or not, he was a great front man. They never would have made it."

But no one had really expected a metal band from Arlington, Texas, to debut at No. 1 on the *Billboard* charts in 1994, when metal looked to be on its way out. The Abbott brothers were used to overcoming adversity, used to convincing all doubters, and more important, used to churning out bone-crushing riffs together. So they kept doing it.

After deciding to start a new band—while drinking beers and watching the New England Patriots beat the Carolina Panthers in Super Bowl XXXVIII on February 1, 2003—Darrell and Vinnie began recording demos at Darrell's home studio. The music that emerged from those probative sessions would have been familiar to most Pantera fans—there was no mistaking a Dime riff—but it was more of a descendant of the duo's now-previous outfit rather than a clone. There was more melody involved in some places; more malady present in others. It was, truly, the sound of a new band, one that would (hopefully) be palatable to the brothers' existing fan base, while (again, hopefully) maintaining its own reason to exist. Darrell would later describe the fresh start as an opportunity to "bust it open a little more and just broaden it up, go for the Baskin-Robbins thirty-one flavors instead of the one."[9]

There were no vocals, but that would change when Pat Lachman, a guitarist who had played with Halford and Diesel Machine and a longtime drinking buddy of Darrell's, heard the demos and immediately wanted in. Though he had never fronted a band before, Lachman proved to be a natural for the role. Rounding out the new group was Bob Kakaha, a Dallas tattoo artist. Thanks to his monstrous bass tone, and possibly due to his tongue-tripping last name, Kakaha quickly earned the handle Bob Zilla from the brothers.

Though Lachman and Kakaha were worthy additions to the lineup, there was no mistaking that this band was the Abbott brothers' show. After all, the news that Rob Halford's former guitarist was in a new band did not inspire breathless, terribly punctuated Internet chatter, and Kakaha's musical résumé was far less interesting than his tattoo portfolio. Lachman and Kakaha were simply the two guys who facilitated the triumphant return of Darrell and Vinnie Abbott. That was the idea. The band—now known as Damageplan—signed a deal with Elektra Records later that year. *New Found Power*, at one point rumored to be the name of the new band, would instead be the title of the group's debut album, released on February 10, 2004.

With a reason to have a guitar in his hands again on a regular basis, the moroseness and frustration that had marked Darrell's unplanned hiatus melted away; whatever anger was left was channeled into the songs with self-explanatory titles like "Fuck You" and "Blunt Force Trauma." His occasional dark moods were replaced by his own newfound power, a sense of motivation that he had lacked even in the Pantera days. Now that Darrell was back in the game, he wasn't happy merely playing; he wanted to win again. "Oh, he was definitely fired up," his friend Scott Minyard says.

"You know, he was a bit of a perfectionist, and he was working very hard on integrating this new band, getting the music to be where he believed it needed to be in order for him to feel proud of what he was doing," English says.

And that took some work and a lot of investment on his part, in terms of time and energy, which he obviously was very willing to give it. But it didn't happen overnight. He put a lot of work into it. I, as a friend, was always supportive and, you know, looking for that hit, that hook, for that thing that made the new band a shooting star. When it came to the company, when they first went out on the road, we made them big banners for the sides of their buses. As a company, we tried to be involved and offer support for the new band.

But internally, you know, he had a lot of challenges. He was coming from Pantera. This is a brand, a franchise that in his world of metal was a difficult one to replace. They made their decision to push forward and depend on their own personalities, their own recognition, and their own capabilities and somehow try to meld the new band together and get to their fan base and see if they would accept the new band in place of the old band.

Very difficult.

Getting to their fan base meant hitting the road. That meant swallowing their pride and reacquainting themselves with small-ish clubs they hadn't played in more than a decade.

16

BREATHING NEW LIFE

On the Road Again

*"I'm looking for a
dare-to-be-great situation."*

LLOYD DOBLER,
Say Anything

Chris Paluska wasn't supposed to be Damageplan's tour manager. He was happy to do it, since he had grown up a huge metal fan in Dallas, making Pantera a "pinnacle band" for him. He had followed the group from *Cowboys from Hell* on, so it "was quite righteous realizing I was going to be working with those guys," he says. But he wasn't supposed to be the group's tour manager.

Bassmanagement, the Dallas-based management concern headed by Paul Bassman, hired Paluska in October 2003, not long after Damageplan joined the company's roster. Bassman and

Paluska had briefly worked together at Last Beat Records and had kept up their friendship after Bassman left to strike out on his own. At Bassmanagement, Paluska became the day-to-day manager for Damageplan, Drowning Pool, and Losa, an upstart band on Metal Blade Records that he had brought to the company. But working with the other two groups paled in comparison to the unique situation he found himself in with Damageplan.

"The first business meeting I ever went to with Paul, we went and met Vinnie and Dime at, I don't know, Texas Land & Cattle or something," Paluska says.

Some restaurant in Arlington. Dime had owed a small commission check to Paul. But instead of just giving him a check, he makes this whole presentation. They were there before us, and we sit down and we're chilling out, ordering drinks and salads and lunch. When the waiter brings the salad plates, there's one with a big plastic rat on it, with a big knife through it, and then the check sitting underneath that. There was a bunch of little inside jokes, with the rat and the knife and the check. He had to give Paul a little bit of money, and instead of having the accountant mail him this check, it's this whole production that was just hilarious. Things like that happened day in, day out.

Though Darrell could still be counted on for a good fake rat prank and was never very far away from a black tooth grin, he had grown much more serious about the business side of his band, as Paluska would find out. He was still the life of the party. But now he knew the party could end at any time, unless he made sure otherwise.

"This was a pretty serious time for them," Paluska says.

They had gone through that whole Pantera (basically) breakup, which for them wasn't a breakup. It was just Phil kind of disappeared and wouldn't talk to them for a couple of years, and those guys just kind of sat around not knowing what to do. So this was really their gusto. They were picking themselves back up, starting a *whole new* project. Man, those guys went back out on the road in a tour bus with ten guys, playing in clubs. They were really swallowing some pride, really trying to make something happen. So they were very motivated, especially Dime. I remember Vinnie commenting on Dime, just as far as, you know, Dime was always just the guitar player and would hang out on the bus, not really that involved with anything. But Dime was really involved with every little aspect. I mean, we'd have daily meetings on the phone and weekly meetings in person. He'd be there with his notebook, with a list of stuff that was longer than ours was. It was fun. It was encouraging. He was really driven and really wanted to make this happen. He was very motivated and tried to keep everybody as motivated.

Somebody had to keep everybody motivated, since the Abbott brothers and most of their road crew had taken the same tumble down the music industry ladder. Sound engineer Aaron Barnes and drum tech John "Kat" Brooks had been with the brothers forever. Pantera had been taken away from them, too. But no one ever stewed about it, least of all Darrell. Not once they were back out on the road, in front of their fans every night.

"Their main attitude was just to roll with it," Paluska says. "One of Dime's famous things was, 'The highs and lows of rock and roll.' Not that it was a low point for them, but as compared to where they were, it would be considered that for sure. It was talked about but it was never dwelled upon. It was the fact, and then the fact beyond that was, 'We're starting something new and we're going to make it happen. We're going to do whatever we got to do to get back where we were.'"

To that end, after *New Found Power* was released in February, Damageplan spent the rest of 2004 in a bus. As the year started to wind down, the plan was to do one more touring cycle before heading back into the studio to record a follow-up. Since the band had had a falling out with its previous tour manager, and since Paluska wanted the education, he decided to tour manage the last leg of Damageplan's road dates. "I really had no idea what it was like out there and what everybody was going through," Paluska says. "So I signed up just for the experience, to be honest. That was a one-time thing. It was the first time I had done any tour managing or anything like it."

After what ended up happening, it's safe to say Paluska will never do any more tour managing. He won't even talk about the end of the trip, that last tragic stop in Columbus. But he can't block out the entire experience either. He doesn't want to. Up until that point, Paluska had been living his dream, circa *Cowboys from Hell*, getting the full Dime experience every day. He was getting paid not only to watch Darrell play guitar every night, but also to hang out with him before and after the show.

"It was awesome, because it was so incredibly consistent," Paluska says. "It was absolutely unbelievable. I had heard reports of—you know, every band that's toured with Pantera is, like, 'Oh, the best live band in the world' and this and that. Dime was just pure artist. Just pure talent. He's not up there worrying about messing up a riff—that's not even on his radar. Just pure, effortless, true talent. And it was completely consistent every night, no matter what the circumstances were the day before or that week. It was the same thing. It was beautiful, actually."

The best part for Paluska, though, was seeing how consistent Darrell was when he wasn't onstage.

"It was nonstop entertainment, but all in a good way," Paluska says. "There was never anything negative. Never any bad vibes. If he was having a shitty day, you never knew. He never brought his stuff that was bothering him out in the open. He wouldn't walk into a room and bum the whole vibe out—you know, like people can get. It was basically the opposite. He was real concerned about fans; that was a big thing to [Darrell and Vinnie]. He was always just kind of, sadly, the Dime that everybody wanted him to be. I'm sure there was points where he was just flat burned out on being this rocker Dime guy. But he never disappointed. He was a complete blast."

But making a habit of never disappointing anyone comes with a price when you've cultivated a reputation as a best-in-show boozehound. "You know what? That was one thing that I noticed that was starting to really become apparent to him as well," Paluska says.

That's kind of the icebreaker that every single fan could think of. They'd walk up to him with a shot. He doesn't want to be the guy that's, like, "Nah." . . . He would never turn anybody down. There have been reports of him being such an alcoholic and such a lush. Yeah, he had fun and he partied, but a lot of it was just entertaining the crowd. Just keeping a good thing going with everybody that's hanging around.

Dime was more approachable, just because he had that reputation, you know, of being a cool guy and he would hang out and talk to people. Vinnie is just as courteous, but he's not as outgoing and he's more kind of business-oriented. He was always there just the same, being just as nice to everybody, but Dime just kind of wore it and lived it.

HOWEVER IT looked or felt, Darrell wasn't starting completely over. He still had his champions. He still won awards. He was still wanted on magazine covers. That's how he crossed paths with Mick Hutson again.

Someone always wanted a picture whenever Pantera (and later, Damageplan) toured through England, and for more than a decade, Mick Hutson usually got the call. He enjoyed photographing the band, mainly because Darrell always made it easy for Hutson to get what he needed, knowing how to ensure he went home with two or three of those wonderful images that jump off the proof sheet. This was particularly true during a show at London's Brixton Academy.

"I had the fish-eye lens on," Hutson says. "He leans right over into the lens with the guitar, and he stayed in that position, playing right into the lens for ages while I shot a good few frames. It turned out really well. . . . He was just very aware of what made a good picture. His perception of always being drunk and being a bit of a fuck-up, I don't think that was accurate at all, actually.

I think he was very aware of what was going on all the time. He was still sharp, and I think he still recognized his performance and what he needed to do."

But it was the last time he was in front of Hutson's lens that sticks out the most in the veteran photographer's mind.[10] Scenes like the one that played out that day tend to get dog-eared in your brain. Or, as Hutson puts it, "The memories of having a really, really fun time driving around London in the back of a stretch Hummer as he was getting *absolutely* arseholed are quite vivid, you know?"

Hutson had been assigned to take the cover photo for *Metal Hammer* magazine's awards issue. The shoot was scheduled for June 7, 2004, the day of the awards ceremony. The plan was to get together three of the winners—Mötley Crüe bassist Nikki Sixx (Spirit of Hammer Award), H.I.M. front man Ville Hermanni Valo (Golden God), and Darrell (Best Guitarist)—in the afternoon, before the festivities that night, and let the magic happen. Which wasn't a problem. Darrell, for one, was so full of magic he could hardly stay upright.

To add to the fun, *Metal Hammer* had provided the trio with a captive audience. Besides Hutson, the stretch Hummer rented for the occasion also included a TV camera crew (meant to shoot Hutson as he shot Sixx, Valo, and Darrell) and one increasingly unhappy driver. Darrell never was one to let down a crowd, certainly not with two willing accomplices on hand, not to mention his favorite silent partner.

"They got progressively drunker and drunker and drunker until they started throwing these champagne glasses around," Hutson says, laughing. "It just got wilder and wilder until champagne glasses are being thrown in mid-air, so I can take photographs of them smashing together. Then they started to stab the leather seats in the back of this Hummer—which didn't go down well with the driver. We then parked up in this kind of car park just next to this park in London to do some shots of everybody hanging around outside the Hummer and all that kind of stuff. Dimebag got in [the Hummer] and tried to drive off, and he could barely stand at that point, which was quite funny as well."

Darrell, fortunately, remained ambulatory long enough for Hutson to stumble upon one of those happy accidents photographers make a living off. Hutson corralled Darrell and Sixx into the same frame as a protestor in the park. The demonstrator was dressed in a monk's habit and held a large homemade sign declaring that rock and roll was the root of all evil.

If only he knew. The *Metal Hammer* award show hadn't started; there would be plenty of wicked deeds yet to come. There had already been plenty of debauchery in the UK that week. Most of the bands scheduled to attend the *Metal Hammer* get-together—Damageplan, Slayer, Slipknot, Korn, Drowning Pool, the Brides of Destruction—had performed at the Download Festival in Donnington, Scotland, the day before. By the time the photo shoot ended, Darrell wasn't in the process of getting drunk. He was in the process of *staying* drunk.

Hutson had seen Darrell in that state often enough to recognize the various phases of his alcohol-induced metamorphosis. "Dimebag, he'd always go through different stages," Hutson says.

At first, he was quiet. And then he would get drunk and he would get quite loud. And then he'd get to the point where he would start hugging you, saying he loved you, you were his favorite photographer in the whole world, all that kind of stuff. Then he would start getting really pissed off with everybody. He got a bit drunk and he was trying to start a fight with everyone. And then, generally, he would just fall into a heap. Definite set of stages of drunkenness. Almost quite shy at the start, and then quite loud, then really loved up, then getting a bit angry, and then just collapse. He always seemed to remember me, though, so that was fine. No matter what stage of drunkenness he was in, he always had to remember who I was.

So Hutson knew, generally, what was coming next. Specifically? No one could ever predict that. Even an expert in game theory would have had his hands full with that equation. When Darrell had a few (or a few too many), the outcome was always mutable, dependent on who and what was around him and what stage he happened to be in.

As the *Metal Hammer* shindig got under way, Darrell was rounding "really loved up" and heading toward "a bit angry." By the time he took the stage to accept his Best Guitarist trophy, he was already there. Darrell slurred and mumbled his way through a short speech that was punctuated by his tossing the prize into the audience. From there, he made his way into the VIP lounge. He grabbed a Gibson Explorer off the wall—the guitar company had a display set up—and began bashing it against a table. To no avail, as it turned out.

"Dime, do I need to show you how to break a guitar?" asked his partner in crime from earlier in the day, Nikki Sixx.

"I got it, Sixx, I got it." He did, finally cracking the guitar in two. With that, Darrell left the room, just as a flabbergasted Gibson representative entered. Sixx, a Gibson endorser, initially claimed responsibility for the act of guitar terrorism. It probably would have worked, too, had Darrell not returned and confessed, telling the fuming rep to "put your dick in your pants"—and the guitar on his bill. (This wasn't the first time he had broken a guitar that didn't belong to him. It was, in fact, a fairly regular occurrence.) Not long after, true to Hutson's play-by-play of a typical Darrell drinking episode, he fell into a heap. "The highs and lows of rock and roll," indeed.

Yet when Hutson looks at his favorite photo of that afternoon's session, it's difficult for him to spot the alcohol, to notice its effects. He knows they're there; he just can't find them.

"Even though he was probably the drunkest I'd seen him in a long time, he looks *brilliant* in this picture," Hutson says. "He doesn't look drunk in the picture; he looks totally, totally on it. And he looks *healthy*, which is another weird thing. He looks really healthy."

DARRELL HAD other reasons to be happy during those last few months, beyond the fact that Damageplan was up and running and he was finally able to be himself again. Chief among those reasons was this: After meeting (and playing shows with) most of his boyhood idols—Judas Priest, Black Sabbath, KISS—Darrell finally had the chance to cross the last one off his list. Not exactly in the way he wanted to, but still. He had tried to do it right, of course, campaigning hard for a chance to open Van Halen's 2004 reunion tour, so he and Vinnie could complete the set and put that Van Halen tour all-access pass next to the ones they'd collected from playing with Judas Priest, KISS, and Black Sabbath. It was not to be.

But when Van Halen came to Texas in Fall 2004, Darrell was onstage. That he was off to the side, out of sight of the crowd and without a guitar in his hand, was irrelevant. The show itself was just icing. The cake was this: He had met Eddie Van Halen for the first time, and during sound check, he had got to play through Eddie's rig. He told Rita later that night, "If I died tonight, it wouldn't matter, because I've done everything now."

Only Ace Frehley and KISS had more to do with Darrell's chosen profession than Van Halen, and the group ran a very close second. It might have even outranked KISS when it came to rating which band had more impact on Pantera as a whole, since the Abbotts had always modeled themselves after Eddie and Alex Van Halen, their guitarist-drummer-brothers predecessors. Darrell even had a recording studio built at his home because he wanted to emulate Eddie, who had long used his 5150 studio to record his namesake band's albums.

Two decades later, Darrell was able to get backstage, and onstage with Eddie's guitar in hand, because he was Dime. But when he *was* back there, he was Darrell Abbott again, teenaged Van Halen fanatic, finger-tapping his way through "Eruption" in his bedroom. Though fans and guitar magazines might consider Eddie and Darrell peers and colleagues, it was difficult for Darrell not to revert to being a star-struck kid in Eddie's presence. Darrell was not one to take the idea of "hero" lightly, which is probably why he routinely gave his fans more than they required from him. He knew what it was like to idolize, and not money, status, or any other kind of success could erase that knowledge.

"He *never* lost that," Scott Minyard says. "He did evolve into somebody a little bit different, but he never lost that eighteen-year-old quality and love for music and love for fun—ever. There's this one picture you gotta see—a friend of mine's got an 8 × 10 of it—and it's Dime backstage, and you can see it in his eye. He's already made it—he's already in Damageplan, he's already done Pantera and succeeded. But he's backstage at Van Halen with a Van Halen set list right there, and you could see him lit up like a little kid. And he never did lose that. He still had that fire. Most people lose it when they get up to that status. The frustrations wear you out."

Darrell left Eddie a voice mail shortly after they met, expressing his gratitude and admiration. Eddie played the message for the crowd at Darrell's public memorial service:

> Ed, it's Dimebag. Hey, man, just wanted to give you a fucking call telling you thank you so fucking much, man, for the most awesome, uplifting, euphoric, spiritual rock-and-roll extravaganza ever. That was fucking pure fucking insanity, man. . . . I just wanted to thank y'all so much for the awesome party. Everybody treated me so fucking great. Your fucking show was goddamn nothing but pure magic. Man! You're playing your fucking ass off! Bad to the fucking bone. Loved everything about it, man. Uh, we got fucking wasted.

DARRELL COULDN'T go very long without someone offering him a shot, but the reverse was also true. If you were pulled into his orbit for whatever reason, unless you had a sobriety chip in your hand you'd have a drink in it. Fan, friend, journalist, whatever—everyone drank. People who hadn't drunk in years would suddenly find themselves double-fisting black tooth grins. It was difficult, if not impossible, to turn him down. Not that many people wanted to.

Juliya Chernetsky, the former host of the metal-centric show *Uranium* on the Fuse network, had a typical introduction to Darrell. She was sent down to Arlington to interview Damageplan. She came back with a hangover and a new friend.

"It was very exciting, because at that point, I was doing what I do for about three or four years and had met absolutely everyone," Chernetsky says. "As much love as I have for the scene, I didn't freak out anymore [when I met someone]. I was fucking freaking out. I was shaking when I met this motherfucker. The first thing he says to me when I walked through the door was like, 'Juliya! Come on in here and do a shot of black tooth! I won't tell you shit till you get drunk!'" She laughs. "That was the first hello I got from Dime."

Chernetsky spent the better part of a week in Texas, on the receiving end of Darrell's brand of southern hospitality, drinking her way through visits to his home, the Clubhouse, his favorite restaurant, and plenty of other places no one involved can remember. She had a few chances to return the favor when Darrell would come to New York, on tour or some other music business.

"Dime would call and be, like, 'We're coming through town. Let's fucking party,'" Chernetsky says. "And I'd be, like, 'Right on,' and start making arrangements, so that, you know, whatever was necessary was there. And then we'd go and get trashed."

Somewhere between "right on" and getting trashed, Chernetsky managed to get Damageplan's last interview—though no one knew it was at the time. On November 29, 2004, she questioned the band on their tour bus before a gig that night at New York's Irving Plaza, the last date of the Devastation across the Nation Tour, a three-band bill that also featured Shadows Fall and the Haunted. Originally, Damageplan was set to return to Arlington after the Devastation tour wrapped up. But the band was offered a gig on the way home, and they needed the money. *New Found Power* was doing OK in record stores, but it hadn't lived up to Pantera standards sales-wise. Since they were going to be home recording, it wouldn't hurt to pick up an extra payday.

Chernetsky didn't ask the band about that. There was no reason to. Besides, she was more fan than journalist, and a friend on top of that. So their conversation ranged from the price of Darrell's cheap leopard slippers ($4.88—he still had the tag on them) to partying on tour ("I think it's escalated," Darrell noted) to various tattoo stories (including a gruesome recounting of Darrell attempting to give someone a Damageplan tattoo).

But one part of the Q&A would turn out to be somewhat chilling, or at least prescient, given what would happen shortly after:

Juliya: Do you think you could lose your respect or reputation as a guitar god? What would you have to do to do that?

Darrell: How could you do that? Once you cut your path you cut your path. I mean—dude, I'll tell ya, anyone who rises above the fence, there's always some dude on the other side with a shotgun trying to blow a couple of bullets at ya, you know? Jack-offs on the Internet or anyone who won't show their face ain't gonna come to the game and tell me to my face or anybody to their face. You know, they're always gonna take cheap shots. But, no, man, every guitar hero I ever loved, I still go back to those old records 'cause, you know, haven't been too many cats in a long time come along.

17

SHEDDING SKIN

Grinding a New Axe and the Birth of Krankenstein

"I want you to hit me as hard as you can."

TYLER DURDEN,
Fight Club

Unfortunately for Larry English, exactly as his job at Washburn had opened the door on a friendship with Darrell it closed it as well. Darrell's contract with Washburn had run its course. Coincidentally, Dean Guitars had been resurrected, and founder Dean Zelinsky was back at the helm. Eager to make a splash, the company took dead aim at reacquiring the services of its most famous endorser. It offered him a contract and a hefty signing bonus to sweeten the pot. On top of that, he would be more-or-less coming home.

As it happened, Washburn wasn't in a very strong bargaining position. English was no longer in artist relations, having taken a promotion to become senior vice president of business development at U.S. Music Corp., the company that owns Washburn as well as Randall Amplifiers, another product Darrell used and endorsed. On the face of it, the fact that his entire guitar-and-amplifier setup was produced by the same company might have made it seem as though Washburn was in better shape than it actually was. But Darrell's relationship with Washburn had spiraled downward since English had left artist relations. While he was still close to English, he was no longer close to the company; he never connected with English's replacements and never really understood why he wasn't working with English anymore.

"It was such a big change," English says. "You know, it's no longer Larry. It's somebody else. He just didn't care about that. He spent all this time building this relationship. That's all he knew about. What he said to me was, 'I feel like I was fired.' So this was a pretty traumatic time."

Beyond that, Washburn also wasn't prepared to offer Darrell a bonus to sign his contract. They never had on any previous resign, and starting now would just be setting a bad precedent, putting the company on the edge of a slippery slope. Had Darrell not already missed out on quite a few paydays thanks to Pantera's interminable hiatus and eventual demise, Washburn might have figured out a way around the bonus. Had Darrell still been working with English, they might have come up with a compromise. He might have stayed just out of loyalty. But English wasn't his guy at

Washburn anymore, and Pantera wasn't his band. He wanted and needed that lump-sum check.

Darrell decided to sign with Dean.

"We talked about it, and what had to happen in order to end the business relationship here, and how do we clean this up, and attending to all the business side of the relationship," English says.

So we went through that . . . and that just changed the condition of our relationship. I can't really remember if we spent any more personal time after that, but I don't think so. I think the next time I saw him was in a coffin. That's my loss. That's the world's loss, really.

Unfortunately, very unfortunately for the folks from Dean, what happened, happened. They, unfortunately, did not have as much time with him as we did. And when I say that, I mean they didn't have as much time to enjoy the relationships, the creativity, the craziness. I feel for them in that they lost out. I'm sorry for me in that I would have liked continuing to be his friend and a person he relied on for forever. I feel bad for the rest of the world, for the people who didn't get an opportunity to share with him, be around him. You can't expect everybody in the world to have done that. The guys who did got a gift. And I was gifted many, many times, and I am thankful.

TOWARD THE end of his life, Darrell's world was in a constant state of flux. He had changed bands, managers, and—maybe most important—guitar endorsements. Another huge development, at least as far as his equipment was concerned, was lost in the news of his switch from Washburn to Dean.

Darrell had used Randall amps since he was a teenager, when he won one—like much of his early gear—in a guitar contest. In fact, the thick and dirty sound provided by Randall's solid-state amps was widely considered the bedrock of Darrell's much-imitated guitar tone. Even by Darrell himself. "Gotta have that Randall Crunch!" he said in the liner notes for *Cowboys from Hell*.

"Solid-state amps are more in-your-face," Darrell once told *Guitar Player* magazine. "I'm not going for soft sounds, and I ain't lookin' for no warm sound. For what I'm doing, I can't get enough fuckin' chunk! I won a Randall half-stack in a guitar contest when I was younger that had a natural nastiness to it. I knew that nobody had really grabbed a hold of that tone, so I built my sound around it."[11]

But when Darrell left Washburn, he left Randall, too, cutting all ties with U.S. Music Corp. He contacted several different companies, looking for a new supplier. Eventually, he settled on Krank, a relatively small outfit, because—as one of its owners, Jody Dankberg, remembers—he "connected" with them. Which should come as no surprise, since that's how Darrell made most of his business decisions.

"It happened really quickly," Dankberg says. "He called us, had us send him some amps. The next thing you know, he was out here a week later." The visit is captured on *Dimevision, Vol. I*: Darrell tests his new amp by playing his iconic "Cowboys from Hell" riff. "Whooo! That's it, brother!" He punches Dankberg's partner, Tony Dow, happily on the arm, then sets off soloing. As if to prove the amp's worth, his riffing sets off a car alarm. Shortly thereafter, Damageplan started its tour, and Krank provided Darrell with his backline. "It was a real whirlwind,"

Dankberg says. "I only knew him a couple of months before he passed away. Everything came together really quickly."

Darrell not only decided to endorse Krank amps, but he also invested in the company. Together, they made plans to design and manufacture what he called the "Krankenstein" amp. Dankberg was just happy to be involved. All of a sudden, one of the guys from a poster on the wall of his teenage bedroom was calling him on a regular basis.

"It was amazing," Dankberg says.

He was a big hero of mine growing up, and so just to have a chance to even know the man was awesome. It was the coolest thing in my life. He was real smart and real serious. He knew a lot about business. He was a real straight shooter. Real honest. You could see why people wanted to do business with him, because he was a real good guy to know. He was real concerned with having a real credible product, something he could stand behind, especially as far as an amplifier goes, where people could actually use his product, as they were using his guitars and his pedals and all that type of stuff. He wanted the same thing with his amp.

DARRELL NEVER got a chance to see how his new relationship with Krank, or his renewed partnership with Dean, would work out. He had taken a chance and truly started over. He was on tour with a different band, playing different (if familiar) guitars out of different amps. It was a new beginning, but the end was near.

18

SLAUGHTERED

Alrosa Villa, December 8, 2004

"The day [Darrell died] was the 9/11 of rock. A little of us died that day, too."

———

DAVID DRAIMAN,
Disturbed

Three minutes. That's all it took. Three minutes, starting at 10:15 P.M., when twenty-five-year-old Nathan Gale got off the first round from his 9-mm Beretta and ending when Columbus police officer James Niggemeyer killed Gale with one blast from his Remington 870 Express shotgun.

At first, everyone thought it was a joke, a hoax, part of the act. Even after the first three shots stopped the show in its tracks. Even after Darrell Abbott slumped to the stage, his final notes giving way to the electric hum of his amplifier. For a beat, everyone stood motionless. Damageplan singer Pat Lachman, who had jumped into the crowd, screamed into the microphone, "Call 911 somebody! Fucking call 911!" That's when they knew it wasn't a cap gun, knew it wasn't all an elaborate charade, much as they hoped it was. Some were laughing, almost reflexively, the kind of bemused chuckle that escapes while watching police chases or skateboard videos or any fucked-up stunt. How could they know it was real? Two years later, every single time I watch the video of the incident, unwittingly captured by the band's own camera, it catches me by surprise—and I know precisely when it's coming and where it's coming from.

I knew what to expect before I ever popped the tape into my VCR. Unlike the people who were there, I had the benefit of hindsight. I combed through hundreds of witness accounts of the shooting, reconstructing those three minutes until I had the timeline down cold.

I could hear the first song of Damageplan's set, "Breathing New Life," thudding through the speakers. I could feel the excitement of the crowd, the release that comes when anticipation is replaced by participation. I could see Nathan Gale appear suddenly from behind the stack of amplifiers at stage left. I could see him jogging across the stage, slowing only when he reached the drum riser. I could see him advancing on Darrell with his 9-mm Beretta in textbook firing position—his right arm extended, his left hand cupping his wrist for support.

I knew the first time I watched the tape that Darrell wasn't making it through that first song. And yet, given the kind of perverse instant replay the Columbus Police Department had provided me with, I hoped I was wrong. I had spent months getting to know Darrell by proxy, constantly talking about him, thinking about him, reading his interviews, watching the home movies he'd made, listening to his music. I was living in a world where I was perpetually in his presence. I spent more time with him than I did with my friends and family. He still felt alive to me.

Then Gale lumbered into the frame, and a few seconds later, it was all over. The standoff would continue for those aforementioned three minutes and a dozen more shots, but Darrell was dead. He was probably gone before he hit the ground. He had suffered gunshot wounds to his right cheek and left ear; the back of his head; and his right hand.

In the video, it's unsettling how perfectly the sequence of events aligned, at least from Gale's perspective. Seconds before Gale made his entrance, the band's security chief, Jeffrey "Mayhem" Thompson, had crossed to the other side of the stage, and Lachman and Bob Kakaha had moved to the front. This arrangement left Gale with an unimpeded path to Darrell: Lachman and Kakaha had their backs turned to him, and Mayhem was now in a position where he could only chase Gale instead of heading him off at the pass. Darrell had moved to the back corner of the stage, around the side of the drum riser. Even if he had been looking up, he would have had only a second, maybe two, to react.

Mayhem caught up with Gale, but by then, he had already shot Darrell in the head at point-blank range. He fired twice more after Darrell fell to the floor, then turned his gun on the assorted crew members and security staff that had followed Mayhem across the stage. Gale shot tour manager Chris Paluska once in the chest before Mayhem grabbed the gunman from behind. He was able to get his gun hand free, however, and shot Mayhem in the chest, back, and upper thigh; Mayhem was pronounced dead at the scene.

It's unclear from the video of the shooting exactly what happened next, and witness accounts are somewhat contradictory. You can clearly see Nathan Bray, a twenty-three-year-old fan, vault over the security barrier and scramble across the stage to where Darrell and Mayhem had fallen. Bray, in fact, was one of the first to act, rushing forward while the majority of the crowd was paralyzed, first by confusion and then by fear. He disappears from sight shortly thereafter, lost in the chaos. Bray's valor was rewarded with a bullet in the chest; he made it to Riverside Hospital but was declared dead at 11:10 P.M.

In the video, you can also see Erin Halk, a twenty-nine-year-old Alrosa Villa employee, and another one of that night's heroes. Instead of following Bray and the others to where the bodies lay, he tried to ambush Gale. You can see the burly, bearded Halk as he makes his way behind the drum riser in an attempt to sneak up on the gunman. He never comes back. Halk suffered multiple gunshot wounds (four in the chest, one in the hand, and one in the leg) as he tried to disarm Gale; he was pronounced dead at the scene.

The rest is left up to the imagination—and the addled memories of those who were there. Another fan, Travis Burnett, made an attempt to subdue Gale; a bullet glanced off his left forearm as he tried to grab the gun. Gale fired on Burnett again, then turned his attention to John "Kat" Brooks, Damageplan's drum tech. Brooks had been behind the amplifiers on Darrell's side of the stage when the shooting started. In shock, he staggered over to the other side after Darrell and Mayhem had been shot; you can see him in the video, his face a mask of pure loss, screaming, "No! No!" But Brooks quickly reentered the fray and, like several others before him, tried to wrestle the Beretta out of Gale's hands. As he struggled with Gale, Brooks was shot twice in the leg.

At this point, Gale—perhaps realizing the police were closing in—grabbed Brooks and used him as a shield as he backed out of the club, jamming the gun against Brooks's temple. That's when Niggemeyer entered Alrosa Villa through a door behind the stage and killed Gale with one shot to the back of the head. Brooks hustled off the front of the stage, half rolling and half crawling, and ran outside and into the band's tour bus.

In the video, you only hear the boom of the shotgun, an appreciably different sound than the pop-pop-pop of Gale's pistol. "You're my witness—I had to do it!" Niggemeyer yells, before entering the frame, shotgun cocked and ready. He was only eighteen minutes into his shift that night; he had just finished roll call at the Eighteenth Precinct substation two miles away when the first 911 call came in through dispatch. He eases up when it becomes clear Gale was the only shooter. Niggemeyer looks haunted by it, even when the scattered fans and security personnel trying to help, trying to make sense of what just happened, trying to do *something*, assure him that he saved a lot of lives with that shot. They're more right than they know: The clip of the Beretta was half-full, and Gale had another box of thirty bullets on him.

That unused cache of ammunition would imply that it could have been much worse, but from another tape that was recorded that night, it's difficult to see how. As disquieting as the video of the incident is, the other recording will stay with me just as long.

Filmed for evidentiary purposes, the tape is a simple documenta-
tion of the aftermath of Gale's attack. The club is completely
empty, save for the bodies. Darrell lies under a white sheet, one
corner soaked in blood, on the floor in front of the stage. Mayhem is onstage with his wallet on his chest, shirtless and shoeless;
his black Adidas sneakers were removed while paramedics tried
in vain to stimulate blood flow back to his heart. Gale is on his
back, lying headfirst down the set of steps leading from the backstage area onto the stage. The cameraman takes in all of this,
pausing to note the shell casings littering the floor, lingering
over every piece of debris that might be construed as evidence.

There is one image on the video that stands out over all others and speaks directly to the events of December 8, 2004, sum-
ming them up in a passing glimpse. As the cameraman pans away
from Gale's bloody body, his lens lights on two objects, thrown
into close proximity by the turmoil that took place in that
cramped area. The way they are juxtaposed, it doesn't seem accidental at all. On one side of the frame is the spent shotgun shell
that ended Gale's life. On the other, and only a few inches away,
is one of Darrell's beloved Dean guitars, broken at the neck, its
now-separate halves twisted awkwardly against each other.

WOULD THAT night have turned out any different if Mayhem
had stayed on Darrell's side of the stage, or Lachman and Kakaha
hadn't moved? It's impossible to say. Damageplan wasn't supposed
to be there at all. It had wrapped up its Devastation across the Nation Tour, with Shadows Fall and the Haunted. It hadn't played at
Alrosa Villa since the *Cowboys from Hell* tour, but the place was
more-or-less on the way home, and the band needed the paycheck;

New Found Power had sold a relatively disappointing 160,000 copies. So, along with the fluky synchronization between Gale and everyone else onstage, the only thing that might have changed is who else died during Gale's assault at Alrosa Villa.

During the investigation of the murders, the Columbus police made an alarming discovery: Gale had interrupted a Damageplan gig once before. Eight months earlier, at an April 5 gig at Bogart's nightclub in Cincinnati, Gale had rushed the stage. He didn't have a gun that time, and it's unclear what, exactly, he planned to do had the security staff at Bogart's not intervened. He refused to leave the stage, latching onto a tower of amplifiers as security guards tried to forcibly remove him, toppling a lighting rig and causing almost two thousand dollars in damages.

The band never stopped playing. Lachman even made light of the commotion when the song was over, jokingly introducing Gale as the fifth member of the band. The members of the band decided not to press charges, since they didn't want to have to come all the way back to Cincinnati just to make a court appearance. Shit happens, they said. Darrell had probably racked up bigger bar tabs. Gale had been removed from the club, the show had kept rolling, and that was good enough. They never expected to see him again.

Why did they? Gale didn't leave behind a note that shed any light on his actions; based on the amount of ammunition he was carrying, he might have believed he would make it out of there to explain it himself. Other than that, there is only hearsay and innuendo.

In the hours after the shooting, it was rumored that, before he shot him, Gale had yelled at Darrell, "You broke up Pantera!" In the days that followed, people sometimes treated this gossip as fact. The revelation that Gale had been obsessed with Pantera only added to this perception. Mark Green, who coached the semipro Lima Thunder football team, for which Gale played on the offensive line, told reporters Gale used Pantera's music to fire himself up before games. Dave Johnson, a high school friend of Gale's, told FOX News that Gale had tried to pass Pantera lyrics off as his own, then claimed that the band had stolen the lyrics from *him* and, furthermore, was trying to steal his identity as well.

Giving further credence to this rumor was an incendiary interview Phil Anselmo had given to *Metal Hammer* for its December 2004 issue, in which he said that Darrell "deserves to be beaten severely."[12] Kat Brooks and Vinnie both mentioned the *Metal Hammer* piece when they were questioned by the Columbus Police Department that night. This, however, was probably unfortunate coincidence more than anything else. Gale reportedly said, "This is for breaking up Pantera," before shooting Darrell, but his statement was never corroborated by anyone at Alrosa Villa, and investigators could find no evidence that Gale had read Anselmo's interview. Clearly, Gale had not picked out Darrell Abbott at random. But what, exactly, had lit his fuse that night is a mystery. He hadn't taken the gun with him to Cincinnati. Why now?

Also deemed coincidental by authorities was the date of the murders. Though the fact that Gale killed Darrell and the others on the same day Mark David Chapman had gunned down John Lennon outside the Dakota apartment building in New York City was certainly attention-grabbing, no one could prove it had played into Gale's thought process—or lack thereof, as the case may be.

There are only a few scattered known truths about Gale's activities and his frame of mind. The Beretta was a gift from his mother, Mary Clark. She had bought it for him for Christmas in 2002; she was proud of him for cleaning up his life—he'd had a drug problem in high school—and enlisting in the U.S. Marine Corps. Clark had put the gun on layaway, and Gale had picked up the gun on December 9, 2002, when he returned home to Marysville, a small town twenty-five miles northwest of Columbus. "I'll never, never be able to live that part down," Clark told Columbus television station WCMH a week after Gale's death.

Gale's stint in the marines was cut short when he was diagnosed with schizophrenia and honorably discharged from service on October 15, 2003. Though he was sent home with medication for the illness, Clark believed he was not taking the pills he had been prescribed. An autopsy would confirm he had no antischizophrenic medication in his system at the time of the shooting.

His demeanor earlier that day, at the Bears Den Tattoo Parlor in Marysville, would have substantiated that claim even without an autopsy. Gale spent a lot of time skulking around the Bears Den, even though customers didn't appreciate the intense and intensely creepy conversations the hulking Gale would frequently try to draw them into. He didn't fit in there, but then, he didn't seem to fit in anywhere. At the shop, he was a beacon of quiet discomfort, trying to find something to hang onto, or someone to hang out with. His last visit to the Bears Den, several hours before the Damageplan gig at Alrosa Villa, was atypical, but not necessarily surprising.

Gale, as usual, was sitting in the tattoo parlor, flipping through a magazine. A thought occurred to him: He asked Bo Toler, the shop's manager, if he could purchase a tattoo gun from Bears Den. Toler told him no, that only licensed tattoo artists were allowed to buy them. Gale returned to his magazine, until he happened to arrive at a page that sent him into a rage.

"You lied to me," he screamed at Toler. "You said I couldn't buy one of these"—he gestured to a picture of a tattoo gun in the magazine—"but it says here that I can!" He became more and more upset, hollering curses at Toler. He slammed the magazine to the floor and stormed out of the building.

DARRELL WAS able to enjoy one last Halloween party before leaving on a tour that never circled back home. With his long, dark hair, navel-brushing goatee, and camo-shorts-and-sneakers attire, Scott Minyard could almost double for Darrell, so for that particular Halloween shindig, he took the easy way out and completed the image. He dyed his beard pink and had an artist friend draw Darrell's tattoos on his arms and legs. When he showed up to the party, he saw that Jeffrey "Mayhem" Thompson—who had long served as a roadie/bodyguard for Minyard's former band, Slow Roosevelt, before signing on with Damageplan—had had the same idea. He, too, was dressed as Darrell. By that point, Darrell's costume had, as Minyard says, "exploded on him," so he was pretty much dressed as Dimebag as well. It made for an interesting scene later that night.

"I stepped outside to get some air, and the limo is backing up in Vinnie's driveway, trying to turn around and get out or whatever," Minyard says.

The window comes down, and Darrell, in the backseat, is, like, "Scott! Get over here!" I'm, like, "What?" I couldn't understand what he was saying; he was so drunk. He goes, *"Hah-*

argh-har." I go, *"What?* I can't tell what you're trying to say." He goes, "Get in the goddamn car!" So I got in the car, and I was sitting, looking out the back window, and Darrell was right across from me. And right beside him was Mayhem. It was just us three in the back, and we're all three Dimes. They were gonna take Dime home—it was time for him to go to bed—but all he wanted me to do was to hear the new Damageplan that was about to come out. They had a whole CD that he'd recorded. No vocals on it. But he wanted me to hear all of it, so we listened to it and blared it all the way to the house to drop him off, and the limo took me back.

It was the last time Minyard had some "Dime Time." After "the bad stuff happened," some of Darrell's friends (including Minyard) went to the Candlelite Inn, a homey little restaurant in Arlington that Darrell and his family had been going to since he was shorter than most of the tables inside. Behind the cash register, there is a platinum plaque for *Cowboys from Hell*. When they came in, the owner, Chris Odell, recognized them as friends of Darrell. The hurt, confused look on his face matched the ones on their faces. He stared at them, arms out, palms upturned: "What happened?"

No one had an answer, and no one does still. All the people who met Darrell remember where they were when they heard the news—to them, it is a combination of the days when John Lennon and John F. Kennedy were shot—and none of them can make any sense of it.

It was especially tough for Minyard; he lost two friends that night. Before Jeffrey "Mayhem" Thompson was hired as Damage-plan's bodyguard, he had served in that same capacity for Minyard's band, Slow Roosevelt. "We weren't able to really pay Mayhem very much—we did every once in a while, when we could. Every time we'd get to the Curtain Club or anywhere in Dallas, and sometimes in Austin, here's Mayhem, helping with equipment." Mayhem even appeared on the cover of Slow Roosevelt's last album.

"That was a real bad December," Minyard says. He learned of the killings as he was leaving a Marilyn Manson gig; he received a text message that simply, frustratingly, read, "Dime's down."

At least Mayhem and Dime both were doing exactly what they loved to do. Dime was playing his guitar. I mean, he was back onstage and doing good—never felt it. Mayhem was doing what he loved to do, which was security for his favorite cats. . . . I was kind of thankful that the whole world kind of stood there and it was a *big deal*. It was huge. You would figure, just because it was metal and sort of underground to most of the world, that it would be just kind of shoved under as a bad something or other that happened in Columbus or whatever. But the whole world stood up.

Dale Brock didn't find out until the next morning. An old friend called him around 7 A.M. to deliver the news, adding credence to the theory that anytime the phone rings before you wake up, it's a call you don't want to get.

"It was so senseless—he was the kind of guy that would have done anything for anybody," Brock says. "Completely, completely senseless. I've had a hard time realizing he's gone. The other day—my wife, she bartended at the Basement back then. She was great friends with them, went out on the road with them a few times; they all loved her. Probably six, seven months after, we were driving through Arlington and thought, 'Hey let's go by and see—.' Had one of those moments. Yeah, it was a really rough day. I had to come home from work. Couldn't deal with it. Terrible, terrible day."

Like Brock, David Karon, who worked with Darrell at Randall and Washburn, didn't find out until the following morning. It was a day he was looking forward to. Now it's one he dreads.

"It was actually my birthday," Karon says. "And I was supposed to get together with Darrell the next night. So it was pretty fucked up. I turned my phone off the night before, because I was celebrating with my girl, and she woke me up the next day and told me. It was pretty rough, especially being the birthday and looking forward to hanging out the next day. It was pretty crazy. . . . Calling all the artists I work with that are friends with him, making sure what the fuck is really going on, because at that time, there was a lot of rumors going around that other people were hurt."

It doesn't make Karon feel any better that his friend finally made everyone stop and pay attention. "I'd rather no one know who he was. I think it was better when him and Vinnie were on CNN talking about Damageplan than being on CNN for his death. I would have rather them have a better PR agent."

Based on her status as one of the most high-profile metal fans around, Juliya Chernetsky was forced into playing the role of PR agent for the entire hard-rock community in the wake of Darrell's death:

The next day, my manager called me and said that CNN wanted to have me come on to talk about what happened and kind of like what this means to our scene and blah blah blah. So I went on CNN and this stupid little hair-sprayed blond bitch was, like, "So, well, you know, does this kind of thing happen all the time in your scene?" I fucking put that bitch straight. I was, like, "Dude, we don't shoot each other, and the person that did this was out of his goddamn mind, and this is not the way it goes down in our scene, and this is not what we're fucking about." And then I had to do a *Uranium* thing, you know, where I kind of talked to the fans about what happened. As important as that is, and was at the moment, and I realize that it was important now that I look back at it, it was the fucking last thing that I wanted to do.

Chernetsky spent the hours after the murder trying to invent scenarios that made more sense than what everyone was saying had happened. "It was kind of like the World Trade Center situation, you know?" she says. "Like, 'Maybe a wing clipped the building.'" But nothing would make it go away, and she was only left asking the same question everyone else was: Why Darrell?

"I truly feel that, of all people, this was the last person—the very, very last of the back page—that I would ever imagine anything like this would ever happen to, because I can't think of a nicer, more happy-go-lucky, more loving individual that I've ever met," Chernetsky says. "We talk about him all the time. I've always felt that he's up there with Randy Rhoads, just fucking rocking out with a guitar."

If that's the case—and, if you believe in heaven, it probably is—then Darrell would probably consider his death worth it. He never would compare himself to Randy Rhoads, never would include himself in his company. But in death, the guitarists are inextricably linked.

"Unfortunately, he is the Randy Rhoads of our era," Slayer's Kerry King says. "He had a longer career, which we're lucky to be a part of that, but . . . I was just talking to my wife the other day about, can you imagine if Randy Rhoads was still around? All the great tunes we would have heard? And, you know, Dime's the same way: There's tons of stuff he still had to give, to throw in the mix. We're all losing out on a lot of killer tunes."

King found out about Darrell's murder as he was walking offstage after a Slayer concert in Billings, Montana:

> I was just walking down the stairs and my tour manager he—I couldn't even tell you the words he told me. You hear that, and you've just got off the frenzy of being onstage, and you think somebody's fucking with you. But then I could see in his eyes that he was serious, and I'm, like, "What are you telling me here?" It's surreal, and unfortunately, it was real. And then you get into all the speculation afterwards, like, "Oh, are you guys gonna raise your security?" I'm, like, "Well, yeah, we kind of *have* to," but do I think it's gonna happen to anybody—you know, like, somebody's picking off metal guitar players or copycats. I really didn't think that because, right away, you knew this was a guy with an issue. It wasn't random. I mean, as much as it was random to you and I, to him it had purpose.
>
> I wish we could have found out what that purpose was.

IN THE years following their reunion at a Nine Inch Nails show, Darrell and Buddy Blaze played an extended game of phone tag, their schedules never managing to align long enough for them to do more than talk to one another's voice mail. That was their way, and always had been. Buddy thought he'd get plenty of other chances to see his friend, to talk to him, because he always did. The music business sent them their separate ways, but it also brought them back together.

In a way, though, they'll always be together, thanks to the Dean ML that Blaze returned to its rightful owner.

"I'm honored that he took that guitar to the heights that he took it," Blaze says.

We'll always be linked forever with that deal. But it was enough to know him. It was really humbling—after Darrell died, Dean [Zelinsky] sent me video that he had. Juliya from Fuse made some tribute to Darrell and they sent me a copy of that. I mean, a bunch of people sent me things, and it was kind of blowing my mind because, within two weeks of him dying, there's, like, four different interviews where he's talking, and he mentioned me in every interview. To know that I was in his thoughts toward the end—and of course, he never knew that was going to be the end—it's kind of humbling. Honestly, he was like my little brother. I always looked at him that way. I was devastated when we has killed.

THE MORNING after Darrell was killed, Ross Halfin posted the following on his Web site:

Woke up to the news about Dimebag Darrell—I took quite a lot of pictures of him, he wasn't the most intelligent human being, but he WAS always nice which counts for a lot in this business. . . . He would always try to get you to do a shot of Jack Daniels with him. I'll put up some photos of the Cowboy From Hell.

"I got, like, two hundred e-mails saying, 'Motherfucker! Asshole! How dare you!'" Halfin says.

You know, I wasn't saying it in a bad way. I meant it in a genuine way. Look, he never pretended he was the most intelligent human in the world. But the point I'm trying to make is, for a guy who was very blue-collar, he was a very nice guy. I never liked his management. His whole management around him were like really protective, keep you away, and make sure you don't do this. But if you actually ran into him, it was, "Hey buddy, you can have whatever you want." He was the nicest guy. And he was like that to everyone. I never saw a really bad side of him. I think, truthfully, his brother Vinnie had a complex. He was always sort of in his shadow. But Dimebag was a genuinely happy guy. He was happy to do what he did. He was happy to be where he was. He was happy that he could play the guitar. And he was happy that they were successful.

Halfin is right. Darrell was as genuine and straightforward as rock stars come. That is, perhaps, the main reason he became one in the first place. Darrell never really cared about being cool or hip or cutting edge. Pantera titled one of its records *The Great Southern Trendkill* specifically so people would understand their stance on the matter. They didn't give a shit what the prevailing fashion happened to be, Darrell most of all. That's not to say he zigged against this trend and zagged against another. After he and the band made the transition from their glitter-dusted early days to cowboys from hell making vulgar displays of power, the rest of their development was a straight line. They didn't really change after that.

Darrell never changed, not after he picked up that cheap Les Paul copy for the first time. He just wanted to play his guitar and live his life as loudly as possible. He just wanted to be himself, and being himself was more than enough to make him a star. He enjoyed the status and worked hard enough to attain it and maintain it, and he did it on his own terms. Some bands make it because they have a good sense of which way the wind will blow. When Metallica finally gave in and openly courted a new audience, Darrell and the rest of the band called them on it. (And looking back, wouldn't Metallica have fared a bit better if they had chosen to embrace Ozzy instead of Perry Farrell? Discuss.) When the Seattle sound was predominant and former metalheads started wearing flannel and whatnot, Pantera said, "Fuck you, we're cowboys from hell, by way of Arlington, Texas"—and it worked. Other guitarists started adopting an anyone-can-do-this slacker aesthetic. Darrell's guitar playing became more intricate and willfully virtuosic. It was fast and loud and cutthroat, but it was skillful, expert, and learned above all else.

While his guitar playing was complicated, Darrell wasn't. He knew his business, and he practiced intently and intensely, but he wouldn't have made it if his instincts weren't so sharp. He just knew. That was the thing. People say he was born to play guitar, and that's true. But what gets missed in the telling is that he was also born with the innate knowledge of what to do with his guitar once he figured out how to play it. He and the band worked hard, but they didn't get where they eventually got because of a plan. They got there because their plan amounted to, "Let's rip it up and keep ripping it up, and eventually people will come around. And if they don't, who gives a shit, as long as the beer is cold, the amps are loud, and there's someone who wants to have their ass kicked by a bad-ass riff."

19

CEMETERY GATES

A Raucous Farewell to
a Cowboy from Hell

*"He came to rock,
and he rocked like no other."*

—

DEAN ZELINSKY,
Dean Guitars

"**D**o you want some candy, little boy?" I hold out my hand while a woman wrapped in animal prints and topped by a novelty cowboy hat drops two pink Starbursts into it. "Vinnie likes the red ones, so I saved all of those."

Dawn Bjornson has already handed out four bags of Starbursts tonight at the Arlington Convention Center—that's her job. "I give candy in Vinnie and Dimebag's name," she explains. She used to do this at local Pantera shows, and then at Damageplan gigs after Vinnie and Darrell formed their new band in 2003.

The presence of strangers with candy—or, at least, this particular stranger—is partly why tonight's event could pass for just another rock show. Then there are the few thousand fans who have been lined up since this afternoon, the ten-deep crowd bellied up to the bars, and the alternating chants of *"Pan! Ter! A!"* and *"Dime! Bag!"* There's also the guest list: Eddie Van Halen and Zakk Wylde; Slipknot's Corey Taylor, James Root, and Paul Gray; former Alice in Chains members Jerry Cantrell and Mike Inez; and Fear Factory guitarist Dino Cazares.

"It feels like we're about to go and see Dime fucking rock," says Ben Doyle, a friend of the Abbotts who worked as a bouncer at the Clubhouse. He's having one last cigarette and shifting uncomfortably in his black suit. "Not even a month ago, I was backstage with him at Freakers Ball," a concert sponsored by local radio station KEGL-FM. "It's just insane. It's absolutely insane that we're here now, doing this."

It's been nearly a week since the murders in Columbus, giving Darrell's fans enough time to move quickly through the five stages of grief and arrive somewhere close to "Party!" Considering he was buried earlier in the afternoon in a KISS Kasket, it's safe to assume Darrell would have wanted it that way.

Not all of the mourners milling around the back of the convention center's grand hall are in such a let's-do-a-shot-for-Dime mood. A few, like Doyle, have come dressed in their Sunday best, but they stick our like narcs at a high school kegger. Many carry small tokens of affection: a handful of roses, a guitar magazine whose cover Darrell had graced. The stage is empty, save for Darrell's legendary "Dean from Hell," propped up under a spotlight. A guy walking around with a thick stack of photos of Dime flags down a TV news crew. "That says it all right there, man," he says, pointing to an 8 x 10 image of the guitarist with his arms raised to the crowd. The cameraman dutifully captures it for the 10 P.M. news.

Everyone cheers up when the night's ringleader, Dr. Rock, a DJ at the Clubhouse who's known the brothers since the days when Dimebag was known as Diamond, takes the stage about thirty minutes late, sporting a white tuxedo and white sneakers. "Vinnie used to tell him, 'Dime, you're gonna be late for your own funeral,'" Rock says. "And guess what? He was." This little anecdote kicks off a very special episode of *Headbangers Ball*.

The first guest, Nick Bowcott, sets the tone by announcing, "Let me get out my script," before taking a slug from a bottle of Heineken. "I was lucky enough to go to a place I call Dime's World on many occasions," Bowcott says. "As a result, my liver is fucked. You know what? I regret not one sip. The guy made me puke on three continents, for Christ's sake—Europe, Asia, and America. I've been hammered with that motherfucker in about eighteen states."

The rest of the evening continues in the same vein: fond memories of Dimebag, usually involving prodigious amounts of booze and curse words. The prototype is Zakk Wylde and Eddie Van Halen's tag-team eulogy, which features more false starts than a Courtney Love concert and the kind of rambling chemistry that just might land them their own VH1 reality show. Slipping onstage unannounced during Wylde's tear-stained salute, Van Halen mumbles, "I thought there was gonna be a band to jam with." Throughout their fifteen-minute speech, Van Halen constantly swipes the microphone from Wylde before he can finish speaking. (Wylde does get out one sentence in its entirety: "It's all about family and it's all about God, and without that, you ain't got shit.") Between shots of an amber liquid and nips from a bottle of wine, Van Halen completes very few thoughts of his own. However, he does bark one instruction four times: "Someone fucking EQ [equalize] this mike!" Aspiring guitar gods, take note: Even in mourning, require perfection from the soundman.

Van Halen gets it together long enough to play a cell-phone message from Darrell that somehow manages to be even more profane than anyone speaking on his behalf.

Later, Rex Brown slips onstage to deliver a few mumbled words. He is a shell of himself, if that. "Rex looked like an old ghost," Terry Glaze would say later, and that pretty much sums it up. He is no doubt haunted by the tragedy in Columbus in a way few others are: There remained a bitter divide between Brown and the Abbotts when Darrell was gunned down. Though his visit to the microphone doesn't appear to be part of tonight's scheduled program—he just sort of stumbled out without much preamble—at least he was allowed to come to the service. Brown's presence throws into even sharper relief the absence of someone else: Phil Anselmo. He is in town and has been for days. But Vinnie and Rita Haney do not want him here, under any circumstances. If Brown and the Abbotts were separated by acrimony, the chasm between Anselmo and the Abbotts was a fiery moat of hatred, thanks, not least of all, to the erstwhile Pantera singer's inflammatory comments to *Metal Edge* magazine. So Anselmo suffers through the service alone, in a hotel room.

Though Van Halen and Wylde's presentation is almost comical, and Bowcott's testimonial is funnier in much more appropriate ways, the three-hour memorial isn't without its moments of poignancy. Stepping onstage to a hero's welcome, Vinnie grabs a life-sized cutout of his brother in one hand and a microphone in the other. "It's been five fucking nights since this stupid shit happened and I ain't heard it yet. I wanna hear it: *Dime! Bag! Dime! Bag! Dime! Bag!*" But he keeps his words short and bittersweet, finishing in tears. "The brightest and biggest star in Texas is shining tonight," he says. "That's my fucking brother Dimebag. Give it up!"

The crowd gets its moment of closure as well, during Cantrell and Inez's acoustic performance of "Brother" and "Got Me Wrong," two Alice in Chains songs. At the end of the latter, Cantrell lets mourners have their turn on lead vocals, and their emotions pour out as they belt the song's final line: "Something's gotta turn out right!"

Tonight, it did.

BONUS TRACK:
LIGHT COMES OUT
OF BLACK

The Legend of the
"Black Tooth Grin"

*"I love being drunk but . . .
I just hate being hungover."*

———

DARRELL ABBOTT

It's backstage during Pantera's *Vulgar Display of Power* tour.
Darrell is talking to a teenager, some kid who's won a contest.
They are discussing important matters: Darrell is teaching the
kid how to make a black tooth grin.

"Pour a little shot of whiskey, like that. And you put just a
dash of Coke. You notice the color?" He holds the plastic cup up
for inspection. "It's not quite black, but we call it a black tooth."
Hands the kid the shot. "Nail it, dude. Dude, nail it back. It ain't
no candy. It's the real shit." It wasn't the first, and certainly not

the last, person Darrell introduced to the pleasures of the black tooth grin.

One can't talk about Darrell Abbott without talking about alcohol, the same way one can't talk about Darrell Abbott without talking about his guitar. Both were part of his daily life. Yet, while his guitar may have had an early lead, alcohol eventually caught up to it.

One can't talk much about Darrell Abbott without talking about alcohol, because he didn't talk much without alcohol. He didn't walk much without alcohol. He didn't play guitar much without alcohol. He didn't do much of anything without alcohol. He was a two-sport athlete, lettering in guitar shredding and drinking marathons. So his life was more-or-less lived between parties, seen through the bottom of a glass. There is a well-known novelty T-shirt that says, "I've got blood in my alcohol stream." On Darrell, that shirt would have read like absolute fact. He woke up with a drink and fell asleep shortly after his last one.

But he rarely drank alone; he always wanted everyone right there with him. He got other people drunk almost as often as he got himself drunk. That was part of his deal. If he was there, then it was going to be a good time. And a good time usually involved drinking prodigious amounts of liquor.

"You can't find anybody that didn't like Darrell," Terry Glaze says. "Darrell would give you the shirt off his back. Darrell was like an angel. If he walked in a room, everybody's going to leave with a smile. You just had to be careful and not let him peer-pressure you into starting drinking."

That was next to impossible for most people.

"Oh, God. He always made sure there was a lot of fucking alcohol going around and everybody was shitfaced," says Juliya Chernetsky, former host of the Fuse network's *Uranium* show.

He was like the ultimate fucking host in terms of everybody getting wasted. That was definitely, I think, priority number one. The first time I came over, there was a big tray, with about twenty shots on it, and nothing happened until you had at least a few. He wouldn't even hear it. He was really fucking good-natured. The goal was always to have a good time. There was no bullshit, no ego. There was no rock-star attitude whatsoever. It was, like, "Hey, man. You're in my fucking house. I got all this booze, and I'm going to share everything I've got with you, until the last drop." I'm not trying to make it sound like an alcoholic thing. I think that was the bonding ritual type of thing. Like, "Let's share this cocktail. Let's share this fucking shot and sit down and have a good time." It was like the bonding torch.

"If you were in the Dimebag cyclone, chances are you had to drink with him someplace," Slayer's Kerry King says. He became one of Darrell's drinking buddies when Slayer toured through Texas in the late 1980s. "You know, when we were on tour together, it was dependent on whose drinks we were drinking—if it was mine, he'd be hungover the next day; if it was his, I'd be hungover the next day. It was just a fun trip."

"A fun trip." "The bonding torch." Most everyone who knew him stops short of referring to his behavior in alcoholic terms. No, he wasn't an alcoholic, they say. He was a pro.

"A very experienced pro," Scott Minyard says. "He drank so much he learned to control it. I've spotted it a few times. Everybody wants to buy him a shot—because he's bought so many shots. I've seen him, not turn the shot down, but take one like that"—Minyard tosses an imaginary shot past his face—"over the shoulder." He laughs. "Because he would already know that he was already gone. But he would almost take offense if you didn't take a shot when *he'd* buy it: 'C'mon, you've gotta drink one. C'mon. Just one more. You've got to!' Anytime they'd roll into the clubs—especially after they had some success, you know, so they had some money in their pocket—up at the bar, usually somebody goes and gets a beer and a shot or a couple of beers. He's got a tray." He laughs. "Trays of shots. Pretty much for the whole club. Willing to give it to anybody. But back in the day, he was pretty much the same way."

Living this way for so long eventually caught up with Darrell. When he joined Pantera, he was impossibly skinny; if you hold up a pair of the spandex pants he wore at the time, they look as though they'd be snug on a small child. More than a decade later—judging by the photo on the back cover of *Vulgar Display of Power*, and taking into account the slimming effect of black clothing—he hadn't appeared to have gained an ounce.

By the time Damageplan's *New Found Power* was released in 2004, however, his face was bloated and his baggy clothes couldn't hide the gut he'd sprouted—not that he ever tried to. Some of the changes in his appearance were due to the natural process of aging. But much of it owed more to fine-aged whiskey. "He wasn't that slim, sleek lead guitar player anymore," Larry English says.

"He drank to excess daily. Every day. And you know that can wear a body down."

Unlike in the typical story of rock star excess, no one ever tried to stop him from drinking to excess daily. No one ever held an intervention or attempted to force him into a rehab program. Maybe it was because he was a fun drunk. Maybe it was because he had enough money to pay for or replace whatever he broke when he was oiled up. Maybe it was because he lived in a world populated by other alcoholics. Maybe it was because that's what was expected of him, to suck it up and rely on his supernatural tolerance and gallons of Pedialyte, his preferred hangover remedy.

"Hangovers hurt every now and then, but what do you do? Throw a couple more doubles back!" Darrell said on a tour stop in New Jersey on the 2000 Ozzfest tour. "Anyway, you've just got to get in a rock-and-roll mode. What's tonight? It's Monday night? Fuck that, it's Friday night all of a sudden! Know what I mean? It's Friday night every goddamn night and it's going to burn. I'm not going to let these people spend all that money, get their hopes up, and wait this long to see our show, and then we say, 'Oh, man, we already did it ten times in a row and now my sides hurt,' or have some other lame excuse. Dude, that ain't going to happen!"

Darrell's commitment to his many fans probably was a big part of why he drank so much, along with the ball-and-chain that was his reputation, but he wasn't on the road all the time. The real reason why no one tried to get Darrell to stop drinking was because everyone who knew Darrell Abbott knew you couldn't change him. If you wanted him to do something, you could only hope that he somehow got the idea on his own. English hoped

Darrell would get the idea to modify his lifestyle. Maybe not stop drinking entirely, but at least drink less, and less often. But that's pretty much all it was—hope.

English says:

I actually felt like I had gotten to the point where I accepted the fact that one of these days, my guy is going to get really, really ill, and that may be what it will take for him to consider a change of life, which would have been entirely radical for him. Entirely. It would have been a persona change. That's big. I did not think that I had any chance of being somebody who could create that kind of change in him. So, did I worry? Yeah, I worried myself sick. But did I try to change it in him? Not directly. And when I say not directly, that means I never sat down with him and tried to counsel him on his drinking and the effects on health. That's really kind of not my place in life.

Instead, what I did do a lot, was try to have good, cohesive business decisions and discussions with him. My hope there was, since he was really into it, and he was like a sponge—he wanted to learn about business as much as possible. He wanted to be up on top of his business, and what it meant to him. I think he really, really liked that help. And I know that when you're drunk, you can't exercise those capabilities. I was hoping that it would mean so much to him that he, at some point, would also hopefully look at that and say, "OK, this is a road I need to be on, and if I keep drinking like this, I can't be on that road." That was kind of the only way I felt, and hoped, that I could make any kind of contribution to him improving that part of his life.

But even though he hoped for a lifestyle change, English admits those hopes never amounted to much. And he wasn't much help, since he never stopped drinking with Darrell.

"Because if you've been around Dime, it's just part of the brotherhood," he explains.

> You can't possibly be a brother and not. Then you're not a brother. It was pretty clear-cut that way. To be with him, to hang with him, to enjoy him, to maximize the relationship, that's what you did. No, I never really saw any glimmer that there was any consideration even of backing off. When he was sober—I don't know if he was ever sober, really. I mean, he'd start banging in the morning. So he'd wake up, in whatever state you wake up in when you're like that, and in order to feel like you're straight, you take a drink. In those times when we'd have those sober and sobering conversations, was he really sober? I don't think so. It became a matter of *drunk to what degree?* It was much more of that. I can remember a particular visit down there—you know, I'd stay in his home and stuff— and getting up the next morning and feeling really lousy. We'd order up some steaks or something. Sometimes he'd cook. Go to Costco and get some steaks and start barbecuing.
>
> And, of course, guaranteed, there would be a black tooth, just to kind of get normal.

That pretty much settles the "Was he or wasn't he?" debate right there. Without disrespecting the dead, it's fairly easy to declare that Darrell was the textbook definition of a functional alcoholic. Why did no one ever call him on it? Why did no one force him into rehab? Why was his behavior celebrated? Why were his misdeeds swept aside with little more than a "Well, you know, that's Dime"?

The likely answer is simple: because he was fun to be around. If he'd been Darrell Abbott, regional manager, that probably wouldn't have flown. But he wasn't that guy. He was Dimebag, King Dime. If you were around him, you wanted him to drink. You wanted him to get you drunk. You wanted to wake up with a face sore from smiling and a liver sore from everything else. The truth is it's quite possible no one really wanted Darrell to stop drinking. It was too much fun to stop.

"Whether I showed up at his house or a hotel or on the bus or backstage, he was always that same guy," English says.

He didn't have this other, second personality. He was just Dime. It was something I felt I could always count on. Hell, there were times I made a fool of myself. It wasn't just him doing the Dime thing. Sometimes you found yourself doing the Dime thing. It can be somewhat embarrassing later. But he would never embarrass you. He just recognized it. He was the same person. There was no fake Dime.

That was clearly part of his persona, his mystique. It was so simple. I think that a lot of people who are extremely talented and artistic and creative like him kind of take a different attitude, where you get a sense of holier than thou or better than thou. Dime, it may not have even occurred to him that he could do that, or wanted to do that. It just never came into play. He was always just a rockin' kid from Dallas. He was having as much fun twenty years later as he did twenty years before. He was, how shall I say this? Infectious. That's the right word. Infectious. You got around him, and he stuck a black tooth in front of you, I *defy* you not to drink it. Because you knew you were going to have a great time right now. Right now. It's like, holy shit, this could be one of the greatest nights of my life starting right now. I never saw anybody turn it down. He was almost pixielike. Like a guy with a devilish gleam in his eye. We're going to have fun tonight.

Epilogue: I'll Cast a Shadow

*Tributes, Lawsuits, and Riffs
from the Great Beyond*

A month after the murders at the Alrosa Villa nightclub in Columbus, Nathan Gale claimed his last victim.

Albert Catuela, who opened Alrosa Villa with his wife, Rosa, in 1974, died at Riverside Hospital on January 9, 2005. He had fallen ill the morning after the shootings, not long after his son Rick—who had taken over the club's operations, along with his brother, John, years earlier—told him what had happened. It was too much for his weakened heart and frail body to take. Catuela was ninety-one.

Alrosa Villa reopened not long after Albert Catuela's death, hosting a sold-out benefit concert for the victims' families. More than three years later, this concert stands out as one of the few highlights of its post–December 8 existence. The club's concert calendar, once full of national and international touring acts, is mostly barren, and the few gigs the Catuelas do manage to book typically feature Ohio-area bands. The club is often dark for weeks at a time.

On the first anniversary of Darrell Abbott's murder, the Catuelas were named in a wrongful death and personal injury lawsuit filed on behalf of Darrell's estate, as well as two of the wounded, Chris Paluska and John "Kat" Brooks. A year later, Jerry and Karen Wessler, who were in the crowd that night, also filed a civil suit against the club, claiming the incident had caused acute and lasting emotional damage. Even if the Catuelas reach settlements in both suits, they will inflict acute and lasting financial damage on the club.

James Niggemeyer, the Columbus police officer who ended Nathan Gale's rampage, was cleared by a Franklin County grand jury and was later nationally recognized for his heroism in the line of duty. Niggemeyer was named one of eight finalists for *America's Most Wanted*'s All-Star award for first-responders. He also received honorable mention for the Police Officer of the Year award sponsored by the International Association of Chiefs of Police and *Parade* magazine, as well as a 2005 Distinguished Law Enforcement Valor Award from Ohio attorney general Jim Petro.

Posthumously, Darrell was honored, too. On November 9, 2006, he was inducted into Hard Rock Café Dallas's Walk of Fame, an accolade that was long overdue. By then, there had been plenty of other tributes.

Dean Guitars went forward with the line of signature Razorback guitars it had been planning with Darrell in the weeks before his murder. The company also made available exacting recreations of two of his most famous axes, the "Dean from Hell" and the sunburst-finish model Jerry Abbott bought for him, with the original KISS sticker Darrell had affixed to the body replaced with a replica that substituted his head for those of all four KISS members. In 2005, Dean partnered with Curse Mackey to create *Six-String Masterpieces: The Dimebag Darrell Art Tribute*. Mackey recruited fifty of Darrell's fans, friends, and fellow guitarists for the touring exhibit. The contributors—which include James Hetfield, Jerry Cantrell, Dave Grohl, Kerry King, Rob Zombie, and Marilyn Manson—used Dean MLs as a canvas, hand-painting homages to Darrell.

Most of the other tributes came, naturally, in the form of music. Nickelback recorded "Side of a Bullet," which featured lyrics about Darrell and—thanks to a cache of circa *Far Beyond Driven* outtakes sent along by Vinnie—a new "Dimebag" Darrell guitar solo. The Abbotts had been friends with Nickelback singer-guitarist Chad Kroeger since his band toured with Jerry Cantrell, and Darrell had contributed guitar to Nickelback's collaboration with Kid Rock on a cover of Elton John's "Saturday Night's Alright for Fighting," which appeared on the soundtrack to 2003's *Charlie's Angels: Full Throttle*. "Side of a Bullet" was released on Nickelback's 2005 album, *All the Right Reasons*.

Another one of Darrell's longtime friends, Black Label Society leader Zakk Wylde, recorded "In This River" and dedicated it to his fallen friend. While Wylde had written the song (which appears on Black Label Society's 2005 album, *Mafia*) prior to Darrell's death, its lyrics still adequately sum up his mood: "All shall fade to black again and again/This storm that's broken me, my only friend." In the video for the song, two kids—dressed like Zakk and Darrell—swim in a river. It ends with the Darrell stand-in being swallowed up by the water.

There were many more songs where that came from. Brides of Destruction, the hard-rock supergroup featuring Mötley Crüe bassist Nikki Sixx and L.A. Guns guitarist Tracii Guns, released the song "Dime's in Heaven" on its 2005 disc, *Runaway Brides*. A Texas country band, Cross Canadian Ragweed, recorded "Dimebag" in honor of the "cowboy from hell on a twisted trail" for its album *Garage*. During the 2005 Gigantour, Dream Theater, Megadeth's Dave Mustaine, Russell Allen of Symphony X, and Fear Factory's Burton C. Bell performed "Cemetery Gates" as a nightly tribute. Dozens of bands dedicated songs and liner-note space to Darrell. Dozens of others—including Alice in Chains, Avenged Sevenfold, Staind, and Anthrax—added Pantera songs (usually "Walk") to their live shows.

Vinnie Paul Abbott made his own return to live music on February 23, 2005, at a benefit for the Dimebag Darrell Memorial Fund, established to cover the funeral and medical expenses incurred by the families of the victims of the Alrosa Villa attack. The show, at Chicago's Aragon Ballroom, featured Disturbed, Anthrax, Drowning Pool, and Soil. Vinnie first joined Anthrax behind the drum kit for "A New Level," then sat in with Disturbed for a version of "Walk." The latter proved too much for him: When the members of the other bands on the bill invaded the stage to scream along with the song's authoritative, two-word, three-syllable chorus—a staple of every Pantera/Damageplan set since "Walk" first appeared on a set list—Vinnie couldn't help but look around for his brother, who enjoyed that moment of fraternity more than anyone else. The weight of the previous three months brought him to his knees when the song was over.

Vinnie made sporadic guest appearances with Black Label Society and Sammy Hagar over the next year or so, but for the most part, he devoted his time to his new record label, Big Vin Records. The label's first two releases—*Rebel Meets Rebel*, the long-awaited collaboration with country iconoclast David Allan Coe, and *Dimevision, Vol. 1: That's the Fun I Have*, a DVD collecting a fraction of the video footage Darrell left behind—were issued on May 2, 2006. Both were tributes to Darrell, but they were more about remembering his life than memorializing his death. The *Dimevision* collection went a long way toward blowing away the dark cloud that had hung over his name for the previous year and a half, showcasing Darrell's status as the original *Jackass*.

In the summer of 2006, Vinnie returned to music full time, teaming up with Chad Gray and Greg Tribbett of Mudvayne and Jerry Montano and Tom Maxwell in a new band they shyly dubbed Hellyeah. The newly formed band recorded its debut over the course of three eight-day sessions—at Darrell's home studio, which had become something of a shrine to him, left almost exactly as it had been when he went on his final tour.

Darrell undoubtedly would have wanted a new band to set up shop in there, and definitely if it was one called Hellyeah and had Vinnie on drums. He would have liked that some part of him continued making music after his death. That, to him, would have meant more than any tear-stained remembrance. He would want people in there spilling shots on the carpet, firing off roman candles in the control room, blowing out amps, pulling pranks, breaking things. He wouldn't want that room to become a mausoleum, a testament to his life. It was built as a testament to the power of heavy metal, everything it had done and everything left to come. He didn't think it would outlive him, but he wouldn't have minded that it did. He would want the party to go on forever.

Van Halen? Van-fuckin'-Halen.

Acknowledgments

First and foremost, this book couldn't have happened without the love and understanding of my wife, Nikki, and our son, Isaac. Without them, of course, I probably wouldn't have had to write it in the middle of the night. It was worth every lost minute of sleep.

My parents, my brother and sister, and the rest of the Crain family deserve their own sentence and their own love and special thanks. As does my second family, Barry Rosen and Susan and Steve Fisch.

The following people all tie for next on the list, for taking my calls, answering my questions, holding my hand, patting my back, kicking my ass, or whatever else was required of them over these past couple of years: Anne Garrett and James Fitzgerald at James Fitzgerald Agency; Ben Schafer, Collin Tracy, and everyone else at Da Capo Press/Perseus Books Group; Josh Venable; Bob Mehr; Terry Glaze; Kinley Wolfe; Tommy Snellings; Buddy, Ken, and Kitty Webster; Scott Minyard; Kerry King; Chris Paluska; Brian Slagel; Jon Wiederhorn; Rick E. Warden; Dale Brock; Paul Rachman; Riki Rachtman; the Columbus Division of

Police; Juliya Chernetsky and everyone at *Uranium;* Corey J. Apling; David Karon; Larry English; Jody Dankberg and all at Krank; Jerry Hudson; Derek Shulman; Jason Janik; Michael Insuaste; Ross Halfin; Mick Hutson; Bugs Henderson; Heidi Ellen Robinson Fitzgerald; Lucy Purdon, Pete Money, and all at Focal Point; Tom Beaujour; Joe Gross; Caryn Ganz (for the original assignment and everything else); Charles Aaron; Chuck Flores; Scott Beggs; Danny Balis; Nicole Simon; Borivoj Krgin and Blabbermouth.net; the entire ZC/07 team and everyone who contributed to the cause; my *D Magazine* family (Tim Rogers, Eric Celeste, Adam McGill, Stacey Yervasi, Sarah Eveans, Laura Kostelny, Elizabeth Lavin, and everyone else); Sarah Hepola; Don Cento; Kris Youmans; Robert Wilonsky and the *Dallas Observer;* Ross McCammon and David Granger at *Esquire;* everyone I've worked with at *Spin,* RollingStone.com, and *American Way;* Skip Hollandsworth; Casey Monahan; Brad Meltzer; Jeff Pearlman; David Hale Smith; Adam Yeargin; Barley House; and the Old Monk.

Last, but certainly not least, I'd like to thank the makers of Dr Pepper and Marlboro Lights.

A Darrell Abbott Discography

PANTERA

Metal Magic (Metal Magic, 1983)
Projects in the Jungle (Metal Magic, 1984)
I Am the Night (Metal Magic, 1985)
Power Metal (Metal Magic, 1988)
Cowboys from Hell (Atco, 1990)
Vulgar Display of Power (Atco, 1992)
Far Beyond Driven (EastWest, 1994)
The Great Southern Trendkill (EastWest, 1996)
Official Live: 101 Proof (EastWest, 1997)
Reinventing the Steel (EastWest, 2000)
The Best of Pantera: Far Beyond the Great Southern Cowboys' Vulgar Hits! (Rhino, 2003)

COMPILATION TRACKS

"The Badge," *The Crow* soundtrack (Atlantic, 1994)
"Cemetery Gates" (Demon Knight edit), *Tales from the Crypt: Demon Knight* (Atlantic, 1995)
"Where You Come From," *Strangeland* soundtrack (TVT, 1998)
"Cat Scratch Fever," *Detroit Rock City* soundtrack (Polygram, 1999)
"Immortally Insane," *Heavy Metal 2000* soundtrack (Restless, 2000)
"Electric Funeral," *Nativity in Black, Vol. 2: A Tribute to Black Sabbath* (Priority, 2000)
"Pre-Hibernation," *SpongeBob SquarePants: Original Theme Highlights* (Jive, 2001)

DAMAGEPLAN

New Found Power (Elektra, 2004)
"Rebel Meets Rebel," *Rebel Meets Rebel* (Big Vin Records, 2006)

SOLO RECORDINGS

"Caged in a Rage," *Supercop* soundtrack (Interscope, 1996)
"Fractured Mirror," *Spacewalk: A Salute to Ace Frehley* (Shrapnel, 1996)
"Heard It on the X" (as Tres Diablos, with Vinnie Paul Abbott and Rex Brown),
   ECW: Extreme Music (1998)

VIDEO COMPILATIONS

Cowboys from Hell: The Videos (Atlantic, 1991)
Vulgar Video (Atlantic, 1993)
3: Watch It Go (Elektra/Asylum, 1997)
(The above are compiled on the 2004 two-DVD collection *3 Vulgar Videos from
   Hell*, released by Atlantic in 1999 and reissued by Rhino in 2006.)
Dimevision, Vol. 1: That's the Fun I Have (Big Vin Records, 2006)

SELECTED GUEST APPEARANCES

Rob Halford, "Light Comes Out of Black," *Buffy the Vampire Slayer* soundtrack
   (CBS, 1992)
Anthrax, "Riding Shotgun," *Stomp 442* (Elektra, 1995)
Anthrax, "Inside Out," *Volume 8: The Threat Is Real* (Ignition, 1998)
Anthrax, "Strap It On" and "Cadillac Rock Box," *We've Come for You All* (Nu-
   clear Blast, 2003)
Nickelback and Kid Rock, "Saturday Night's Alright for Fighting," *Charlie's
   Angels: Full Throttle* soundtrack (Sony, 2003)
Nickelback, "Side of a Bullet," *All the Right Reasons* (Roadrunner, 2005)

BOOTLEGS

Pantera: The Early Years (1984, exact date and location unknown)
A Pair of Early Pantera Shows (Fort Worth, TX, Dec. 31, 1986, and Dallas, TX,
   July 2, 1988)
Before We Were Cowboys (The Basement, Dallas, TX, Dec. 20, 1988)

Showdown (Dallas, TX, 1989, exact date and location unknown)

Diamonds & Rust (Diamond Ballroom, Oklahoma City, OK, Dec. 1, 1991)

The Hell With It (Irvine Meadows, Irvine, CA, Mar. 14, 1992)

High Voltage (The Palladium, Hollywood, CA, June 27, 1992, and Santa Monica Civic Center, Santa Monica, CA, May 2, 1994)

Live in Pittsburgh (Pittsburgh, PA, Apr. 4, 1993)

Four Cowboys From Hell (Concert Hall, Toronto, Ontario, Mar. 6, 1993)

Live Beyond Driven (San Antonio, TX, May 5, 1994)

Slaughtered Show (Osaka, Japan, May 1994, exact date and location unknown)

No Compromise, No Sellout (Monsters of Rock Festival, Donnington Park, UK, June 4, 1994)

Live in Chandler (Compton Terrace, Chandler, AZ, July 20, 1994)

Support the Madmen (Nassau Coliseum, Uniondale, NY, Aug. 18, 1994)

Live in the UK, (Brixton Academy, London, UK, Sep. 12, 1994)

Live in Poughkeepsie (Mid-Hudson Civic Center, Poughkeepsie, NY, Mar. 7, 1995)

Happy New Year's Fort Worth (Tarrant County Convention Center, Fort Worth, TX, Dec. 31, 1995)

Live in Peoria (Peoria Civic Center, Peoria, IL, Nov. 16, 1996)

We Ain't in Kansas Anymore (Memorial Hall, Kansas City, KS, Nov. 30, 1996)

Sandblasting Sacramento (Memorial Auditorium, Sacramento, CA, Nov. 17, 1997)

Dynamo Open Air '98 (Dynamo Festival, Eindhoven, Germany, May 30, 1998)

102 Proof (Parque Sarmiento Stadium, Buenos Aires, Argentina, June 9, 1998)

Ozzfest 2000 (Ozzfest, Cincinnati, OH, Aug. 8, 2000)

Live in Sunrise (Sunrise Musical Theater, Sunrise, FL, Apr. 1, 2001)

Selected Bibliography

Abbott, Darrell, Vince Abbott, Pat Lachman, and Bob Kakaha. Interview with Juliya Chernetsky. 29 Nov. 2004.

Abbott, Vince. Interview with Detective Christopher Rond. 8 Dec. 2004. Columbus Division of Police Case File, PIS #2004–16.

Barnes, Aaron. Interview with Detective Stephen Glasure. 9 Dec. 2004. Columbus Division of Police Case File, PIS #2004–16.

Big Story Weekend. Fox News. 11 Dec. 2004.

Bjornson, Dawn. Personal interview conducted by the author. 14 Dec. 2004.

Blaze, Buddy. Telephone interview conducted by the author. 28 Apr. 2006.

———. Telephone interview conducted by the author. 20 May 2006.

Bowcott, Nick. "Blood Brothers." *Metal Hammer.* Jan. 2006: 40+.

———. "Cowboys from Hell." *Guitar World.* June 2006: 62+.

Brock, Dale. Personal interview conducted by the author. 2 Mar. 2006.

Brooks, John. Interview with Detective Althea Young. 9 Dec. 2004. Columbus Division of Police Case File, PIS #2004–16.

Carlson, Peter. "Guitar World: 25 Years of Resonant Distortion." *Washington Post.* 4 Jan. 2005: C1.

Carpenter, Mitchell. Interview with Detective John Weeks. 9 Dec. 2004. Columbus Division of Police Case File, PIS #2004–16.

Chernetsky, Juliya. Telephone interview conducted by the author. 1 May 2006.

Clark, Mary. Interview with Detective Russell Redman. 9 Dec. 2004.

Damageplan Band Stage Video from Alrosa Villa. 8 Dec. 2004. Columbus Division of Police Case File, PIS #2004–16.

Dankberg, Jody. Telephone interview conducted by the author. 18 Dec. 2006.

DeRogatis, Jim. "Behind the Scenes at a Rock Concert; A Really Big Show Goes on before the Band Plays." *Chicago Sun-Times*. 17 July 1994: 1.

Dimevision, Vol. 1: That's the Fun I Have . . . Red Ezra, Rita Haney, and Bobby Tongs. 2006.

Doyle, Ben. Personal interview conducted by the author. 14 Dec. 2004.

English, Larry. Telephone interview conducted by the author. 18 Dec. 2006.

Epstein, Dan. "Guitarists Gone Wild." *Guitar World*. Dec. 2004: 70.

———. "Lady Dime." *Revolver*. June 2006: 58.

Evidentiary Map of 5055 Sinclair Road, drawn by W. A. Snyder. Columbus Division of Police Case File, PIS #2004–16.

Ferman, Dave. "Pantera: The People Have Spoken." *Fort Worth Star-Telegram*. 12 July 1996: 7.

Futty, John. "Interviews with Victims Detail Horror of Concert Shootings." *Columbus Dispatch*. 20 Oct. 2005: 1C.

———. "Shooter Had Prior Tussle." *Columbus Dispatch*. 13 Apr. 2005: 1A+.

———. "3 Minutes of Hell." *Columbus Dispatch*. 16 Jan. 2005: 1A+.

Futty, John, Evan Goodenow, and Aaron Beck. "A Nightmarish Scene." *Columbus Dispatch*. 10 Dec. 2004: 1A+.

Geist, Brandon. "By Demons Be Driven." *Revolver*. Feb. 2006.

Gill, Chris. "This Love." *Guitar World*. Mar. 2008: 52+.

Glaze, Terry. Personal interview conducted by the author. 15 Apr. 2006.

Graham, John. Interview with Detective Russell Redman. 9 Dec. 2004. Columbus Division of Police Case File, PIS #2004–16.

Gubbins, Teresa. "Split Decisions: Brothers Forge Ahead after the Breakup of Pantera." *Dallas Morning News*. 29 Oct. 2004: 33.

Gulla, Bob. "Pantera: Ten Hellacious Riffs." *Guitar One*. Dec. 2004: 37+.

Gundersen, Edna. "Pantera: Texas band Sticks to Its Roots." *USA Today*. 6 Apr. 1994: 10D.

Halfin, Ross. Telephone interview conducted by the author. 15 Oct. 2006.

Heinlein, Detective Rob. E-mail to Detective William Gillette. Columbus Division of Police Case File, PIS #2004–16.

Henderson, Bugs. Telephone interview conducted by the author. 4 Aug. 2006.

Hiatt, Brian. "Disturbed Get Revenge." RollingStone.com. 6 Oct. 2005. http://www.rollingstone.com/news/story/7687833/disturbed_get_revenge.

Hudson, Jerry. Personal interview conducted by the author. 22 July 2006.

Hutson, Mick. Telephone interview conducted by the author. 4 Sept. 2006.

Jenkins, Ronald. Interview with Detective Christopher Rond. 9 Dec. 2004. Columbus Division of Police Case File, PIS #2004–16.

Karon, David. Telephone interview conducted by the author. 9 May 2006.

King, Kerry. Telephone interview conducted by the author. 18 Apr. 2006.

Langer, Andy. "Bare Assets." *Texas Monthly.* May 2000: 84+.

Lewis, Bradley J., and Collie M. Trant. *Coroner's Report: Finding of Facts and Verdict.* Rep.No. 04–3819. Franklin County Coroner's Office. Columbus Division of Police Case File, PIS #2004–16.

Longworth, M., and T. DeFosse. *Incident Report: 04/05/2004.* Rep.No. 40402555. Criminal Investigation Section, Cincinnati Police Department. Columbus Division of Police Case File, PIS #2004–16.

Mancini, Robert. "Dimebag Darrell: A Brother Remembers." MTVNews.com. 5 Dec. 2005. http://www.mtv.com/bands/d/damageplan/qa_feature_120805/.

Marx, Matthew. "Officer Honored for Heroism at Nightclub." *Columbus Dispatch.* 16 Sept. 2005: 6B.

Minyard, Scott. Telephone interview conducted by the author . 11 May 2006.

———. Interview conducted by the author. 12 July 2006.

"Mother of Shooter Says He Had Paranoid Schizophrenia." Associated Press State and Local Wire. 16 Dec. 2004.

Niggemeyer, James D. Interview with Sergeant Eric I. Pilya. 9 Dec. 2004. Columbus Division of Police Case File, PIS #2004–16.

"Nightclub Founder Dies a Month after Shooting There." Associated Press State and Local Wire. 11 Jan. 2005.

Paluska, Chris. Telephone interview conducted by the author. 18 Dec. 2006.

———. Interview with Detective William Gillette. 10 Dec. 2004. Columbus Division of Police Case File, PIS #2004–16.

Pantera. *Hot & Heavy.* Video and raw footage.1983.

"Pantera." *Behind the Music.* VH1. 11 May 2006.

"Pantera: Rock Group's Music." *Guitar Player.* May 1994: 20.

Perlah, Jeff. "Hell on Stage." *Onstage.* Jan. 2001: 46+.

Rachman, Paul. Telephone interview conducted by the author. 15 Jan. 2007.

Rachtman, Riki. Telephone interview conducted by the author. 10 May 2006.

Real Estate Search by Owner Name. Tarrant Appraisal District. 5 Jan. 2007. http://www.tad.org/datasearch/re_owner_search.cfm?matches.

Rebel Meets Rebel. *Rebel Meets Rebel.* Vinnie Paul and Dimebag Darrell, 2006.

Reed, Penny. Interview with Detective Philip Paley. 9 Dec. 2004. Columbus Division of Police Case File, PIS #2004–16.

Recording Industry Association of America US Sales Search. 1 Mar. 2006. http://www.riaa.com/gp/database/search_results.asp.

Russell, Deborah. "Pantera Pursues Touring with a Vengeance." *Billboard*. 20 June 1992: 16.

Sangiacomo, Michael, and Damian Guevara. "Attacker Wanted Friends but Just Didn't Know How." *Plain Dealer* (Cleveland). 10 Dec. 2004: A1.

Scene Video by Homicide Squad at 5055 Sinclair Road. 2004. Columbus Division of Police, PIS #2004–16.

Sheets, David. Interview with Detective Philip Paley. 9 Dec. 2004. Columbus Division of Police Case File, PIS #2004–16.

Shulman, Derek. Telephone interview conducted by the author. 15 Jan. 2007.

Slagel, Brian. Telephone interview conducted by the author. 27 July 2006.

Snellings, Tommy. Interview conducted by the author. 15 Apr. 2006.

"SOiL." *Revolt*. 11 Feb. 2007. http://www.revolt-media.com/guest/?cat=21.

Toler, Bo. Interview with Detective William Gillette. 28 Apr. 2005. Columbus Division of Police Case File, PIS #2004–16.

Warden, Rick E. Telephone interview conducted by the author. 20 Jan. 2007.

Webofhair. "Pantera Live 1989 Practice with Kerry King, Part 2." 12 Feb. 2006. http://www.youtube.com/watch?v=ofxuhny6iwa.

———. "PanterA 1989—Dimebag Darrell & Kerry King Practice." 12 Feb. 2006. http://www.youtube.com/watch?v=a8r0tj11pdw.

———. "PanterA 1989 Practice with Kerry King, Part 1." 12 Feb. 2006. http://www.youtube.com/watch?v=vq4kkqluzxc.

Webster, Ken. Telephone interview conducted by the author. 20 June 2006.

Webster, Kitty. Telephone interview conducted by the author. 12 Sept. 2006.

Wiederhorn, Jon. "Back in the Saddle." *Revolver*. June 2006: 57+.

———. "Night Riders." *Revolver*. Mar. 2007: 60+.

———. Telephone interview conducted by the author. 15 Aug. 2006.

Wild, Ulrich. Telephone interview conducted by the author. 3 Mar. 2006.

Notes

NOTES TO SIDE 1

1. Its official title was the Texxas World Music Festival. Absolutely no one, outside of the organizers, called it by that name.

2. "Dimebag Darrell: Requiem for a Heavyweight." 1 Feb. 2005: 50.

3. Hart went on to front another local band, Boss Tweed, which had a hand in Darrell's original stage name. "They were the original metal band in Dallas–Fort Worth," Rick E. Warden says. "[Drummer] Lance Williams came out of a casket. They played, like, Holocaust songs and stuff. Nobody did that back then; they were the only ones. Darrell respected that and he thought that name Lance was cool. It happened to be his true middle name. Well, when the album came out, there it was: *Diamond Darrell Lance*. We were like, '*Diamond?* What is this "Diamond Darrell Lance" stuff?'" He laughs. "We were like, 'I ain't calling you 'Diamond.' I'll call you 'Dime.' I'll call you 'Dimebag.'"

4. Brown joked about this in a circa *Reinventing the Steel* interview with the Web site DrDrew.com, answering "Steve Buscemi" when asked who he thought would play him in a Pantera film.

5. Boulder, CO: Westview Press, 1996.

6. Darrell's ever-shifting moniker wasn't completely solidified until the mid-1990s. "The first time they ever did *Headbangers Ball*, the people at MTV said that they didn't want to use the word 'Dimebag,'" says the show's original host, Riki Rachtman. "So he was 'Diamond' Darrell. I don't know if you knew that or not, but that's kind of funny. I couldn't say *dimebag*. At that time, nobody was sure if they were going to be huge or not—and that was, of course, a producer's call. It had nothing to do with me." Darrell didn't start officially calling himself "Dimebag" until around the time of *Far Beyond Driven*.

7. Lance Williams. May 1983: 4.

8. Preston Versailles. Nov. 1983: 5.

9. "Dimebag's Girlfriend on His Murder: 'I Take Comfort in Knowing That He Didn't See It Coming.'" http://www.roadrunnerrecords.com/blabbermouth .net/news.aspx?mode=Article&newsitemID=52240. Blabbermouth.net. 13 May 2006.

10. http://www.decibelmagazine.com/features/oct2007/down.aspx. Oct. 2007.

11. "On Behalf of Darrell Lance Abbott, Pt. 1." 21 Jan. 2005. http://www .philanselmo.com.

12. "Ridin' High: Bernard Doe Reports on the Non-Stop Power Metal Force from Texas—Pantera." June 1988.

13. *Power Metal* also includes the Darrell-sung "P*S*T*88"—"Well, actually it's called 'Pussy Tight,' but we decided to doll it up a little," Darrell told *Metal Forces*—a tribute to porn flicks. "We figured that there hadn't been any band since the Mentors who have jammed up anything like this, so we thought it'd be a real good subject to cover!" Quoted in "Ridin' High: Bernard Doe Reports on the Non-Stop Power Metal Force from Texas—Pantera." June 1988.

14. "Ridin' High: Bernard Doe Reports on the Non-Stop Power Metal Force from Texas—Pantera." June 1988.

NOTES TO SIDE 2

1. Gould would later leave the company, but Concrete would serve as Pantera's management until O'Brien left the business a decade or so later.

2. Some believe Darrell never would have joined someone else's band, Megadeth or anyone else, under any circumstances. "To me, for the life of me, why on earth would Darrell—maybe Mustaine's not picking up on it—but why would Darrell want to be in Megadeth?" Buddy Blaze says. "I can't see Darrell answering to anybody, let alone Dave Mustaine. I couldn't imagine that. I could see him being flattered that somebody like Dave would have wanted him in the band. But as far as I know, the likelihood of that was zero."

3. Atco released Tangier's debut for the label, *Four Winds*, in 1989; it reached No. 91 on the *Billboard* charts. *Stranded* followed in 1991, never rising above No. 187 in *Billboard*'s rankings. The band was never heard from again.

4. He would go on to record four Pantera albums in all (*Cowboys from Hell, Vulgar Display of Power, Far Beyond Driven,* and *The Great Southern Trendkill*), overseeing a six-year stretch that was easily the most fruitful of the group's twenty-year run.

5. It might have been even rougher if, as Rita Haney claims, the mixing engineer hadn't toned down Darrell's riffs. The demos for the album were "more brutal," she says.

6. *Cowboys from Hell: The Videos.* 1991.

7. "A Conversation with Rex Brown." 12 Dec. 2007.

8. "Suicidal Tendencies Leads Metal Slugfest." 31 Aug. 1990: 12F.

9. Well, it was at the time. MuchMusic has since moved its headquarters to New York City and changed its name; you now know it as Fuse.

10. "Judas Priest Singer Rob Halford Remembers Dimebag Darrell." http://www.roadrunnerrecords.com/blabbermouth.net/news.aspx?mode=article&newsitemid=30259. Blabbermouth.net. 11 Dec. 2004.

11. "Judas Priest Singer Rob Halford Remembers Dimebag Darrell." http://www.roadrunnerrecords.com/blabbermouth.net/news.aspx?mode=article&newsitemid=30259. Blabbermouth.net. 11 Dec. 2004.

12. *Cowboys from Hell: The Videos.* 1991.

13. The movie with Kristy Swanson, not the TV series with Sarah Michelle Gellar.

14. "Judas Priest Singer Rob Halford Remembers Dimebag Darrell." http://www.roadrunnerrecords.com/blabbermouth.net/news.aspx?mode=article&newsitemid=30259. Blabbermouth.net. 11 Dec. 2004.

15. "Texas-Based Pantera Puts Some Heart into Its Power as It Tries to Take Out the Thrash." 15 May 1991: F5.

16. Halford appreciated touring with Darrell and Pantera in Europe as well. He left Judas Priest not long after and formed a new band, Fight, which took many cues from his former traveling partners.

17. *For Those About to Rock: Monsters in Moscow.* 1992.

18. Some of those early shows turned up in Rachman's outstanding 2006 documentary, *American Hardcore*, including an interview with Philip Anselmo. "I certainly could have interviewed Darrell for that, too," Rachman says.

19. "I Remember You, Dimebag Darrell." 30 Dec. 2004. http://www.sebastian bach.com/archives/dimebag.html.

20. This show was also notable for kicking off a firestorm of controversy when Bach was photographed postgig wearing a T-shirt that said, "AIDS Kills Fags Dead." "When we finished, I was totally hot and sweaty," Bach told *Metal Hammer* magazine in 2006. "The guys from L.A. Guns were all backstage, so I said, 'Gimme a fucking shirt to put on.' Gerri Miller from *Metal Edge* magazine is there asking for a picture of all of us, so I just pick up this hideous fuckin' shirt that some fan had thrown up onto [the] stage and put it on. We all knew

it was the worst shirt of all time. It wasn't some campaign that I went on." Quoted in "Sebastian Bach Says He Lied When He Said He'd Stopped Drinking." Blabbermouth.net. 21 Oct. 2006. http://www.roadrunnerrecords.com/blabbermouth.net/news.aspx?mode=article&newsitemid=60702.

21. Gene Stout. "Decibels Will Be Dancing in Seattle." 28 Feb. 1992: 9.

22. "Top Five Dimebag Riffs." 5 Dec. 2005. http://www.mtv.com/bands/d/damageplan/news_feature_120505/index2.jhtml.

23. "Pantera's 1992 Vulgar Display of Power Set the Standard for Nineties Metal to Come." July 2000: 36.

24. "Pantera; Rock Group's Music." May 1994: 20.

25. *Dimevision Vol. 1: That's the Fun I Have.* 2006.

26. Atlantic merged Atco with EastWest in 1991, forming Atco/EastWest; a year later, the name Atco was ditched altogether.

27. "Pantera 'Driven' to Harder Sound; EastWest Trusts Fans Will Embrace New Set." 24 Feb. 1994: 12.

28. "Pantera; Rock Group's Music." May 1994: 20.

29. At one time, NAMM was an acronym that stood for the National Association of Music Merchants. The longer version of the name fell out of use as the organization developed into a worldwide concern. Yet even though the group behind what has become the largest music product trade show in the world is officially called the International Music Products Association, its annual gathering is still universally referred to as "the NAMM show." Confusing, yes, but easier than trying to convince everyone to start saying "the IMPA show," I guess.

30. You could have, if only briefly: The image appeared on the vinyl version of *Far Beyond Driven*, and was subsequently banned.

31. "Band Defined by a Word: 'Hostile.'" 14 Apr. 1994: C20.

32. Now called the First Midwest Bank Amphitheatre, the venue has also been known as Tweeter Center Chicago and the New World Music Theatre.

33. "Metal with No Middle Ground." 3 Feb. 1995: 35.

34. "Seating Dispute Cancels Concert." 2 Feb. 1995: B4.

35. Well, I'm sure it seemed like that to many people. It's difficult to accurately gauge the size of an angry mob.

36. http://www.roadrunnerrecords.com/blabbermouth.net/news.aspx?mode=Article&newsitemID=52240. 13 May 2006.

37. "Animal House." June 1996.

38. "Damageplan." *Headbangers Ball.* 24 Jan. 2004.

NOTES TO SIDE 3

1. *Dimebag Darrell's Riffer Madness.* New York: Warner Bros., 2003.

2. "Sylvia Rhone Leads Elektra's Turnaround." 9 Nov. 1996.

3. There is the silhouette of another guitar at the bottom, featuring the Razorback body style Darrell was developing with the company before he died.

4. "I Remember You, Dimebag Darrell." 30 Dec. 2004. http://www.sebastian bach.com/archives/dimebag.html.

5. Mike Heika. "For Pantera, Writing Stars' Tune Was Net Gain." 11 Dec. 2004.

6. "TSG Backstage: Metallica." http://www.thesmokinggun.com/backstage tour/metallica/metallica1.html.

7. Kerby, Jeff. "Kerby's Exclusive Interview With Damageplan Drummer Vinnie Paul." *KNAC.com.* 2 June 2004. <http://www.knac.com/article.asp?articleid=3056>

8. "Pantera's 1992 Vulgar Display of Power Set the Standard for Nineties Metal to Come." July 2000: 36.

9. "Pantera Gives—and Gets—Energy." 20 Mar. 2001: 4E.

NOTES TO SIDE 4

1. "A Conversation with Rex Brown." 12 Dec. 2007.

2. "Heavy Metal Maestro." 24 May 2002: 20+.

3. "Heavy Metal Maestro." 24 May 2002.

4. "Kerby's Exclusive Interview with Damageplan Drummer Vinnie Paul." 2 June 2004. http://www.knac.com/article.asp?articleid=3056.

5. "The Process of Weeding Out." Sep. 2003.

6. "Ex-Pantera Drummer: 'Philip Anselmo Was Afraid of Success.'" Blabber mouth.net. 25 Nov. 2003. http://www.roadrunnerrecords.com/blabbermouth.net/ news.aspx?mode=Article&newsitemID=16971. Revolver excerpt.

7. "Ex-Pantera Singer Philip Anselmo: Vinnie Paul Is a 'Crybaby.'" Blabber mouth.net. 18 Dec. 2003. http://www.roadrunnerrecords.com/blabbermouth .net/news.aspx?mode=Article&newsitemID=17500. SMNnews.com excerpt.

8. "Dimebag Darrell Says He Tried to Help Philip Anselmo Beat His Drug Problem." Blabbermouth.net. 24 Jan. 2004. http://www.roadrunnerrecords.com/ blabbermouth.net/news.aspx?mode=article&newsitemid=18464. Guitar World excerpt.

9. *The Biz.* CNNFN. 1 Apr. 2004.

10. A far more random memory from Hutson's time spent with Darrell: "I once gave him a picture of Paul McCartney, because he seemed to profess a love of Paul McCartney at one point. Which I thought was really quite odd, actually. I did a big print of Paul McCartney for him and Phil Anselmo, because apparently they loved the Beatles. I would have thought if they were going to pick a band from England at the time; I would have thought they would have gone for something like, you know, the Kinks or the Rolling Stones, something like that. The Beatles, I found that quite surprising. I thought they would have gone for something with sort of a harder edge in terms of sixties bands, as opposed to something that my mum likes."

11. "Dimebag Darrell: Requiem for a Heavyweight." 1 Feb. 2005: 56+.

12. "Philip Anselmo: 'Dimebag Darrell Deserves to Be Beaten Severely.'" Blabbermouth.net. 1 Dec. 2004. http://www.roadrunnerrecords.com/blabber mouth.net/news.aspx?mode=article&newsitemid=29847. *Metal Hammer* excerpt.

Index

About the Author

Texas-based author Zac Crain was music editor for the *Dallas Observer* and is currently a senior editor at *D Magazine*. His writing has also appeared in *Esquire, Spin,* RollingStone.com, and *American Way*. He ran for mayor of Dallas in 2007, using a logo pilfered from AC/DC.